Medical Malpractice —

A Physician's Guide to Navigating the Minefield of Medical Malpractice Law

Darryl S. Weiman, M.D., J.D.
Professor, Cardiothoracic Surgery
University of Tennessee Health Science Center
Chief, Surgical Service, VAMC Memphis

www.MedicalMalpracticeAndTheLaw.com

Creative Team Publishing
San Diego

© 2014 by Darryl S. Weiman.

All rights reserved. No part of this book may be reproduced, stored in a retrieval system or transmitted in any form or by any means without the prior written permission of the publisher, except by a reviewer who may quote brief passages in a review distributed through electronic media, or printed in a newspaper, magazine or journal.

Disclaimer: The opinions and conclusion expressed in this book are strictly those of the author and do not necessarily represent or express the policies and procedures of the U.S. Department of Veterans Affairs or The University of Tennessee Health Science Center

Hardcover Edition

ISBN: 978-0-9897975-8-0

PUBLISHED BY CREATIVE TEAM PUBLISHING
www.CreativeTeamPublishing.com
San Diego

Printed in the United States of America

Prologue

"Malpractice litigation is usually less about right and wrong than it is about moving money around."[1]

I am a Cardiovascular and Thoracic surgeon and a Professor of Surgery at a major teaching university. Although I enjoy taking care of patients and performing operations, I'm miserable when I get involved in a malpractice action, whether it's against me or another physician.

Unfortunately, malpractice actions are all too common in our society. An analysis of the 2012 data from the National Practitioner Data Bank shows there was a total of 12,142 payouts for medical malpractice where some liability was assessed to the health care practitioner. (Diederich Healthcare's "2013 Medical Malpractice Payout Analysis," written by Molly Gamble, May 3, 2013) The cost of these payouts was $3.6 billion. Since 78% of claims did not result in payments, doing the math shows that there were about 55,190 claims for that year. About 7.4% of all physicians get served with a malpractice claim every year. (Jena AB, Seabury S, Lakdawalla D, Chandra A: Malpractice risk according to physician specialty, New England Journal of Medicine. 365(7): 629-36, 2011). This is a surprisingly high number.

In the state of Tennessee, statistics show that a cardiac surgeon is sued on the average of once every three years. I have been named in several lawsuits in the course of my career and I've never believed that any were justified. In fact, I've even been sued when the patient had a good result.

Initially, I didn't fully comprehend the legal process I had to face in dealing with these actions. Interrogatories, depositions, proceedings in court, legal definitions were all beyond my knowledge base. I soon realized that, as a surgeon, I was at a definite disadvantage in the legal arena. Since opposing attorneys knew the rules, they had a clear advantage in the legal combat that these actions often become.

In the midst of one of the malpractice claims against me, I told my wife that she needed to go to law school to get a legal education so that one of us could better understand what was going on. With two young daughters ages three and four, she was not receptive. "I'm a Mom now," she said. "If you want a legal education, you need to do it yourself."

However, her permission was predicated on the condition that I maintain my practice as a surgeon and I would not be allowed to study until the girls were put to bed in the evenings. I agreed.

I went through the normal process of applying. I took the Law School Admissions Test (LSAT), applied to the only law school in Memphis, and went for the interview. I had to get my college transcripts out of microfiche since I had graduated over twenty years earlier. The law school also asked that I send in my medical school transcripts. I did.

I did well on the LSAT and my college and medical school records were solid so I was not too surprised that I got accepted.

It took me four years to finish law school. I had to go part-time to maintain my practice. For the first year, the professors would call me "Mr. Weiman," just like they addressed all students with the Mr. or Ms. descriptor. After the first year grades came out, they started to address me as Dr. Weiman. I guess they wanted to see if I was serious in the undertaking before they would be willing to acknowledge that I was a medical doctor.

I knew I wasn't going to give up my career as a surgeon, but I did want to learn as much as possible about the law and then, hopefully, convey some of this knowledge to my colleagues so that they could better participate in the legal process and have a better understanding of how to competently manage a malpractice claim against them.

While maintaining a full-time practice as an academic Cardiovascular and Thoracic surgeon, I successfully navigated through law school, took the Bar Exam in the State of Tennessee, and passed. During my law school coursework, I maintained my position as a Professor of Surgery at the same University. Currently, I take care of patients with diseases of the chest, do research, and teach medical students and residents. The only difference now is that some of my research and teaching is in the field of Health Care Law.

It's true, with knowledge comes power. I designed this book to help the health care provider to better cope with the legal process that they will be confronting in a malpractice action. Most books written about malpractice law have been written by practicing attorneys. My perspective is different because of my medical background, my direct experiences of being sued for malpractice, being deposed and testifying in court, working with attorneys as a medical expert witness, and my legal education.

As the state legislatures and the United States Congress are actively debating various aspects of malpractice reform, doctors who have more knowledge of the system should be better able to participate in the legal debates dealing with reform. This book also looks at various aspects of malpractice reform and provides the basic legal knowledge that physicians may need to participate intelligently in the debate.

The great Supreme Court Justice Oliver Wendell Holmes said in a dissenting opinion in *Abrams v. U.S.*, 250 U.S. 616 (1919), the "ultimate good desired is better reached by free trade in ideas — that the best test of truth is the power of the thought to get itself accepted in the competition of the market." This was a case dealing with free speech. The original ruling was against political radicals who were opposed to the United States getting involved in World War I. Justice Holmes changed his mind feeling that the court was acting too harshly against a man who was only publishing leaflets expressing his opinion of the War.

I hope my colleagues find this book useful. I enjoyed writing it.

It's true, with knowledge comes power.
I designed this book to help the health care provider to better cope with the legal process that they will be confronting in a malpractice action.

Medical Malpractice —

A Physician's Guide to Navigating the Minefield of Medical Malpractice Law

Darryl S. Weiman, M.D., J.D.
Professor, Cardiothoracic Surgery
University of Tennessee Health Science Center
Chief, Surgical Service, VAMC Memphis

www.MedicalMalpracticeAndTheLaw.com

Facts will always win out over put downs, innuendos, and unjustified allegations. Facts are the basis of any persuasive argument. As John Adams—a noted attorney before he became President of the United States—said, "Facts are stubborn things."

Perception is important.
Always answer truthfully.

Endorsements on Behalf of
Medical Malpractice —
A Physician's Guide to Navigating the Minefield of Medical Malpractice Law

Dr. Glenn Whitman
Associate Professor, Johns Hopkins School of Medicine
Director, Heart Transplant and the Cardiac ICU,
Johns Hopkins Hospital,
Baltimore, Maryland

Dr. Weiman walks his colleagues through the burdensome, frequently unjust task of defending ourselves when faced with a lawsuit. Using cardiac surgery as an example, he points out that a physician will face a suit one out of every three years in practice. Understanding the foundations and process of a lawsuit give us the keys to preventing them and, when necessary, defending ourselves successfully.

Unquestionably, this book represents a body of knowledge physicians would rather not spend time learning. However, the material covered should be part of every physician's lexicon. This easily understood book explains the processes involved in a lawsuit, from beginning to end, giving the reader an awareness of the relevant legal issues, enabling us to converse with our representatives as well as adversaries knowledgably, in a manner that can only serve our profession and our individual cause well.

The prose flows well, the arcane legal terms are demystified. Dr. Weiman provides the reader with an understanding of a process that otherwise frequently makes little sense. His stepwise approach to a lawsuit, pinpointing key elements as he takes us through the process, is a time saving, efficient guide with which we should all be fluent.

Medical Malpractice – A Physician's Guide makes for easy reading; its directed approach to teaching us what we need to know distills a vast body of knowledge, quickly putting the most important issues at our fingertips.

Dr. Weiman deserves applause and appreciation for what he has given us.

*****

Endorsements

Mark K. Ferguson, MD
Professor, Department of Surgery and
The Cancer Research Center Head,
Thoracic Surgery Service Director,
Residency Program in Cardiothoracic Surgery
The University of Chicago Medicine & Biological Sciences

Medical Malpractice is a wonderful compendium of medical-legal facts and fallacies that every physician will benefit from. Dr. Weiman brings his considerable experience as a cardiothoracic surgeon and educator in medicine and the medical-legal environment to a volume that is full of practical advice. He provides a careful presentation of facts and lucid explanations of what, to a lay person, appears to be an arcane and convoluted legal system. Nothing is "dumbed down;" the assumption is that readers have more than a casual interest in the topic and more than average intelligence.

This well organized book anticipates the needs of physicians throughout the process and provides the information necessary for physician defendants to manage a trying situation with insight and, hopefully, aplomb. It is readable, informative, and very helpful. This is the perfect book for physicians who are faced with legal challenges to their professional activities.

*****

Endorsements

Frederick L. Greene, MD FACS
Levine Cancer Institute, Charlotte, NC and
Adjunct Professor of Surgery, University of North Carolina School of Medicine

Darryl Weiman, a medical educator, practicing cardiothoracic surgeon, service chief, and a lawyer well-versed in malpractice law has authored a book specifically aimed to help physicians maneuver the mine field of tort law as it pertains to medical malpractice. Dr. Weiman is a unique individual who was not only concerned about the problems that physicians faced in courts of law, but wanted to understand the nuances of malpractice issues from the inside. He, therefore, matriculated in law school with the specific purpose of understanding every facet of this process which he has now brought forward in *Medical Malpractice – A Physician's Guide*.

Dr. Weiman takes us from the beginning of the process, introducing us to the lexicon of terms frequently both foreign and confusing to the practicing physician. In well-referenced chapters he covers every conceivable nuance of the malpractice process while making this a readable and highly educational process for physicians who need to know.

If a physician is one of the 7 to 8% who will find themselves in a malpractice claim each year, this treatise is mandatory for understanding not only what is expected, but

Endorsements

arms the physician with important information on preparing and bearing up through the process. This book also carefully outlines the peer review process and helps us to understand what is privileged and protected information as we convene in our healthcare institutions.

We should all be grateful to Dr. Weiman for creating this primer that will be mandatory reading for those physicians who might find themselves in the vortex of a malpractice case. As Dr. Weiman tells us, "knowledge is good." This book helps us to understand the very fluid nature of medical liability and to enter into the world of a malpractice claim armed with essential background material.

As Dr. Weiman reminds us, the Chinese philosopher, Sun Tzu, wrote: "So it is said that if you know others and know yourself, you will not be imperiled in a hundred battles." *Medical Malpractice – A Physician's Guide* will undoubtedly arm us and help us prepare for any conflict that we might face if we find ourselves as a defendant.

*****

Foreword

E. Ratcliffe Anderson, Jr., MD
Lieutenant General, USAF (Ret.)
Former Surgeon General of the United States Air Force
Former CEO of the American Medical Association

Being served with a malpractice suit is one of the most stressful administrative problems that a health care provider may face in his career. Interrogatories, production of documents, depositions, and in court testimony are issues not usually taught during professional medical training. As such, the provider is working with no real knowledge base in a situation which may have significant financial implications.

Finally, we have a health care provider, a noted Cardiothoracic Surgeon, who has obtained a legitimate legal education, passed the Bar exam for the State of Tennessee, and is now writing so that his colleagues will have a starting point to better handle the headaches of dealing with the adversarial process that a malpractice case is likely to become.

Dr. Darryl S. Weiman is a Professor of Surgery who obtained a law school degree. Remarkably, he did this while maintaining his surgical practice. Obviously he could only attend law school as a part-time student and, originally, he anticipated that the project would take six years. He accomplished the schooling in four years, something not unexpected from a cardiothoracic surgeon.

The book is presented in three sections. The first deals with the legal definitions, rules, and processes associated with the beginnings of a malpractice action. This section includes discovery, defenses, and damages. The second section deals with the trial itself from jury selection, opening statements, presentation of the case, jury instructions, and closing arguments. Post-trial motions and appeals are also presented. The final section deals with pertinent legal issues relating to a medical malpractice action. These include alternative methods of dispute resolution and the possibility of Health Courts as a future method of resolving medical misadventures.

Dr. Weiman writes in a clear and concise manner and he explains the applicable case law and statutes along with the processes in a way that we can understand. His personal stories from his own cases where he was a defendant to cases where he has served as an expert witness add to the educational experience of the reader.

Unfortunately, being a health care provider requires a knowledge base beyond that of medicine and surgery. Having a medical practice also requires an understanding of running a business and knowledge of applicable law. *Medical Malpractice – A Physician's Guide to Navigating the Mine Field of Medical Malpractice Law* provides a starting point to answer the fundamental questions that a provider will need as he works through a malpractice action.

Thank you, Dr. Weiman for taking on this project. The knowledge, education, training, and experience portrayed will help all of us. It is about time that one of our own has learned how to get through the process and has expertly provided that knowledge to the rest of us in an understandable way.

Dr. Weiman still makes his living as a cardiothoracic surgeon. He does not practice law but he is licensed to do so if he chooses.

This book should be in the personal library of all health care providers, not just physicians, surgeons, and nurses. I hope that you never have to use this book, but if you ever are served with a malpractice suit, this will be a good starting point for your own legal education.

Dedication

This book is dedicated to those who have devoted their lives to taking care of patients.

We strive to provide the best care possible yet deal with the reality that bad outcomes can and do occur.

Table of Contents

Prologue 3

Endorsements 13

Foreword 19

Dedication 23

Section One: Medical Malpractice

Chapter 1: Medical Malpractice — A Definition 33
    The Medical Expert Witness 36
    Non-expert Testimony 46

Chapter 2: Negligence 53
    Ordinary Negligence 53
    Res Ipsa Loquiter 58
    Medical Negligence 62
    Gross Negligence 65

Chapter 3: Duty Owed	71
Chapter 4: Standard of Care	81
Causation	86
Foreseeability	88
Chapter 5: The Discovery Process	97
Service	97
Discovery	100
Interrogatories	102
Affidavits	104
Depositions	105
Evidence	112
Chapter 6: Defenses	123
Contributory Negligence	123
Comparative Fault Doctrine	128
Statute of Limitations	130
Statute of Repose	140
Chapter 7: Damages	145
Punitive Damages	147
Ordinary Damages	151
Pain and Suffering	152

Section Two: The Trial

Chapter 8: The Jury — 159
    Jury Selection — 159
    Preliminary Instructions of Law — 164

Chapter 9: Opening Statements — 169

Chapter 10: Plaintiffs — 175
    Plaintiffs Case-in-Chief — 175
    Motions after Plaintiffs Rests — 191

Chapter 11: Defendants — 195
    Defendant's Case-in-Chief — 195
    Objections — 196
    Motions after Defendant Rests — 206

Chapter 12: Plaintiff's Rebuttal and
    Defendant's Surrebuttal — 209

Chapter 13: Instruction Conference — 211

Chapter 14: Closing Argument   213

Chapter 15: Before the Jury Deliberates   215
    Jury Instructions   215
    Jury Deliberation and Verdict   227

Chapter 16: Conduct of the Attorneys   231

Chapter 17: After the Trial   235
    Post-Trial Motions and Appeal   235
    Conclusion of the Trial   237

Section Three: Other Legal Issues Pertaining to Medical Malpractice

Chapter 18: Fault, Liability, and Strict Liability   239
    Fault   239
    Liability   240
    Strict Liability   240

Chapter 19: Commentary on the American College of Surgical Expert Witness Affirmation   247

Chapter 20: *Daubert v. Merrell Dow Pharmaceutical, Inc* 257

Chapter 21: Federal or State Court 269

Chapter 22: Locality Rule 275

Chapter 23: Doctrine of Informed Consent 281

Chapter 24: Emergency Medical Treatment and Active Labor Act (EMTALA) 295

Chapter 25: Borrowed Servant Doctrine 307

Chapter 26: Good Samaritan Rule 313

Chapter 27: Dynamite Charge 321

Chapter 28: Lying Under Oath 327

Chapter 29: Conflict of Laws 331

Chapter 30: Provider Regulation under Medicare and Medicaid	339
Chapter 31: Confidentiality of Peer Review	351
Confidentiality of the Personnel Files Of Residents	356
Peer Review and Privileging	361
Chapter 32: Morbidity and Mortality Conference: What Is Discoverable	367
Chapter 33: Rules of Professional Responsibility For Lawyers	379
Chapter 34: Removing Medical Malpractice from The Courts	389
Administrative Agencies	393
Arbitration	402
Mediation	403
Collaborative Practice	407
Chapter 35: Health Courts	411
Compensation Models	416
Other Courts	417

Chapter 36: Going Bare	425
Chapter 37: Conclusion	429
The Author	439
Acknowledgements	441
Citations	443
Index	455
Products and Services	467

Section One: Medical Malpractice

Chapter 1:
Medical Malpractice — A Definition

Simply put, medical malpractice is a *tort*. A tort deals with civil and not criminal wrongs. Examples of torts are defamation, trespass, assault, and negligence. All of the torts have their own elements and definitions, but the one thing they have in common is that some person has sustained a loss that was due to some act--or failure to act-- by some other person who should have known better.

Many people, including physicians, don't know there is a difference between criminal law and civil law. There was a surgical journal that used to have a section dealing with malpractice cases. After the case was presented, they would ask the readers to decide if the medical practitioner was guilty or not guilty. The definition of *guilty* in the legal sense is an adjective meaning, "having committed a crime; responsible for a crime."[2] The editors of the journal were using the wrong legal word because, in general, malpractice is not a crime. In layman's terminology, the word is often used to describe those responsible for a civil wrong but, perhaps the word *liable* would have been better. The public shouldn't think that malpractice is a criminal act for which a physician would be at risk of not only monetary penalties, but jail time as well.

Do torts only happen between people? The law isn't that simple. Entities, such as corporations, are also considered to be "persons." This is how a person injured in a car crash can bring suit against the auto maker who may have made a defective car which may have contributed to the injuries. Remember the Ford Pinto which had a rear mounted gas tank? People injured from the exploding gas tank in rear end collisions were able to bring suit for a defective design of the car.

Medical malpractice includes any conduct by a medical practitioner who is providing medical care that is *liability producing*. This means that the practitioner may have to pay monetary damages to the injured party. More often the terminology used is *medical negligence* by a medical professional. The system that has developed over the years is a means of *loss allocation* that is based on fault—whereby an injury has occurred to a patient which was due to care that fell below the standard of care expected of a health care professional of like or similar specialty. In many states, this is a local standard of care which means it had to happen in the same or similar type of community where the injury occurred. This "locality rule" is a means of recognizing that the standard of care may be different from place to place, usually depending on what type of facilities are available to the practitioner.

A malpractice action usually starts with a complaint being filed in a court which is believed by the plaintiff, acting through his attorney, to have jurisdiction for the case. In the complaint, the plaintiff describes the nature of the claim and the *remedy* sought. The complaint and any other papers filed in the court in support of the action are called *pleadings*. The remedy sought is usually in the form of money to be given to the plaintiff.

After the complaint is filed, a copy of the complaint is then *served* on the defendants. The complaint is accompanied with a summons which informs the defendant of the actions he needs to take and the time frame in which he has to take those actions. Usually, the summons tells the defendant he needs to answer the complaint and if he doesn't answer in the indicated time frame, the plaintiff will be granted a judgment by default. The defendant, usually through his lawyer, will need to file an *answer* to the complaint. The answer will admit, deny, or plead ignorance to each of the allegations in the complaint. If the defendant fails to answer the complaint in the required time-frame, he may lose the case right off the bat.

Now that the parties are involved in the process, the next phase of the malpractice action is *discovery*. In the *discovery* process, the strengths and weaknesses of each party's cases are learned, as well as other parties or witnesses who may be helpful in the action. Interrogatories, depositions, affidavits, and admissions are all part of the discovery process.

Whenever the State is involved in taking some of your property, the Constitution of the United States along with the State constitutions require that *due process* occur as a matter of fairness to you, the defendant. *Due process* requires you, as the defendant, be notified of the pending suit and be afforded a fair hearing on the merits of the case before the judgment on the claim is made.

The Medical Expert Witness

An expert witness is a person who by knowledge, education, experience, training and/or skill, can assist the *trier of fact* in understanding the evidence or to determine a fact in issue. A "trier of fact" is either a jury or a judge. Since most lay people don't have a deep understanding of medicine and surgery, it's not surprising that medical experts are needed to help the jury or the judge understand the *standard of care* and *causation issues* which are required elements of a malpractice action.

Since most malpractice actions are resolved on the issues of *standard of care* and *causation*, the case will often come down to a battle between the expert witnesses. The plaintiff's expert must define what he thinks the standard of care is, and he must also convince the jury that the defendant, by acting negligently, violated that standard. He must also testify it was that breach of the *standard of care* which was the cause, the *proximate* or *legal cause*, of the patient's injury.

Of course, the defendant's expert witness, which can be the defendant himself, but is usually an outside expert to help allay the conflict of interest concerns the jury might harbor with the defendant acting as his own expert, will argue that the *standard of care* was met, or, if the standard was not met, the *causation* was not due to that breach of the *standard of care*. The case is often decided on the battle of the experts.

Under Tennessee law, it's first required that the expert will *substantially assist* the jury. The court decides if the proposed expert can *substantially assist* the jury. In making this determination, the court must look at several nonexclusive factors which were delineated in the federal case of *Daubert v. Merrell Dow Pharmaceuticals*.[3]

The Supreme Court took on the case of *Daubert* to rule on the standard needed to admit expert scientific testimony in federal trials where expert testimony was needed. In this case, Daubert and Schuller were minor children that were born with serious birth defects. They and their parents brought suit against Merrell Dow in the California state courts alleging that the birth defects were due to Bendectin, an anti-nausea drug manufactured by Merrell Dow that was taken by the mothers during the pregnancies. Merrell Dow removed the suit to the federal court system on diversity of citizenship grounds. Removing a suit to a federal court is a strategy used by defendants who believe they will be treated more fairly by a federal judge, appointed for life, as opposed to a state judge who must face re-election to maintain his position.

After the discovery process, Dow moved for *summary judgment* on the grounds that there was no admissible evidence showing Bendectin caused birth defects in humans. Supporting the summary judgment motion was an affidavit of Steven Lamm, a physician and epidemiologist who was deemed to be an expert on risks of chemical exposures.

Dr. Lamm reported he had reviewed over 30 published articles dealing with over 130,000 patients and none of them found Bendectin had caused any malformations in fetuses. He concluded that ingesting Bendectin in the first trimester of pregnancy did not cause birth defects as was claimed by plaintiffs.

The plaintiffs countered Dr. Lamm's affidavit with eight experts of their own. However, these experts relied on in vitro test tube and animal model tests which were done in preparation for the trial, all of which claimed to show

Bendectin caused birth defects. They also claimed to have reanalyzed the published human epidemiologic studies, and they drew different conclusions from the scientists who did the original studies.

The District Court granted the motion for summary judgment *holding* that scientific evidence can only be admitted if it is based on principles which have general acceptance in the scientific field where it is proffered. The Court felt the plaintiff's studies, which were basically done for the purposes of the trial and had never been peer-reviewed and published in the appropriate scientific literature, could not be used to establish *causation*. The animal studies, the test tube studies, and the similarities of Bendectin to other chemicals known to cause birth defects, were thus ruled inadmissible.

The Court of Appeals for the Ninth Circuit agreed based on *Frye v. United States*.[4] The *holding* of Frye was that expert opinion based on scientific technique would not be admissible unless the technique was *generally accepted* as reliable by the appropriate scientific community. The Court also refused to admit a reanalysis of the epidemiologic data that had never been subjected to a peer review and was, thus, never published.

The U.S. Supreme Court decided to *grant certiorari*, meaning they would take the case to clarify for the courts the proper standard for admission of expert testimony in the federal courts.

In its decision, the Supreme Court first noted that the *Frye* test, which came into effect in 1923, was the dominant standard for admitting any new scientific evidence at trial. *Frye* was a *general acceptance* test and it came from a trial which was concerned with the admissibility of evidence that was derived from the systolic blood pressure deception test—which was a precursor to a polygraph machine.[5] In *Frye*, the evidence of the *deception* test was not allowed to be admitted because the test had "not yet gained such standing and scientific recognition among physiological and psychological authorities as would justify the courts admitting expert testimony deduced from the discovery, development, and experiments thus far made."[6]

The Court in *Daubert* ruled the Federal Rules of Evidence overruled *Frye*. Rule 402 of the Federal Rules of Evidence states, "All relevant evidence is admissible, except as otherwise provided by the Constitution of the United States, by Act of Congress, by these rules, or by other rules prescribed by the Supreme Court pursuant to statutory authority. Evidence which is not relevant is not admissible."[7]

The question now facing the courts is how to decide if the expert witness's testimony is relevant. If it is relevant, then by the rules, it should be admitted. The Court answered this question by going to Rule 702 which deals specifically with expert testimony. Rule 702 says, "[i]f scientific, technical, or other specialized knowledge will assist the trier of fact to understand the evidence or to determine a fact in issue, a witness qualified as an expert by knowledge, skill, experience, training, or education, may testify thereto in the form of an opinion or otherwise."[8]

Would this new rule in assessing the validity of expert testimony assure that the truth will be found? Not necessarily.

Galileo Galilei was an astronomer and physicist who lived from 1564 until 1642. By viewing the heavenly bodies with a telescope of his construction, he came to the conclusion the earth and the other planets revolved around the sun. This sun-centered theory, also called the heliocentric theory, first proposed by Copernicus, was not *generally accepted* at the time. In fact, the Roman Catholic Church considered this theory to be heresy. Pope Urban VIII told Galileo he could only write about the theory so long as he would treat it as a mathematical proposition and not as scientific fact.

Galileo defied the church by writing a book about the theory called *Dialogue Concerning the Two Chief World Systems*. Shortly after the book was published, Galileo was called to Rome, faced the Inquisition, and was found guilty of heresy. He probably would not have been allowed to be an expert witness under the *general acceptance* doctrine of

Frye, but he may have been allowed to testify if his work had been published in peer-reviewed journals, and used methods that were accepted by the scientific community at the time.

However, since the telescope was new, and the theory was not yet published in peer-reviewed journals, it is more likely that Galileo would not have been allowed to testify as an expert, although he would be considered to be an expert by today's standards. The point is, even if the purported expert is right, he may not be allowed to testify by the court if he does not pass the *Daubert* test.

The court, meaning the judge, must still come to a conclusion whether or not it can ascertain the certainty of a matter put forth. Somebody must win and somebody must lose. As such, the courts are looking for finality. The truth may have to come later. Of course, by then it's probably too late to do the losing party any good.

Since *general acceptance* is no longer the rule to determine the reliability of the basis for an expert's opinion, it appears the traditional barriers to expert testimony are no longer standing. As such, the Court ruled the *Frye general acceptance* standard was incompatible with the *Rules of Evidence* and would no longer be applicable—at least in federal courts. From *Daubert* on, the judge was given the job of ensuring the expert's testimony was both relevant to the case at issue and was based on a reliable, accepted scientific foundation. The goal of the new standard set by the *Daubert* decision was to keep junk science out of the courtroom, and it probably was an advance in that direction, but it's an aspiration that may never be actually attained. Junk science today may be accepted fact in the future.

What if, like Galileo, the expert witness is ahead of his time and his opinions, although they will be proven to be right in the future, are not the present standard?

Back in the late '70s at the University of Chicago, the standard operation for a patient with breast cancer was a mastectomy. Any surgeon who did not at least remove the breast would have been considered to be negligent. If an expert at trial were to claim a breast sparing operation was safe and a good alternative to mastectomy, it is likely his testimony would not have been allowed under the rules. Breast sparing operations were not generally accepted because there was little experience with the procedure as it pertained to cancer, the procedure was not being taught to the residents, there was no training, and skill was not determinative.

With the passage of time, breast sparing operations for breast cancer have become the standard. The expert who would not have been allowed to testify in the '70s would most likely be allowed to testify now. This is just one of many examples which demonstrate the problems with the standards set up by *Daubert*, and it also demonstrates one of the serious shortcomings of our legal system. The law and science are always changing; a verdict today may not be consistent with a verdict in the future. We hope that our legal system would be consistent, but often it is not.

Even though the necessity to come to a definitive answer can lead to erroneous and unfair decisions, it is, in the opinion of many, the best legal system for dispute resolution. In our legal system, Galileo would have at least been allowed a *Daubert* hearing in front of a judge before he was thrown to the wolves.

Does the law require the expert witness to practice in the same specialty as the defendant? In Tennessee, it doesn't. However, the expert witness "must be sufficiently familiar with the standard of care of the profession or specialty and be able to give relevant testimony on the issue in question."[9] Check your state for its rule.

In the recent case of *Markina Westmoreland et al. v. William L.Bacon, M.D. et al.*[10] the Court found the plaintiff's expert was not qualified to testify because the expert's affidavit did not demonstrate the he was sufficiently "familiar with the recognized standards of acceptable professional practice applicable to Defendants' specialties of hematology and orthopedics."[11] In this case the Plaintiff's expert was an emergency room specialist. The Court wrote, "Tenn. Code Ann. [section] 29-26-115(b) does not require that an expert witness practice the same specialty as the defendant;

nevertheless, the expert witness "must be sufficiently familiar with the standard of care of the profession or specialty and be able to give relevant testimony on the issue in question." *Cardwell,* 724 S.W.2d at 754. Therefore, "where an expert has a sufficient basis on which to establish familiarity with the defendant's field of practice, the expert's testimony may be accepted as competent proof even though he or she specializes or practices in another field." *McDaniel,* 2009 WL 1211335, at 8.[12] So long as the court deems the testimony relevant and the expert is deemed competent on the issue, the testimony will be allowed to reach the jury.

The fact that experts may testify against experts of another specialty or field is known as *fungibility* of experts and this is permitted under Tennessee's Medical Malpractice Act. The Court went on to say, "[a]lthough *fungibility* of experts is allowed, "where an expert is unfamiliar with the practice of another field and with its standard of care. . .," it would be inconsistent "with the terms or policy of the Medical Malpractice Act to permit. . .generalized evidence." (citing *Cardwell,* 724 S.W.2d at 754-55.[13]) In this case, the Court found the emergency room specialist did not demonstrate the requisite knowledge to comment on the standard of care of an orthopedic surgeon or a hematologist.

"Our courts have repeatedly rejected efforts to adopt a general standard of care to which medical doctors could testify, holding it is both contrary to the express provisions of Tenn. Code Ann. section 29-26-115(b) and a significant departure from the case law of this State. *Cardwell*, 724 S.W.2d at 754. As stated in *Cardwell*, Tenn. Code Ann. section 29-26-115(b) "was enacted in part to prevent further erosion of the competency requirements for expert witnesses in malpractice actions" and it would be inconsistent with the Medical Malpractice Act to permit "generalized" evidence to establish a standard of care in a locality. Id. at 754-55."[14] The Court of Appeals of Tennessee held that the lower court did not abuse its discretion in finding that the Plaintiff's expert witness was not competent to testify under the law. In *Cardwell*, the Defendant won.

Non-expert Testimony

What about testimony from witnesses who are not medical experts in a malpractice action? As is true in any trial, testimony from lay witnesses will be allowed so long as the evidence they are presenting is relevant to the case and is not unduly prejudicial to the defendant. The judge decides if the testimony would be prejudicial and what would cause "undue prejudice" is very subjective. For example, testimony that describes in detail, a clinical condition with extreme pain, a foul smelling wound, or gross drainage, may be considered prejudicial since it could cause an emotional response in a juror that could be unfair to the defendant.

In general, a lay person is allowed to testify about things they perceived through their own senses. Usually they testify as to what they saw and heard but, sometimes they testify to what they tasted, smelled, or touched. They are not allowed to testify in regards to what is considered expert opinion testimony.

In *Hensley v. Cerza*,[15] the patient was about to undergo a resection of a substernal goiter. The anesthesiologist had some difficulties in placing a double-lumen endotracheal tube and in an effort to pass the tube, a long laceration of the trachea was made. This was a life-threatening injury and a cardiothoracic surgeon had to be called in to repair the trachea through a right-sided thoracotomy. Obviously, this was a very serious injury. The patient brought suit alleging that the anesthesiologist breached the standard of care by using too much force to try and get the endotracheal tube into a too small trachea.

During the trial, the plaintiff put a nurse and a scrub technician on the stand and they testified they saw the defendant encounter resistance as he tried to place the tube and that he then used excessive force to push the tube through the resistance. Although the court allowed these witnesses to testify that they saw the anesthesiologist's hand "turn white" and "he grunted" as he pushed the tube in, it disallowed the testimony that he appeared to encounter quite a bit of resistance, that he increased the amount of force that he used, and that he finally crammed the tube down.

On appeal, the appellate court ruled the trial court had erred when it disallowed this testimony. The appellate court wrote, "Under Tenn. R. Evid. 701(a), lay opinion testimony is permissible if 'rationally based on the perception of the witness' and 'helpful to a clear understanding of the witness's testimony or the determination of a fact in issue.'"[16] The statements excluded by the trial court describe the amount of force used by [the anesthesiologist] in pushing the tube down [the patient's] throat."[17] Since both witnesses had seen other anesthesiologists place this kind of endotracheal tube, they had the knowledge and experience to compare this intubation to others. This evidence would have been based on their perceptions and would have been helpful to the jury in understanding what happened during the intubation. Thus, the testimony, by law, should have been allowed into evidence.

The trial court had excluded the testimony because they felt the "opinions regarding the force exerted and the resistance encountered by [the anesthesiologist] were expert opinions a nurse and scrub technologist were not qualified to offer."[18] The appellate court, in its disagreement, explained there is a difference between describing a perception of the amount of force applied and an opinion as to whether the amount of force was too much or within the standard of care. "Lay opinion is proper as to the former, but not as to the latter."[19] The appellate court ruled that the testimony of the nurse and the scrub technician should have been allowed to reach the jury.

However, the court also ruled the mistake of the trial court was not enough to affect the outcome of the case. The defendant won anyway. They reasoned the testimony allowed to be heard by the jury was sufficient to give them an accurate picture of the amount of force the anesthesiologist used in placing the tube. The plaintiff's expert witness testimony had testified it was his opinion too much force had been applied in placing the tube and the use of this force led to the tearing of the trachea. A breach of the standard of care and causation was presented to the jury, and they rejected it in drawing their conclusions.[20]

Vocabulary

tort
guilty
liable
liability producing
medical negligence
loss allocation
locality rule
remedy
pleadings

served
answer
discovery
due process
trier of fact
standard of care
causation issues
proximate or *legal cause*
substantially assist
Daubert v. Merrell Dow Pharmaceuticals
summary judgment
holding
Frye v. United States
generally accepted
grant certiorari
deception
Dialogue Concerning the Two Chief World Systems
Rules of Evidence
Markina Westmoreland et al. v. William L. Bacon, M.D. et al
Cardwell
McDaniel
fungibility
Hensley v. Cerza

Citations

[1] Waters JW. A Surgeon's Little Instruction Book. Quality Medical Publishing, Inc., St. Louis, Missouri, 1998.
[2] Black's Law Dictionary, Seventh Edition, Bryan Garner editor-in-chief.
[3] 509 U.S. 579(1993).
[4] *Frye v. United States*, 54 App. D.C. 46, 47, 293 F.1013,1014 (1923).
[5] Id.
[6] Id.
[7] Federal Rules of Evidence, Rule 402.
[8] Federal Rules of Evidence, Rule 702.
[9] *Cardwell v. Bechtol*, 724 S.W.2d 739, 754 (Tenn. 1987).
[10] *Westmoreland v. Bacon, M.D.*, No. M2009-02643-COA-R3-CV Filed January 31, 2011.
[11] Id. at 5.
[12] Id at 7.
[13] Id. at 8.
[14] Id.
[15] In the Court of Appeals of Tennessee at Nashville, May 13, 2010, No. M2009-01860-COA0R3-CV Filed August 25, 2010.
[16] Id. p.5.
[17] Id.
[18] Id.
[19] Id.
[20] Id. p. 9

Chapter 2: Negligence

Ordinary Negligence

The distinction between ordinary negligence and medical malpractice is important but not always an easy distinction to make. Under Tennessee law, medical malpractice has specific requirements that must be met by the plaintiff that are not needed under an ordinary negligence cause of action. These include the three-year *statute of repose*, the *notice requirements*, *a certificate of good faith*, and the need for *expert testimony* on the elements needed to prove malpractice.

Sometimes, plaintiffs file a *cause of action* alleging ordinary negligence and the courts have found the claims to really be for medical malpractice. When this happens, the plaintiff is at risk for losing the case at a summary judgment based on the fact they don't have expert testimony to support the claim or because the *statute of repose* has run out. Now, with the new notice requirements for a medical malpractice claim, the plaintiff is also at risk of having the case thrown out because they did not provide the *implicated health providers* with written notice sixty days before the suit was filed, or for failing to file a certificate of good faith with the complaint.[21]

In *Graniger v. Methodist Hospital Healthcare Systems, Inc.*[22] the plaintiff presented to the hospital with a chief complaint of pain and swelling of the legs. After being examined by a physician, she fell while trying to get off of the examining table and broke her wrist. A suit was filed alleging ordinary negligence, not malpractice. The court disagreed and without the required expert testimony, the plaintiff lost. The court held that the main issue was whether or not the patient needed assistance in getting off of the table and that issue was based on her medical condition. As such, it was a medical question beyond the usual knowledge base of an ordinary person.

The court said, "Medical malpractice cases typically involve a medical diagnosis, treatment or other scientific matters. The distinction between ordinary negligence and malpractice turns on whether the acts or omissions complained of involve a matter of medical science or art requiring specialized skills not ordinarily possessed by lay persons or whether the conduct complained of can instead be assessed on the basis of common everyday experience of the trier of fact."[23]

In *Johnsey v. Northbrooke Manor, Inc.*,[24] the plaintiff filed suit against the nursing home where her husband was a resident, after he either fell, or was dropped, while bathing. The nursing home argued the case was one of medical negligence and the plaintiff could not prove the elements needed under this standard. The trial court awarded the summary judgment.

The appellate court agreed the case was one of alleged malpractice because the support and care needed in bathing this type of patient was based on his medical condition (severe dementia). However, they disagreed with the summary judgment holding that there was enough expert testimony as to causation and standard of care that the case should have gone to the jury for a decision.[25] The decision of the circuit court was reversed and the case was *remanded* – returned to the lower court for reconsideration.

In *Katrina Martins v. Williamson Medical Center*,[26] the patient, who had just given birth to her second child, fell while walking across her hospital room. She sustained severe injuries to her head and face. The plaintiff filed suit alleging the employees of the hospital were negligent in permitting the patient to walk unassisted and were also negligent in letting her fall to the floor.

The hospital filed a *Motion to Dismiss* the complaint stating the *cause of action* was based on medical malpractice and failed to meet the requirements of the Tennessee Medical Malpractice Act. The trial court agreed and granted the *Motion to Dismiss*.

The plaintiff appealed, but the appellate court agreed with the trial court. Relying on the complaint from the plaintiff, the appellate court said, "The complaint alleges facts relating to services requiring specialized skill and training, such as recognizing the potential for a post-delivery fall and preventing injuries there; the duty attendant to such services is the professional duty arising from the rendition of medical care covered by the malpractice act."[27] Since the assessment of a post-delivery patient's ability to walk without assistance requires specialized skill and training that is not ordinarily possessed by lay persons, this case was one of medical negligence.[28]

Physicians and nurses are not alone when it comes to risk in medical negligence cases. If this is not recognized by plaintiffs, they can lose their case if they deem it to be ordinary negligence and they're wrong. In *Holt v. City of Memphis*[29] the court held the *standard of care* for paramedics needed to be established by expert testimony. In *Holt*, a patient in respiratory distress refused to be transported to the hospital. The plaintiff, in this case the patient's son, later alleged the paramedics were obligated to transport his mother to the hospital despite her objections, because she was in respiratory distress and there was a state regulation that said patients in respiratory distress, over the age of fifty-five, *should* be transported to the hospital. The plaintiff relied on this regulation to prove his case.

The court noted the regulation didn't state the patient *must* be transported even though she refused. The defendant's expert testified the paramedics cannot force a competent patient to be transported to the hospital under the applicable *standard of care*. Since plaintiff had no expert to rebut the *standard of care* issue, they lost.[30]

In *Mooney v. Sneed,* the Tennessee Supreme Court defined *health care practitioners* to be anyone who is subject to being sued for medical malpractice.[31] As a corollary, the appellate court of Tennessee ruled that all claims against *health care practitioners* are subject to the stringent requirement of needing expert witnesses to testify as to standard of care and causation such as in *Holt v. City of Memphis*.[32]

This doesn't mean a *health care practitioner* can never be sued under an ordinary negligence theory. Plaintiffs and their attorneys need to be prepared for the court to decide either way. Although plaintiff's attorneys tend to err on the side of retaining expert witnesses on any claims which involve health care providers, there are still situations where the defendant can be sued under an ordinary negligence theory.

In *Peete v. Shelby County Health Care Corp.*,[33] the plaintiff brought suit after she was injured when a portion of an orthopedic suspension bar fell on her head while a hospital worker was dismantling it. The employee was not actually doing anything to the patient so there was no need to exercise a medical judgment which would have triggered the need for expert testimony. In this case, the court agreed that this act was a matter of ordinary negligence.[34]

Res Ipsa Loquitur and Prima Facie

Res ipsa loquitur is Latin meaning *the thing speaks for itself*. In torts, it is the doctrine providing that, in some circumstances, the mere fact of an accident's occurrence raises an inference of negligence so as to establish a *prima facie* case.[35] *Prima facie* is the common law doctrine of the minimal amount of evidence that the plaintiff must show in order to get his case into court. *Res ipsa*, on the other hand, means the facts are so compelling the plaintiff does not need to show any more facts in order to shift the burden of proof on to the defendant.

In medical malpractice, *res ipsa* doctrine applies to the cases where it seems pretty obvious a negligent act occurred. The instrument or lap pad left in the abdomen after an operation is the classic example. For this type of event, expert testimony usually isn't needed for standard of care or causation issues as the jury with common sense and past experience can infer the event was caused by the defendant's negligence.

In order to invoke the doctrine of *res ipsa loquitur*, the plaintiff must show that the injury was of a type that would not ordinarily occur unless someone has been negligent. This inference of negligence doesn't mean that there are no other possible causes of the injury, but the plaintiff only needs to show that it is the most probable cause.

The exact nature of the act that caused the injury doesn't need to be proven. For example, if a lap pad is left in the abdomen after an abdominal exploration, it won't matter if it was put in by the surgeon, a resident, or a nurse. It is sufficient to show the event would not have occurred unless someone on the operating team had been negligent.

The next element the plaintiff must show under the doctrine of *res ipsa loquitur* is the plaintiff's injury must have been caused by some instrument or condition that was under the *exclusive* control of the defendant. In medical malpractice cases, this isn't a difficult element to prove.

Some state courts have removed the requirement of exclusive control because there are situations where it's unknown who actually caused the injury, yet as a matter of fundamental fairness, *res ipsa* should apply. In *Ybarra v. Spangard*,[36] Ybarra, the plaintiff, was admitted to the hospital with a diagnosis of appendicitis. The surgeon assigned to

Mr. Ybarra, Dr. Spangard, performed an appendectomy. After the operation, Ybarra developed sharp pain between the neck and right shoulder and went on to develop paralysis and atrophy. Ybarra brought suit based on *res ipsa loquitur* against the physicians and the nurses, all of whom may have had a role in positioning him for the operation.

The defendants argued *res ipsa loquitur* didn't apply since there was no assertion that any particular defendant was the cause of the harm as there were several people and instrumentalities involved. Since any of them could have been the cause of the injury, they felt the *res ipsa* doctrine could not apply. The trial court agreed with the defendants.

On appeal, the judgment was reversed. The appellate court held the doctrine of *res ipsa loquitur* does apply when a plaintiff undergoing a medical procedure sustains an injury to a body part as long as it's a body part not undergoing treatment.

In California, neither the number of defendants nor their relationship to the plaintiff will determine if the doctrine of *res ipsa loquitur* applies. If the patient is unconscious and he sustains an injury in the course of his treatment, all parties who had control over the patient may be held accountable under the *res ipsa doctrine*.

By pleading the *res ipsa loquitur doctrine*, the plaintiff shifts the burden from himself to the defendants. The defendants would then have the burden of determining the negligent party.

The last element that the plaintiff must show under the *res ipsa* doctrine is he didn't do anything that contributed significantly to the act that caused the injury.

If the plaintiff is able to show the doctrine applies, it doesn't necessarily mean that the defendant has lost the case. This evidence is only circumstantial and the defendant will have the opportunity to show he wasn't the cause of the event and, therefore, was not negligent.

In the case of the lap pad left after an abdominal exploration, if the pad was left in to help control bleeding from a lacerated liver with the surgeon planning to re-explore and remove the pad after the bleeding had been controlled, this wouldn't be a negligent act. If the lap pad was left in during a subsequent operation and the defendant could prove the lap pad wasn't in the abdomen after his operation, he could prove the negligent act wasn't his. A simple radiograph of the abdomen after the first operation would suffice so long as the lap wasn't seen in the film.

The point of these examples is to show how the doctrine of *res ipsa loquitur* shifts the burden of persuasion to the defendant to show he wasn't negligent. If the defendant did perform the act which subsequently caused the patient harm and he has no good explanation as to why it happened, it's time to think about settling the case before it gets to the jury.

Medical Negligence

Once it is determined the claim is being made for medical negligence, then the laws applying to medical malpractice will come into play. In Tennessee, the plaintiff must prove by a preponderance of the evidence that the defendants failed to act in accordance with the recognized standard of acceptable professional practice in the defendant's community or in a similar community at the time of the alleged negligence. The plaintiff must also prove that as a proximate result of the defendant's medical negligence, the plaintiff suffered injuries which would otherwise not have occurred.[37]

In a medical negligence action, expert testimony is necessary to establish what the standard of care is for a particular procedure or medical situation and whether or not the physician's—or other health care provider—actions met the standard in question. Expert testimony is also required to prove that it was the defendant's negligence which caused the patient's injuries. Remember, in an ordinary negligence cause of action, expert testimony is not required.

In Tennessee, the law specifies the requirements which must be met for a person to qualify as an expert witness. "No person in a health care profession requiring licensure under the laws of this state shall be competent to testify in any court of law to establish the facts required to be established by subsection (a), unless the person was licensed to practice in the state or a contiguous bordering state a profession or specialty which would make the person's expert testimony relevant to the issues in the case and had practiced this profession or specialty in one (1) of these states during the year preceding the date the alleged injury or wrongful act occurred."[38]

While many states may have recognized that there may be a national standard of care, Tennessee isn't one of them. Since medical education is relatively standardized with a uniform licensing exam and since most board certifications are national in nature, the movement away from a community standard is growing. Therefore, it is imperative your legal counsel is up-to-date on what constitutes the standard of care for your state.

The Tennessee Supreme Court has not made the change to national standard of care because the Court feels the change should come from the legislative body. Until that legislation is passed, the Court will continue to follow the law as it is written since it is constitutional.

Tennessee also has the unusual condition of requiring the expert witness to have been practicing in Tennessee or a bordering state. This puts a geographical burden on the plaintiff to find an expert to support his position. The requirement is also applicable to the defendant's experts, but there are usually more experts willing to testify for the defendants so it is not as much of a burden. It's easier to be a defendant's expert where you are not testifying against a fellow clinician.

In medicine, there are often different views on how to treat a particular medical condition. The law recognizes this *two schools of thought* situation. Just because one particular treatment is not the majority view of the community does not mean the standard of care is not being met. In *Gresham v. Ford*, the court stated, "where two or more schools of thought exist among competent members of the medical profession concerning proper medical treatment for a given ailment, each of which is supported by responsible medical authority, it is not malpractice to be among the minority in a given city who follow one of the accepted schools."[39]

It is wise to keep the *two schools of thought* doctrine in mind when opposing attorneys are questioning their expert witnesses. Some expert witnesses have stated the standard of care is what the "majority" of physicians would do in the same or similar circumstances, but this isn't the definition of standard of care. The standard of care is what a "reasonable" practitioner would do if faced with the same or similar circumstances. The lawyers know the definition, but the witnesses don't. Lawyers who are using the expert to support their case will often conveniently ignore this misstatement of the law in hopes of getting it to the jury without challenge. A medical practitioner named as a defendant would be wise to not let this statement go unchallenged. You can use this mistake to your advantage as it will reflect poorly on the quality of the witness. Always stay alert in case your attorney is not.

The plaintiff also has the burden of proving that it was the breach of the standard of care which led to his injuries. Expert testimony is also required to prove this *causation* element in a malpractice action.

Gross Negligence

There are cases where a medical expert witness has claimed the defendant was *grossly negligent*. In this context they were trying to emphasize the defendant was very negligent. What they didn't understand is the law actually defines *gross negligence* to mean "[a] conscious, voluntary act or omission in reckless disregard of a legal duty and of the consequences to another party, who may typically recover exemplary damages. Other terms used for gross negligence are reckless negligence; wanton negligence; willful negligence."[40] In the many cases where this term was used, it's clear the witness did not really mean the defendant was intentionally trying to harm the patient, but that's exactly how the law looks at it.

When this misuse of words occurs, it's rare the plaintiff's attorney tries to correct the witness. Normally it is because it opens the door for the plaintiff to try for *exemplary damages* – damages which are intended to punish and therefore act as a deterrent to a defendant who acted deceitfully, with malice, or with recklessness. It's basically saying the defendant was intentionally trying to hurt the patient. The damages now in play may be significantly higher than the damages of the usual medical malpractice suit which is usually limited to costs and pain and suffering.

In some states, exemplary damages may triple the amount of the award and may even make the defendant liable for the costs which exceed the coverage of the malpractice insurance. The malpractice carrier may only cover for negligence and not gross negligence.

In one particular case, the plaintiff's attorney made a threat to amend his original complaint to include an allegation of gross negligence. In this instance, he was trying to get the defendant to settle so the defendant would not be liable for the exemplary damages that wouldn't have been covered by his malpractice carrier. It made sense to settle for the upper limits of his malpractice coverage so as not to be at risk of what could have been very high, bankruptcy-causing out-of-pocket costs. Fortunately for the defendant in this case, the amendments were never made as the resulting judicial hearing would have made the plaintiff look bad in front of the judge.

Clearly, the defendant needs to read the deposition transcripts and the allegations closely and he should communicate with his attorney if he comes across any allegation stating his actions were grossly negligent. Steps can be taken to get these words clarified or even stricken by the judge at a separate hearing so the risk of being liable for these exemplary damages will be off the table.

Forty-three states and the District of Columbia do allow for punitive damages in a malpractice action. Five states do not allow for punitive damages in any negligence action. Illinois and Oregon, for example, don't allow for punitive damages in malpractice actions. Know what your state allows and doesn't allow. This will help you greatly when you are named as a defendant.

In states where punitive damages are allowed, most require the standard of proof be by *clear and convincing* evidence which is a higher burden than the *preponderance of the evidence* burden which is present for the plaintiff in a regular malpractice action. In Colorado, the burden on the plaintiff is even higher in that gross negligence needs to be proven by the *beyond a reasonable doubt* standard which is usually reserved for a criminal action.

In the *burden of persuasion*, the level of evidence that must be proven for various actions is a matter of law. In the *preponderance of evidence* standard, the plaintiff must convince the *trier of fact*, either a judge or a jury, *by a more likely than not* standard of their case. The plaintiff only needs to convince the jury that there is over a 50% chance the defendant acted in such a manner as to be liable for malpractice.

The *clear and convincing* standard which most states require to prove *gross negligence* is a much higher burden—it means the defendant must be about 80% likely to have committed the act. The most stringent burden of persuasion is the *beyond a reasonable doubt* standard which is usually the standard in a criminal action where the defendant is at risk of losing his freedom or even his life.

Vocabulary

statute of repose
notice requirements
a certificate of good faith
expert testimony
cause of action
implicated health provider
Graniger v. Methodist Hospital Healthcare Systems, Inc.
Johnsey v. Northbrooke Manor, Inc.
remanded

Katrina Martins v. Williamson Medical Center
Motion to Dismiss
Holt v. City of Memphis
standard of care
Mooney v. Sneed
health care practitioners
Peete v. Shelby County Health Care Corp.
Res ipsa loquitur
prima facie
exclusive
Ybarra v. Spangard
nonsuit
res ipsa doctrine.
two schools of thought
Gresham v. Ford
gross negligence
exemplary damages
clear and convincing
preponderance of the evidence
beyond a reasonable doubt
burden of persuasion

Citations

[21] Tenn. Code Ann. section 29-26-122.
[22] *Graniger v. Methodist Hospital Healthcare Systems, Inc.,* No. 02A01-9309-CV-00201, 1994 WL 496781 (Tenn.Ct.App.)
[23] Id.
[24] *Johnsey v. Northbrooke Manor, Inc.,* No. W2008-01118-COA-R3-CV.
[25] Id.
[26] *Katrina Martins, et al. v. Williamson Medical Center,* No. M2010-00258-COA-R3-CV (Tenn.Ct.App. 2010).
[27] Id.
[28] Id.
[29] *Holt v. City of Memphis,* No. W2000-00913-COA-R3-CV, 2001 WL 846081 (Tenn. Ct. App.).
[30] Id.
[31] *Mooney v. Sneed,* 30 S.W.3d, 304, 307-08 (Tenn. 2000).
[32] *Holt v. City of Memphis,* 2001 WL 846081 (Tenn. Ct. App.)
[33] *Peete v. Shelby County Health Care Corp.,* 938 S.W.2d 693, 696 (Tenn.Ct.App. 1996).
[34] Id.
[35] Black's Law Dictionary, Bryan Garner, editor-in-chief.
[36] *Ybarra v. Spangard,* 154 P.2d 687 (Cal.1944).
[37] Tenn.Code Ann. Section 29-26-115.
[38] Id.
[39] *Gresham v. Ford,* 241 S.W.2d, 408 (Tenn. 1951).
[40] Id.

Chapter 3:
Duty Owed

One of the elements that must be proven in a malpractice action is the *duty owed* by the practitioner to the plaintiff. It is fairly obvious the healthcare provider must have a duty to the patient but history shows this wasn't always the case. In fact, a duty was not owed unless there was a contract. If there was no contract, the doctor—or other health care provider—did not have to take care of a patient even if it was an emergency.

In the case of *Hurley v. Eddingfield* from the Indiana Supreme Court in 1901,[41] Charlotte Burk, the patient, was being taken care of during her pregnancy by her family doctor, George Eddingfield. When Burk went into labor, she had complications and was seriously ill. Dr. Eddingfield was notified, but he refused to come. A messenger was sent several times to Dr. Eddingfield to notify him of the grave condition of both Ms. Burk and the baby and they even tendered him payment for his fee. Without any reason whatsoever, Dr. Eddingfield refused to come to her aid. In fact, there was nothing going on at the time that prevented Dr. Eddingfield from coming. Burk and her baby both died and their heirs sued.

The court in the late 1800s ruled there was no duty for Eddingfield to care for this woman and unborn child because there was no contract between the parties even though he was the family doctor and was taking care of her during her pregnancy. Today, this isn't a contract law issue and there are statutes, precedent, and licensure requirements which would make Eddingfield's actions indefensible. Now when a court or legislature says a doctor must take care of a patient in need, they are generally relying on what they feel is best for society as a whole. This is a great example of how the expectations of society have changed in regards to the duties of medical professionals over the years.

In a malpractice case, the plaintiff must still prove the health care practitioner owed him a *duty of care*. This is a required element in a malpractice action and, like the other required elements, must be proven by a preponderance of the evidence standard. As professionals, physicians and nurses owe a duty of care to their patients to act in such a way as to meet the standard of care of their profession. In Tennessee, there is an added requirement to meet the standard of care of like professionals in the same or similar community where the treatment is being performed.

In a malpractice action today, the *duty of care* element is rarely litigated because, in most cases, once a practitioner has agreed to take care of a patient, they have implicitly agreed to the duty to provide competent care. They have agreed to perform in such a way as to reasonably ensure no harm will come to the patient under their care. In a sense, they have agreed to do what a reasonable provider would do if faced with the same or similar circumstances i.e., they will not act negligently. By today's standards, Eddingfield would have to render care to his patient with whom he had an ongoing doctor-patient relationship.

Though rare, a practitioner can be confronted with the scenario where he has not yet agreed to care for a particular patient when something happens. In *Millard v. Corrado*,[42] a surgeon was sued by a patient that he never took care of. On November 5, 1994, 63-year-old Millard was involved in a motor vehicle accident. Dr. Corrado was the general surgeon on call for the Audrain Medical Center (AMC). Unfortunately for Ms. Millard, Dr. Corrado had assigned his duties to an orthopedic surgeon, Dr. Ben Jolly, so that he could go to an American College of Surgeons local meeting. Dr. Jolly did not have privileges to do general surgery. Dr. Corrado had not notified anyone else that he would not be taking call.

Ms. Millard's accident occurred 14 miles from AMC and 25 miles from the University of Missouri Medical Center. At the scene of the accident, the emergency medical technicians were not able to measure a blood pressure or feel a pulse so they chose to transport Ms. Millard to the nearest hospital which was Audrain. The EMTs arrived on the scene of the accident at 10:28 a.m. They arrived at Audrain at 11:07am. At Audrain, intravenous fluids were started and a chest radiograph was obtained. The chest film showed an increased density in the left chest which was felt to be a hemothorax. The emergency room physician examined Ms. Millard and he concluded there was intra-abdominal bleeding for which a general surgery consult was indicated.

Two pages went out for Dr. Corrado but they weren't answered. At 12:00 noon, air transport was requested so as to expedite a transfer to the University of Missouri, but the helicopter was grounded by inclement weather. At 12:07 p.m., Dr. Jolly came to the ER, saw the patient, and agreed she needed an abdominal exploration—but he didn't have the privileges to perform the surgery.

At 12:23 p.m., Dr. Corrado responded to the previous pages. In discussing the situation over the phone, Dr. Corrado agreed that the patient should be transferred to the University of Missouri. Transportation arrangements were made and Ms. Millard arrived around 1:45 p.m. to the University of Missouri. She underwent operative exploration at 2:15 p.m., about 4 hours after the accident. In the operating room, surgeons removed her left kidney, gall bladder, part of the colon, and part of the small bowel.

Ms. Millard subsequently brought suit alleging that "as a direct and proximate result of the delay in treatment caused by Dr. Corrado's absence, (she) sustained aggravation of the injuries she sustained in the accident and additional serious injuries."[43]

Defendant Corrado filed a motion for summary judgment because, he argued, he was entitled to a judgment as a matter of law because the plaintiff had failed to establish there was ever a patient-physician relationship. Without the doctor-patient relationship, Dr. Corrado's stance was he had no *duty of care* to Ms. Millard. Without a *duty of care* established by Ms. Millard, she could never prove that necessary element and, thus, could never win a malpractice action against Dr. Corrado. Dr. Corrado's position seemed pretty solid and the trial court agreed. The court granted the motion and entered a judgment in favor of Dr. Corrado.

Every party involved in a suit has the right to appeal a trial court's decision and this is exactly what Ms. Millard did. On appeal, the Missouri appellate court ruled in favor of Ms. Millard. The court held a duty is created by the physician who agrees to be available without reservation to treat emergency patients. The court stated that the public policy of the State of Missouri and the foreseeability of harm to patients in the position of Ms. Millard support the recognition of a duty flowing from Dr. Corrado to Ms. Millard.[44]

The appellate court further stated that "on call" physicians owe a duty to reasonably foreseeable emergency patients to provide notice to the hospital when they will be unable to respond to calls. The court felt the duty to provide adequate notice will not have a detrimental impact on the ability of hospitals to attract physicians to accept "on call" assignments.[45] The appellate court reversed the judgment of the trial court and sent the case back for further proceedings, i.e., a trial for the malpractice claim raised by Ms. Millard.

In a concurring opinion, one of the judges referred to the Restatement (Second) of Torts, Section 324A, which states, "(o)ne who undertakes, gratuitously or for consideration, to render services to another which he should recognize as necessary for the protection of a third person or his things, is subject to liability to the third person for physical harm resulting from his failure to exercise reasonable care to protect his undertaking."[46]

Under this section, it was clear the plaintiffs produced substantial evidence showing Dr. Corrado's actions led to a delay in Ms. Millard's care which did increase her risk of harm. As such, the appeals court concluded that Dr. Corrado was not entitled to a summary judgment.

In coming to its decision, the court took into consideration many public policy factors. These factors included: a goal to prevent future harm; the consideration of costs and who would be in the best position to take on the costs; the economic burdens placed on the actors and the community; the moral blame that society places on the conduct in question; the foreseeability of harm and the degree of certainty that the protected person suffered the injury; and the social consensus that the interest is worth protecting.

In this particular case, the court decided that Dr. Corrado, in fact, owed a *duty of care* to Ms. Millard and this duty was contractual in nature. AMC expected the "on call" physicians to respond in a reasonable time, i.e. thirty minutes. "On call" physicians also owed a duty to AMC to notify the hospital if they were unavailable to take the call. Since physicians were not required to take call, the duty to be available to treat was based solely on the physician's pre-existing contractual obligation to the hospital.

With the possible legal ramifications of taking call, many physicians only agree to take call for pay. The hospitals are required under the Emergency Medical Treatment and Active Labor Act (EMTALA) to have physicians available to provide *stabilizing* care. In order to meet their statutory requirements, some hospitals pay over one thousand dollars per day just to have a surgeon take call.

Some hospitals require their physicians take call in order to be privileged at the hospital. Many physicians will ignore this responsibility or just work at hospitals that do not require call responsibilities. Those physicians just starting their practice often will be willing to take call as a means to build their practice. This is a good financial incentive but, as call pay became an issue, these new practitioners have tried to participate in call for pay. The bottom line is even without the establishment of a patient-physician relationship, a duty can still be present for a physician who is taking call at a hospital.

There are other states that have followed the same reasoning as Missouri. It would be wise for any physician whose name is on a call list to learn what his duty will be to the yet unknown patients he may be called to see. Check the rules/guidelines of your state.

Vocabulary

duty owed
Hurley v. Eddingfield
duty of care
Millard v. Corrado
stabilizing

Citations

[41] *Hurley v. Eddingfield,* 59 N.E. 1058, (Ind. 1901).
[42] *Millard v. Corrado,* Mo. App.E.D (1999)
[43] Id.
[44] Id.
[45] Id.
[46] Restatement (Second) of Torts, section 324A.

Chapter 4: Standard of Care

In order to win a malpractice action under a negligence theory, the plaintiff must show, by a preponderance of the evidence, four things. First, the plaintiff (patient) must show the defendant (health care practitioner) had a duty to the plaintiff. This is pretty clear cut as the plaintiff is often the patient of the defendant and the duty is usually conceded. Second, the plaintiff must show the defendant acted in a negligent manner—a manner that was below the *standard of care* for the defendant. Most malpractice actions are won or lost on the second element—proving the *standard of care* and proving the defendant, by acting negligently, didn't meet the standard. Third, the plaintiff must show he suffered an injury. Finally, the plaintiff must prove that the injury was due to the negligent act of the defendant—in the law this is known as the *legal cause, or proximate cause*, of the injury.

The *standard of care* in the medical malpractice setting is what a reasonable health care provider—usually a physician—of the same specialty would do if faced with the same or similar circumstances. Some states have decided the professional standard would be in terms of the average practitioner in the specialty of the defendant. Other states have decided the standard would be what the minimally competent practitioner would do. The states that follow the latter doctrine note that some doctors with less than the average knowledge, education, experience, training, and skill may still be competent and qualified to practice without negligence so that is the standard the defendant should be held to.

In general, you, as the defendant, will be compared to your peers of the same specialty. In some states like Tennessee, there is also a community standard whereby the practitioner will be held to the standard of his community or a similar community. This locality rule is meant to help protect physicians practicing in rural communities which may not have the facilities and support personnel present in the big cities.

At a recent continuing legal education seminar dealing with malpractice theories and strategies, the audience was made up of lawyers with only one physician. One of the presenters, a well-known plaintiff's attorney in Memphis, told the audience to look for deviations in guidelines and use those deviations as evidence the *standard of care* was not met. The example he used was the Advanced Cardiac Life Support (ACLS) guideline for the initial management of the acute coronary syndrome. In the guideline, a patient who presents with an acute coronary syndrome should be treated with four things noted by the acronym MONA: **m**orphine for the pain; **o**xygen so that more oxygen will be available for delivery to the oxygen starved heart muscle; **n**itrates to increase blood flow to the heart muscle; and **a**spirin to prevent the platelets from plugging up the coronary any more than it already was when the patient presented.

The plaintiff's attorney stated as far as he was concerned, any health care provider who did not follow the MONA paradigm was liable for malpractice because this is the *standard of care*.

Remember, by law the *standard of care* is what a reasonable health care provider would do if faced with the same or similar circumstances. If the patient in question was not the ideal patient for whom the paradigm was written, then, maybe, a reasonable provider may not follow the paradigm.

It may be contraindicated to give the patient morphine if his blood pressure is low or he is allergic to morphine. You may not want to give extra oxygen to a patient with chronic obstructive pulmonary disease (COPD) whose respiratory drive is dependent on low oxygen. If you give him supplemental oxygen, he may stop breathing altogether.

As for nitrates, if you have a television, you may have seen the commercials advertising for drugs used to treat erectile dysfunction, which warn the patient these drugs may be dangerous if the patient is already taking nitrates as this could lead to a dangerous fall in the blood pressure.

The issues are similar for aspirin; you should not give aspirin to a patient who has gastrointestinal bleeding since the aspirin may make the bleeding worse, and you should not give aspirin to a patient who is allergic to that medication. The point is the paradigms that are written for various disease states are for the *ideal* patient who presents with a particular disease. It's rare to see an *ideal* patient with anything, and this is where medical judgment comes into play.

If health care could be handled by paradigms, there would be no need for physicians to take a medical history, do a physical exam, order blood work and other tests, and come to a diagnosis so appropriate therapy can be started. Sometimes, even after examining the patient, doing the blood work and getting the results of tests, physicians are still uncertain what needs to be done. When this occurs, they need to give themselves a little time to think about the case — to formulate a plan for the patient. During this treatment planning stage, your knowledge, education, training, experience, and skill come into play. The law recognizes this as *judgment* and the law gives this due respect.

This is also why the law says nothing about paradigms in defining the *standard of care*. Most of the guidelines have disclaimers which concede that the ultimate judgment as to the care of an individual patient should be made by the provider who has the information of the specific circumstances relating to their patient. As such, the management of the patient may not follow the guidelines and yet still be appropriate. Plaintiff's attorneys usually ignore the disclaimers.

The burden of proof is on the plaintiff to show the *standard of care* was not met. In order to do this, he must get an expert to testify as to what the *standard of care* is, and also that the defendant, by acting negligently, did not meet the *standard of care*.

Defendants must also state what they believe the *standard of care* is and they must also show they met the standard. For the defendants, this proof is usually pretty easy to obtain. First, there are usually many experts willing to testify on behalf of defendant practitioners. Also, the defendant himself may testify as to the standard because he has the knowledge, education, training, experience, and skill to be deemed qualified to state what the standard is. Because the burden of proof is on the plaintiff, the defendant may not even need to present any expert testimony and may not even need to testify himself if the plaintiff is not able to meet his burden.

Causation

One of the things a plaintiff must prove during a malpractice action is that the breach of the *standard of care* was the *legal* cause of the injury to the patient. In the law, the *legal* cause is often called the *proximate cause* – meaning the cause was legally sufficient to result in liability.

Causation is sometimes downplayed in a malpractice action and this can be a critical mistake on the plaintiff's part. The plaintiff has the burden of proof to show that as a proximate result of the defendant's negligent action or omission, the plaintiff suffered injuries that otherwise would not have occurred. This proof requires the testimony of an expert witness who must testify that the alleged negligence *more probably than not* caused the plaintiff's injuries.[47]

The plaintiff's expert witness must also state that the injury occurred to a *reasonable degree of medical certainty* meaning that it was more likely than not to be a result of this breach. Testimony that merely suggests that the plaintiff would have had a better chance for a better result will not be enough to meet the burden of proof on this causation element.[48]

"[P]roof of causation equating to a *possibility*, a *might have*, a *could have*, is not sufficient, as a matter of law, to establish the required nexus between the plaintiff's injury and the defendant's tortuous conduct by a preponderance of the evidence in a medical malpractice case. *Causation* in fact is a matter of probability, not possibility, and in a medical malpractice case, such must be shown to a reasonable degree of medical certainty."[49]

Merely testifying to a reasonable degree of medical certainty stating the injuries were a result of the breach of the *standard of care* isn't enough to establish the necessary link which is required by law. Be aware of the expert who uses the proper legal words to establish the case. He was probably instructed to use these words by the plaintiff's attorney. The expert must also provide some reasonable basis for the *causation*.

The Court in *Taylor v. Jackson-Madison County General Hospital* wrote, "Although [the expert] initially testified to a reasonable degree of medical certainty that the conduct, acts, and/or omissions of the Defendant's employees caused [the plaintiff's] injuries, we find, upon closer examination of [the expert's] deposition, that [he] ultimately failed to establish *causation* to a reasonable degree of medical certainty that any of these alleged breaches of duty actually caused the subsequent harm to [the plaintiff]. Specifically, on cross examination, [the expert] failed to sufficiently link the alleged negligent acts by Defendant's employees to the injuries suffered by [the plaintiff] to meet the required burden of proof."[50]

The expert in *Taylor* was trying to say that giving a drug sooner would have increased the chance for a better result. This *better chance* theory is not enough, in general, to prove *causation* because it is unlikely to rise to the level of more probable than not. Keep this in mind when you are listening to the expert's testimony and be sure to discuss the *better chance* theory with your attorney if the issue arises.

Foreseeability

To be considered the *legal cause*, the injury that occurred must have been foreseeable as a consequence of the breach of the standard of care. This foreseeability factor has long been a mainstay in America's jurisprudence whereby it was deemed to be unfair to hold someone liable for the results of an event that he could not have reasonably foreseen. In other words, it would not be fair to punish someone for an event he could not have predicted.

The necessity of *foreseeability* dates back to *Palsgraf v. Long Island Railroad Co.*,[51] coming out of the New York Supreme Court. It was decided by a future Supreme Court justice Benjamin Cardozo. The details of Palsgraf are as follows: A passenger was rushing to get on a slowly moving train. Two guards, employees of the railroad, tried to help get the passenger onto the train—one pulling and one pushing. The guard's efforts to help the passenger caused a package that the passenger was holding to drop. Unfortunately, and unknown to the guards, the package contained fireworks which exploded when the package hit the platform. The shock of the explosion apparently caused a scale at the other end of the platform to fall down, although other reports say that a passenger who was startled may have knocked over the scales, which injured the Plaintiff, Mrs. Helen Palsgraf. Palsgraf sued the railroad alleging her injury resulted from the negligent acts of the employees. It should come as no surprise that she went after the railroad with its deep pockets as opposed to suing the passenger.

The trial court, on a verdict from a jury, found for Palsgraf. On appeal, the intermediate appeals court affirmed. The Long Island Rail Road appealed again. The Court of Appeals, which is the highest court in New York, reversed and dismissed Palsgraf's case. In what is now a classic decision written by Cardozo, and taught in all law schools, the court made clear that the relationship of the guard's action to Palsgraf's injury was too remote to make the railroad liable. In the opinion, Cardozo wrote "there was nothing in the situation to suggest to the most cautious mind that the parcel wrapped in newspaper would spread wreckage through the station. If the guard had thrown it down knowingly and willfully, he would not have threatened the plaintiff's safety, so far as appearances could warn him."[52]

It is the concept of *foreseeability* in tort law that will limit the liability to the consequences of an act that could not be reasonably predicted. Otherwise, the liability of an act could be far-reaching in scope as consequences could still be occurring although distanced in space and time. One should not be held liable for a result that could not have been foreseen.

Interestingly, three judges on the case did not agree with Cardozo. The dissenters argued that Palsgraf's injuries could be traced to the wrongs of the guards and that alone should be enough to find negligence. They did not believe *foreseeability* was a necessary element in proving a negligence action. Since their opinion was not the *holding*, it does not have the force of law and in fact, is considered to be wrong. One of the reasons judges write dissenting opinions is to provide a foundation for future courts to use in case they want to change the law with a new *holding*.

As for now, *foreseeability* is still a requirement to assess liability in a negligence action.[53] Even though Mrs. Palsgraf lost her case, her name lives on in American jurisprudence and her case is studied by all fledgling law students for its cause and verdict.

Sometimes plaintiffs will drop their case if the issue of *causation* turns out to be determinative. This happened with a morbidly obese patient who had a long history of recurrent pneumonias. During the work-up of one of his pneumonias, a CT scan was obtained which demonstrated an anterior mediastinal mass. The differential diagnosis included the "four Ts": teratoma, thymoma, thyroid tumors, and "terrible" lymphoma. Further evaluation led to the diagnosis of thymoma. Since it could not be determined whether the thymoma was malignant or not, the surgeon recommended and the patient agreed to undergo a resection via a sternal splitting incision, aka, median sternotomy. The thymoma was determined to be benign.

Unfortunately, several of the sternal wires which had been placed to reconnect the sternum, broke a few days after the operation. The usual course of events would be to take the patient back to the operating room to rewire the sternum. In this particular case, the surgeon chose to not repair the sternum and knowingly decided to let the healing proceed to a non-union. The patient was not informed of the possible consequences and the primary care providers were not informed of what to look for so that a rewiring could have been done if the possible complications were to occur.

About one year after the operation, a chest radiograph was obtained which, on the lateral view, showed that one of the wire fragments was pointing directly at the front wall of the heart. The surgeon was not aware of the findings of this radiograph.

Several weeks later, the patient started complaining of chest pain. Evaluation by his primary care providers included an electrocardiogram and cardiac enzymes, all of which were normal. No one considered that the wire pointing at the heart was a potential source of disaster until after the patient arrested and died. An autopsy showed that the right ventricle had been lacerated by the wire. The autopsy showed that this laceration had occurred over several days as there were cells at the site which take several days to show up. The wire was rubbing the heart and tearing it until the accumulated blood led to tamponade and death.

During the discovery phase of the lawsuit, the plaintiff learned from his experts that laceration of the heart from a broken sternal wire must be exceedingly rare as the experts had never heard of this happening before. A search of the surgical literature also failed to reveal a previously reported case of this happening. Since this complication had never happened before, how could it have been foreseeable? Even though it seemed inherently obvious a wire pointing at and in close proximity to the heart could lead to a cardiac laceration, it would have been difficult to convince the jury that the failure to rewire the sternum in a timely fashion was the legal cause of the patient's death. Remember, the plaintiff must prove all elements of the malpractice action in order to win. In this particular case they could prove that a duty was owed, a breach of the standard of care occurred, and that the patient suffered an injury, but they could not prove this particular injury was foreseeable; the plaintiff dropped the case.

A recent decision coming out of the Court of Appeals of Tennessee further clarifies the importance of *causation* in a malpractice action. In *Carol E. Miller v. Joel S. Birdwell, M.D. et. al.*,[54] the plaintiff alleged medical malpractice against three doctors who were involved in treating her ankle injury. The initial evaluation led to the diagnosis of an ankle sprain. They had obtained and reviewed ankle films in the usual projections and their initial reading was consistent with a sprain as they saw tissue swelling but no obvious fracture. As luck would have it, the treatment was the same for either a fracture or a sprain — they immobilized the ankle and gave her crutches and instructions to not bear any weight on the foot.

One week later, another set of ankle films was obtained. These films were read as a possible fracture of the calcaneous. She was then referred to an orthopedic surgeon who put her in a cast. All physicians involved in her care advised non-weight bearing which, apparently, she didn't follow. By not following the physician's instructions, the plaintiff had some comparative liability, but this issue was not addressed by the court as they were able to rule on causation alone.

The foot eventually had to be amputated. Of note, she was a diabetic and on dialysis for kidney failure, so there were other issues that could have led to the amputation. It was unclear from the legal opinion as to when the amputation occurred but a footnote says "... it may have been up to four years later."[55]

The defendant doctors each filed a motion for summary judgment but the trial court denied all of these motions. The defendants appealed. The defendant's argument centered on the issue of causation in that even if they missed seeing the fracture on the initial ankle films, the treatment was appropriate. In other words, even if there was a breach of the standard of care by not reading the films correctly, the patient was not harmed by the breach because the treatment was the same for a fracture or ankle sprain. Thus the breach is not what led to the amputation.

The defendants made affidavits asserting their claim. After the affidavits had been made alleging that the missed reading of the ankle films was not the proximate cause for the amputation, the burden shifted to the plaintiff to have her own expert testify otherwise. This contrary testimony would have shown that there was a dispute of material fact which would have forced the court to proceed to trial and this is what the trial court ruled.

On appeal, the appellate court ruled the plaintiff had failed to demonstrate, by expert testimony, that it was the breach of the standard of care which led to the amputation. All of the proffered expert testimony only alleged there was a breach, but there was no statement that the breach is what caused the amputation. As such, the appellate court ruled that the trial court was in error and the defendants were entitled to the summary judgment ruling. By not proving the causation element as was required in the malpractice action, the plaintiff lost the case.

Vocabulary

standard of care
legal cause
ideal
judgment
Causation
more probably than not
reasonable degree of medical certainty
Taylor v. Jackson-Madison County General Hospital
foreseeability
Palsgraf v. Long Island Railroad Co.
holding
Carol E. Miller v. Joel S. Birdwell, M.D. et. al.

Citations

[47] *Kilpatrick v. Bryant,* 868 S.W.2d 594, 602 (Tenn. 1993).
[48] Id.
[49] *Taylor v. Jackson-Madison County General Hospital,* 231 S.W.3d 361, 374 (Tenn. Ct. App. 2006)(citing *Kilpatrick v. Bryant,* 868 S.W.2d 594, 602 (Tenn. 1993).
[50] Id. at 375-76.
[51] *.Palsgraf v. Long Island Railroad.* 248 N.Y. 339; 162 N.E. 99
[52] Id.
[53] It is sometimes said that surgeons may be wrong but they are never in doubt.
[54] No. M2009-01730-COA-R9-CV- Filed June 23, 2010.
[55] Id. at p.2.

Chapter 5:
The Discovery Process

Service

When a patient or a patient's legal representative decides to sue a physician for malpractice, one of the first things they do is get a lawyer. If the lawyer agrees the patient may have grounds for initiating an action, they will file a complaint with the court of their choosing. Choosing a court in which to bring the suit is a strategic decision which may be based on differences in law, procedure, or a history of jury verdicts which have been favorable for plaintiffs.

A *complaint* is the initial pleading that will officially start the civil action, which in this case is a malpractice suit. In some jurisdictions, a *complaint* is called a petition. The *complaint*, which is filed with the court, will usually state the grounds for the patient's belief that *malpractice* has occurred, the reasons the court chosen has jurisdiction, and a demand for some form of *relief* from the court usually in the form of a monetary payment.

Once a *complaint* has been filed, it is incumbent for the court, as a state actor, to let the defendant know he is being sued. The reason for this notice requirement can be found in the Constitution of the United States either under the Fifth Amendment or the Fourteenth Amendment depending on whether the suit has been filed in Federal, Fifth Amendment, or State, Fourteenth Amendment, court. These amendments make it clear that a *property interest*, in this case money, cannot be taken by the Federal or State governments without *due process of law*. Even though it's really the plaintiff who is trying to take money from the defendant, since the courts are being used as the means of *taking* the money, the court, as a *state actor*, must abide by the rules found in the Constitution.

The Supreme Court of the United States has held that *due process* includes at least notice of the pending suit and a fair hearing. *Service* of the *complaint* on the defendant will fulfill the *notice* requirement. The requirements for adequate *service* vary among the states. They also vary in regards to what type of action is being taken by the plaintiff. For example, in the *malpractice* arena, Tennessee recently clarified that *service* can be personal or via mail. Personal *service* is pretty clear cut. If you are served with papers, you are stuck. It's hard to say you weren't given sufficient notice when a process server can certify that he hand delivered the papers to you. Mail service, on the other hand, was an area of confusion until recent laws have shed light on the areas of ambiguity.

In Tennessee, mailing the notice of a *malpractice action* will be enough to meet the *statute of limitations* and *repose* so long as it is done in compliance with the state statute. The statute requires the letter be sent to the provider's current business address and/or the address listed on the Tennessee Department of Health website for the provider. The letter should be sent by certified mail with a return receipt requested. The return receipt will be evidence that the letter was sent appropriately. A Certificate of Mailing by the United States Post Office will also provide sufficient proof that the papers were mailed. If the letter serving notice of the lawsuit comes back undelivered, the plaintiff must make one more effort to give notice to the defendant under the Tennessee law. However, the *statute of limitations* was extended by the first mailing. A *last chance* letter must be sent to the office where the provider last took care of the plaintiff. This letter has the same requirements of proof as the original mailings.

Since the laws dealing with notice are different from state to state, it is important that you have a lawyer deal with this critical aspect of the suit. Note exactly how you received the notice of the suit and be sure you note the exact day of notice. Your lawyer will need to have this information as it may serve as a means to have your case decided in your favor very early in the process; such as would occur after the statute of limitations has run out on the case. It is also absolutely critical to notify your malpractice carrier as soon as you receive the notice. There are time requirements for your response, usually thirty days, and it would be in your best interest for your lawyer to have the time he needs to make an appropriate response. If you decide to ignore what's happening in hopes that the lawsuit will disappear, a judgment will be made for the plaintiff and you may never have the chance to present a defense. These judgments will be reported to the National Practitioner Data Bank.

If the notice requirement of *due process* has been met, the process of the fair hearing then ensues. You are now heading to a trial of your peers, but before a trial, there will be *discovery* where both sides will try to find the facts needed to help their case before it gets to trial. Both parties will spend a great deal of time and money to learn the facts of the case.

Discovery

It used to be that the parties would go to trial without having the opportunity of knowing what information the opposing party had. Today, the modern rules of *Civil Procedure* allow for a more open discovery process whereby the parties will have ample opportunity to learn all of the facts relevant to the litigation long before the case ever gets to trial. In the Federal courts, the *Federal Rules of Civil Procedure* makes it a requirement for the parties to provide their opponent with the relevant documents they have in their possession. These documents must be handed over without the opposing party asking for them. Most state courts also allow for broad discovery which is designed to prevent one side from hiding relevant information from the other, but the information usually has to be requested before it is handed over. This, of course, requires that the requesting party has some knowledge of what they are looking for.

A party can further investigate information that their adversary may have by several means. All of these methods have requirements described under the rules of *civil procedure*. A party can interview the other party under oath during a proceeding called a *deposition*. They can present the opposing party with written questions called *interrogatories* which must be answered truthfully. They can demand that all documents and physical evidence relevant to the case be produced so that they can study it, and they can even require the opposing party to undergo a physical or psychiatric exam if it were likely to reveal relevant information.

Interrogatories

Shortly after you get notice that you are being sued, the plaintiff's attorney will send you a set of questions which you will be expected to answer. This is part of the pre-trial discovery process. You must answer the questions under oath and the answers you provide can be used as evidence at the trial.

It's very important you answer all of the questions and that they are answered in the time frame set by law, usually thirty days. Sometimes, the plaintiff's attorney who has prepared the questions will use words which can be used against the answering party, so it's critical your attorney is with you to help with formulating the answers.

"How often do you beat your wife?" is an example of a question whose premise assumes that wife-beating occurs. It may be appropriate to object to the questions as being irrelevant or too vague, lacking clarity, and it is even acceptable for you to claim an inability to answer if you don't have the information needed to answer appropriately. If you don't know the answer, say so and move on. Don't make up an answer that you think will help your case. The answers you give to the interrogatories must be truthful and if they aren't, you can be held accountable.

Most states put a limit on the number of questions that may be asked in the interrogatories so they can't be used as a means of oppressing or badgering the answering party. Even if the state has limits on the number of questions, the asking party can get a court's permission to ask more if they can show that there is a legitimate need to do so.

As soon as you receive the interrogatories, get them to your attorney so that he can respond in the specified time frame. Many defendants put off giving their lawyer the plaintiff's interrogatories because they hope the case will just go away. This rarely happens and you hurt your case by not getting your attorney these questions as soon as your receive them.

If the questions are related to documents that you may not have, it is acceptable for you to designate which documents have the answer. This will force the asking party to do the work necessary to find the answers in the documents themselves. You don't have to do the work for the side taking you to court.

If you do object to the question being asked, then you don't need to answer until the court rules on the validity of the question. However, you must document the objection. If you don't provide any objection or answer, the court may construe the question against you. For example, "On the day in question, did you negligently perform a hernia repair on Mr. Smith?" If you choose not to answer the question, the court may decide that you have admitted the negligence.

Good attorneys try to frame the questions to be as distinct and capable of a definite answer as possible. They try to write the questions so they can't be evaded by an unwilling witness. Leading questions should be avoided, but some lawyers do this on purpose hoping that the answering party will make a mistake that they can use to their advantage in the future.

Affidavits

An affidavit is "[a] voluntary declaration of facts written down and sworn to by the declarant before an officer authorized to administer oaths."[56]

Some evidence is submitted by affidavit and it is commonly used in pre-trial matters such as motions for summary judgment. The affidavit should have the date the statement was made, the address of the *declarant*, the *declarant's* signature or mark, and where the affidavit was made. If the statement is based on the *declarant's* information or belief, it should state the source of the information and the reasons that the *affiant* has to believe the information. With this information, the court should be able to draw its own conclusions as to its veracity. An affidavit based on **knowledge** of the *declarant* will have more weight than one based on information or belief.

An affidavit is considered to be a weak form of evidence because it's not written in court and the *declarant* is not subject to a cross-examination witnessed by the judge and jury. If the witness is present during the trial, they will be expected to testify and the affidavit will be inadmissible except to impeach the witness who says something at trial that contradicts what is in the affidavit.

There is no standard form or language that is required for an affidavit, but it's important the facts are clearly stated. There should be no legal arguments or unnecessary statements in the document. The *affiant* is responsible for the accuracy and the truth of the statement. If the statement is false in any part, the *affiant* could be prosecuted for perjury. As in all court proceedings, it's important to be absolutely truthful.

If the affidavit is determined to be admissible, it's not considered to be conclusive evidence of the facts purported to be true in the statement. The weight afforded this evidence is still up to the judge or jury to decide. Unless there is a statute in the jurisdiction stating otherwise, an oath affirming the truthfulness of the facts stated in the document must be given by the *affiant* to a proper official who is qualified to administer the oath.

Depositions

Any party in the malpractice action is allowed to take the sworn testimony of any witness, opposing party, or an expert expected to be used at the trial by the opposition.

The witness will be placed under oath to tell the truth and then the lawyers from each party will be allowed to ask questions. There is no judge present at the *deposition* so any objections will have to be ruled on at a later time. Usually, the objecting attorney will place the objection into the record and then the witness will be allowed to answer. If the objection is later sustained, the answer will not be allowed to be used at the trial.

The questions and answers at the *deposition* will be recorded by a court reporter and the transcript of the proceeding will be given to either party provided they pay the fee for the transcript. Some depositions are video recorded and the video can be played to the jury if the witness is unable to attend the trial. This is more effective than just having someone read the transcript to the jury. The jury can actually see the witness, evaluate his demeanor, the tone of voice and get a sense of the timing of the answers so as to get a better feel for the witness's credibility.

There are many ways the *deposition* can be used at the actual trial. It can be used to impeach the witness if he says something at trial that contradicts what he said at the *deposition*. It can be used to refresh the witness's memory as many trials occur years after the *discovery process* and, if the witness is not available, it can be read into the record so that the jury can hear it, or see it if a video recording was made.

Depositions are a great opportunity for an attorney to learn about the adversary's case, and get a feel for the performance and credibility of the witness. Although a majority of medical malpractice cases get resolved before they ever get to trial, it's rare for the resolution to occur before the depositions of the plaintiff, defendant, and the plaintiff's expert. If the plaintiff's expert isn't as knowledgeable as they could be it's unlikely that the plaintiff's attorney will be willing to take the case to trial and will push hard for a settlement. Remember, if he goes to trial and loses, he will take a financial beating, especially if he took the case on a contingency basis.

As a discovery tool, the *deposition* will also be useful in gathering information that may not be in the medical records, obtain useful admissions from the witness that you will not then have to elicit at trial, and box the witness in as to what they can say at trial. It is very common for the opposing attorney to close his questioning by asking the witness if there are any other issues that he will be testifying to at the trial. If the witness says "no" then he will not be allowed to bring up new issues at the trial unless the opposing attorney "opens the door" to new testimony by asking a question that he should not have asked—questions that are beyond the scope of what was asked at the deposition.

There is a great deal of strategy that goes into taking and defending *depositions*. Many experienced lawyers will get right to the heart of the matter and ask as few questions as possible to get the information they need so as to win their case—or at least have a good chance at a settlement. This "short and sweet" approach is possibly due to the fact that the witness, if it is the expert witness of the opposition, must be paid by the deposing attorney's side. Also, lawyers usually want answers only helpful to their cases and not waste time on answers that will not make a difference as to the outcome.

If you are involved in a malpractice action either as a defendant, expert witness, or as a plaintiff, you will probably be deposed. I cannot overemphasize the necessity that you answer honestly. This is paramount. If the opposing attorney can show that you're lying, your credibility will be destroyed and you should be prepared for some punishment by the court.

Besides being honest, there are other things to keep in mind during the deposition. Always be professional and polite. A *deposition* is stressful but you should maintain your cool and answer to the best of your ability. The jury knows that you are stressed and they will respect you more if they see you are being courteous—even to your adversary. Dress appropriately and be on time. Don't try to be funny or sarcastic with the opposing attorney. Every word you say is being recorded by the reporter and often the transcript is asked to be read back at trial—you want to make sure your words are appropriate.

If you are asked a question and you don't remember the answer, it's alright to say you "don't remember" or "don't recall." It's the rare individual who can recall what he was thinking at a particular time many years ago. It's probably not a good idea to guess at what you could have been thinking. The opposing attorney may ask you to look at the medical record and then ask if you can now come up with the answer. It's unlikely that the chart review will allow you to remember what you were thinking years ago so it's best to point out that a review of the chart won't be enough for you to recreate the thought pattern you might have had during that time period.

The opposing attorney may be persistent and present you with a hypothetical patient who is similar to the plaintiff and then ask your opinions as to diagnosis and treatment. As a physician, you should point out that the presence of the patient—one that you can actually talk to and possibly examine—is critical to making a diagnosis and outlining treatment and without the patient you are reluctant to give an answer based on limited knowledge.

If your case involves a missed diagnosis which led to harm to the patient, some attorneys will persist in trying to get you to admit to a mistake. They will do this by posing a theoretical question dealing with signs and symptoms of the plaintiff and ask you to give a differential diagnosis. For example, let's say the patient had an aortic dissection and the diagnosis was not made until he was already dead.

The attorney might ask you for a differential diagnosis for a patient who presents with substernal chest pain, shortness of breath, and tachycardia.

Faced with this scenario, the inclination is to say "it could be an aortic dissection." This is especially true in light of the fact that you already know that's what the plaintiff had. It would be truthful and better for your case if you don't jump ahead. Provide the attorney with a list of conditions which meet the proposed criteria so that the jury can actually see the case is not as simple as the plaintiff is trying to portray. In this example, the list could include myocardial infarction, pulmonary embolus, aortic dissection, pneumonia, pancreatitis, a duodenal or gastric ulcer with perforation, costochondritis, and perhaps a sternal or rib fracture, etc.

Don't start offering opinions without examining the theoretical patient. Don't let the opposing attorney force you to make suppositions as to what the patient might have had since you are only being given limited information which was not the situation when you were actually taking care of the patient. Remember to only answer the question you've been asked. Many defendants feel if they give a long, detailed explanation that goes beyond the scope of the question, they will educate the attorney as to their thought process and make him realize that you are a knowledgeable, reasonable, and prudent physician. This is unlikely to happen and you may even be hurting your case. Actually, the more information you provide to the plaintiff's attorney will just provide him with more material with which to ask you more questions.

If you are asked a "yes" or "no" question, you don't need to provide any explanations. For example: if you're asked if you remember seeing the patient on a particular day when there is no note by you or your team and you really don't remember, then "no" is the answer. If you say, "No, but it could have been one or two times and I just didn't document it," you will be opening yourself up to another line of questioning dealing with your documentation habits. Answer as briefly and as succinctly as possible. Don't volunteer information.

During a deposition where you aren't really intent on educating the jury, some lawyers will advise you to use medical terms in your answer so as to force the opposing attorney to use his limited knowledge and look to you for help. This may not be the best strategy. Instead, always answer in a way that would be understandable to the lay person who will be a member of the jury. Again, your deposition testimony may end up being read back to you at trial, and the jury may not appreciate it if they perceive you as talking down to them.

Another strategy that plaintiff's attorneys use is to try and get codefendants to start pointing the finger at each other. Pointing the finger at a codefendant is unlikely to help your case and the codefendant may even point the finger back at you. When this occurs, plaintiffs will then sit back and watch the defendants fight it out knowing that they are going to win the case and get a monetary award from at least one of the defendants. If you can, present a united front and don't answer in a way that makes your codefendants look bad.

Evidence

During the course of a malpractice action, evidence will be sought by both parties. The evidence will be used to try and convince the *trier of fact* to rule in favor of one party or the other. The judge will only allow the jury to see or hear evidence that is deemed *relevant*. *Relevant* evidence is evidence that has "any tendency to make the existence of any fact that is of consequence to the determination of the action more probable or less probable than it would be without the evidence."[57]

Not surprisingly, there are *rules of evidence* which must be followed in order to get the evidence to the jury or the judge. All *relevant evidence* is *admissible* unless there is some rule saying it is not. If this sounds confusing, you are right.

A physician in Philadelphia was sued by a patient who had a terrible complication from the pacing leads that are routinely placed at the conclusion of an operation on the heart. In this particular case, the atrial leads punctured the sigmoid colon as they were brought out from the chest to the usual position on the upper abdominal wall. The sigmoid colon was in a very abnormal position and the physician had no way of knowing this prior to his directing the leads out. The patient ended up getting an infected sternum and a colostomy. Several operations were needed to correct the problems, but he did recover. A suit was brought against the doctor alleging he was negligent in bringing out the pacer leads and this is what caused the harm to the patient.

The plaintiff's expert witness turned out to be one of the cardiac surgeons who had trained one of the defendant's partners in New York. This surgeon brought out the leads in exactly the same fashion as the partner did. The partner brought this information to the defendant's attorneys who ended up putting the partner on the stand to testify as to how the leads were placed by the plaintiff's expert. How could the expert claim the defendant was negligent if he put in the leads the same way himself? The intent of this testimony was to show that the complication would have happened even if the plaintiff's expert was doing the case.

During the direct examination, every time the defendant's attorney asked the defendant's partner to describe how the plaintiff's expert placed the pacing leads, the plaintiff's attorney would object since it was not relevant and the expert was not on trial. Amazingly, the judge would *sustain* the objection and the partner was never allowed to testify on this subject.

It's taught in law school that this particular point can be put into the record by claiming it reflected on the credibility of the expert. As the jury had the responsibility of determining credibility, this information would have met the *relevance* requirement. How could the expert say the defendant was negligent for doing the exact same thing he did on all of his own heart cases? In the heat of the trial, the defendant's attorney could not get this argument past the judge so he dropped the issue. Fortunately, the jury found for the defendant anyway.

The rules will not allow *relevant evidence* to come in if this *relevant evidence* will lead to unfair prejudice, confusion of the issues, or a waste of time. The judge is the one who decides if the *evidence* meets any of these exclusionary criteria. For example, it would be a waste of time to have several expert witnesses says the same thing as to the *standard of care*; the judge will generally allow only one expert witness for this function.

We have all seen television shows dealing with the legal profession where we have learned hearsay will not be allowed. Hearsay is an out-of-court statement (assertion) made by a person which is submitted in *evidence* as *proof of the matter* asserted. Generally, hearsay will not be allowed in as *evidence* since the opposing side will not have the opportunity to question the person making the statement. This lack of *cross-examination* will not allow the opposing party to ascertain the level of certainty of the statement nor establish the credibility or lack of credibility of the *declarant*. This inability to question the person making the statement means that the level of reliability cannot be explored, and thus it would not be fair to let it in. However, there are hearsay exceptions which have been deemed to be so reliable that the inability to cross-examine is considered to be not enough to keep out the statement.

Each state has its own rules as to hearsay exceptions, and the states may even define hearsay differently. First look at the Federal Rules of Evidence as they pertain to hearsay so that you can better understand the complexity of this issue. Rule 802 of the Federal Rules of Evidence is the Hearsay Rule, "[h]earsay is not admissible except as provided by these rules or by other rules prescribed by the Supreme Court pursuant to statutory authority or by Act of Congress."[53] Basically, the Rule says hearsay will not be allowed into evidence unless the rules state that it is not hearsay to begin with or there is another rule which will allow a particular form of hearsay into evidence—these are the exceptions of the hearsay rule. Unfortunately, it's not clear.

Rule 801(d) helps define what is not hearsay. "A statement is not hearsay if it is a prior statement by a witness and you can now cross-examine the witness in regards to the statement, and the statement is inconsistent with the declarant's testimony, and was given under oath subject to the penalty of perjury."[59] This rule is consistent with the idea that fairness will be attained so long as the witness making the statement can be cross-examined under oath[60] so inconsistencies can be unmasked and credibility of the *declarant* can be assessed by the *trier of fact*.

Rule 801(d) goes on to say that "admission by a party opponent, either his own words or words of a person authorized by the opponent to make the statement or a statement by a party's agent concerning a matter within the scope of the agency during the existence of the relationship; or a statement by a co-conspirator of a party during the course and in furtherance of the conspiracy" will not be considered to be hearsay.[61] These are not *exceptions* to the Hearsay Rule because they are not even *hearsay* to begin with.

Rule 803 deals with the *hearsay* exceptions when the *declarant* availability does not matter:
(1) *Present sense impression* — describes an event while it is occurring or immediately thereafter;
(2) *Excited utterance* — relates to a startling event made while the *declarant* was under the stress of the event;
(3) A statement dealing with the *declarant*'s state of mind to prove the fact remembered or believed. These would relate to things like *intent, motive, pain,* and *bodily health*;

(4) Statements made for purposes of medical diagnosis or treatment. These statements are deemed to be reliable because the *declarant* is unlikely to mislead the health care provider who is taking care of him;

(5) *Recorded recollection.* This would be a *record of a matter* that the witness once had knowledge of, but has now forgotten. It needs to be shown that this document was made when the matter was fresh in the witness's memory;

(6) *Records of a regularly conducted activity.* Records that would routinely be kept in the course of a regularly conducted business activity such as bills of sale, minutes of committee meetings, etc.;

(7) *Absence of information* that would usually be present in records kept under provision (6) above. This lack of information can be used as *evidence* to prove a matter or event did *not* occur;

(8) Public records and reports. These are generally felt to be reliable and there should be no need for cross-examination;

(9) Records of vital statistics;

(10) Absence of a public record or entry — again deemed to be reliable *evidence* that a particular event or activity did not occur;

(11) Records of religious activities such as births, marriages, divorces, and deaths;

(12) Marriage, baptismal, and other similar certificates;

(13)   Family records such as facts contained in a family bible, inscriptions on a ring, tombstone, or crypt;

(14)   Records pertaining to a piece of property;

(15)   Statements in documents affecting an interest in property;

(16)   Statements in ancient documents. These documents need to be shown to be at least 20 years old;

(17)   Market reports and commercial publications;

(18)   *Learned treatises* — to the extent an expert witness says he has relied on them, or called to the experts attention on cross-examination;

(19)   Reputation concerning personal or family history;

(20)   Reputation concerning boundaries or general history;

(21)   Reputation as to character among associates or in the community;

(22)   Judgment of a previous conviction. This can be used to *impeach* a witness;

(23)   Judgment as to personal, family, or general history or *boundaries*.

The common characteristic of all of these exceptions is the inherent reliability of the statement or documents such that *cross-examination* is really not needed to assess credibility. It has been deemed to be fair to let in this evidence even if *cross-examination* is not possible.

Rule 804—*Hearsay* exceptions where the *declarant* is unavailable.
- (1) Former testimony given as a witness at another hearing of the same or a different proceeding so long as the party against whom the testimony is now offered had the opportunity to develop the testimony by direct, cross, or redirect examination;
- (2) Statement under belief of impending death. The statement must be related to the cause or circumstances of what the *declarant* believed to be impending death. This exception came into play when the victim of foul play was able to identify the assailant before he died and the statement would clearly meet the hearsay definition;
- (3) *Statement against interest.* This statement must be against the *pecuniary* or *property* interests of the *declarant* such that a reasonable person in the declarant's position would not have made the statement unless it was true;
- (4) Statement of personal or family history; concerning *declarant*'s own birth, adoption, marriage, divorce, legitimacy, relationship by blood, or marriage, or ancestry. This exception will be allowed even if the *declarant* had no means of acquiring personal knowledge of the matter stated;
- (5) Transferred to Rule 807;
- (6) *Forfeiture by wrongdoing.* This deals with the statement offered against a party who then engages in some

wrongdoing to try to make the *declarant* unavailable as a witness.

Rule 807—Residual exception. This particular rule will allow statements not specifically covered by Rules 803 or 804, but having equivalent circumstantial guarantees of trustworthiness to be admitted into evidence. However, the statement will not be admitted unless the proponent makes it known to the adverse party sufficiently in advance of the trial or hearing so as to allow the adverse party to prepare to meet it. Name and address of the *declarant* must be included in the particulars of the notice.

Vocabulary

complaint
relief
property interest
due process of law
taking
state actor
notice
service
statute of limitations
last chance
discovery
Civil Procedure
Federal Rules of Civil Procedure
deposition
interrogatories
declarant
affiant
discovery process

Citations

[56] Black's Law Dictionary, Seventh edition, Bryan Garner, editor-in-chief.
[57] Article IV, Rule 401. Definition of "Relevant Evidence" in Tennessee Rules of Evidence.
[58] Federal Rules of Evidence Rule 802.
[59] Federal Rules of Evidence Rule 801(d).
[60] Id.
[61] Id.

Chapter 6: Defenses

Contributory Negligence

Contributory negligence is careless conduct by the injured party which was a contributing factor in the injuries that he incurred. Under a doctrine of common law, the injured party would not be entitled to collect any damages from the party who allegedly caused the injury. Contributory negligence has the potential of being a very harsh rule where the injured party is at risk of getting no compensation even if his own part in his injury is miniscule.

In *contributory negligence*, the conduct of the plaintiff must fall below the legal standard of protecting oneself from an unreasonable risk of harm. For many years, the fact that the plaintiff may have been a responsible party in his injuries was an absolute defense and was a bar to any recovery in a legal action. Because of the possibility of unfair results, many juries tended to ignore the rule and, as a result, many states have done away with this doctrine and have adopted a *comparative negligence* test in which the jury would decide on the relative percentages of negligence between parties so as to apportion the damage recovery.

Much like ordinary negligence, *contributory negligence* will not allow any recovery for the plaintiff if he is found to be partially responsible for the injury. Today, there are only five jurisdictions which still use the contributory negligence doctrine—Alabama, District of Columbia, Maryland, North Carolina, and Virginia.[62]

In most jurisdictions, if a person is injured while trying to rescue another person or property from danger, the rescuer will not be liable for contributory negligence unless the conduct is reckless—meaning that the conduct was "[c]haracterized by the creation of a substantial and unjustifiable risk of harm to others [and oneself] and by a conscious—and sometimes deliberate—disregard for or indifference to that risk."[63]

In *Eckert v. Long Island Rail Road Co.*,[64] Eckert saw a boy sitting on the railroad tracks as a train was fast approaching. Eckert was able to throw the boy off of the tracks but he was killed by the train during the rescue. Eckert's estate sued the railroad claiming that the train was traveling too fast in a residential neighborhood. The railroad claimed that the death was a result of Eckert's *contributory negligence* when he rescued the boy and put himself in harm's way.

After a trial, the jury found for Eckert. On appeal, the appellate court affirmed the ruling. On further appeal by the defendant, the State's highest court affirmed, holding that there will be no negligence if a person risks his life for another unless the act was done under such circumstances as to be reckless in the judgment of reasonably prudent persons.

In *Baltimore & Ohio R. Co. v. Goodman*,[65] Goodman pulled up to a train crossing and proceeded to cross even though his view was obstructed. He was struck and killed by the oncoming train. The court ordered a directed verdict for the railroad holding that Goodman was *contributorily negligent* and that no reasonable jury could have found for the plaintiff under the facts of this case. A *reasonable* person would not have pulled onto the tracks unless he was sure a train wasn't approaching.

In *Alexander v. Kramer Bros. Freight Lines, Inc.*,[66] Alexander brought suit after he was injured in an accident with Kramer's truck. The defendants claimed *contributory negligence* as a defense. The trial court found for the plaintiff and the appellate court affirmed. The court held that while the plaintiff has the burden of proof to show that he was **not** contributorily negligent, Alexander met that burden. While this appears to be counterintuitive, it is in line with the burden of proof always falling on the plaintiff. The jury apparently had enough information at trial to draw the conclusion that the plaintiff was not *contributorily negligent* since Alexander won the case.

In *Butterfield v. Forrester,* one of the seminal cases dealing with contributory negligence, Butterfield was injured by a pole that Forrester had laid across the road. It was twilight and Butterfield was riding a horse at a high rate of speed and he did not see the pole in time.[67] The trial court gave a judgment to Forrester. The trial court held that Butterfield was *contributorily negligent* because a rider using ordinary care would have been able to see and avoid the pole.[68] The verdict was affirmed on appeal.

In another case right out of the law school textbooks, *Brown v. Kendall,*[69] Kendall was injured while he and Brown were trying to separate their dogs who had gotten into a physical altercation. Kendall was struck in the eye by a stick that Brown was using to get the dogs to stop fighting. The jury verdict was for Brown. The appellate court overturned the verdict and remanded—meaning they sent the case back to the trial court for a new trial. The court held that the injured party could not recover if both parties are negligent, if both parties had used reasonable care, or if the injured party was negligent and the defendant was not.[70] The jury should have been so instructed which is why it was sent back for a new trial.

Another interesting case was *Martin v. Herzog*.[71] In this case, Martin was driving a buggy but he did not have his lights on as the law required. Herzog, who was driving on the wrong side of the road, did not see Martin in time. Martin was killed in the collision. The jury found for the plaintiff but the appellate court reversed.

The state Supreme Court affirmed the appellate court decision holding that Martin's violation of the law—by not having his lights on—was negligence per se and the jury should not have ignored that duty. The state supreme court held that if the lights were on, defendant would have been able to avoid the collision. In other words, the lack of the lights was also the proximate cause of the accident. Martin was liable for the *contributory negligence* because it was his conduct that was the cause of the injury. While this decision seems harsh on its face considering Martin died and Herzog was driving on the wrong side of the road, it takes into account that Martin could have avoided the collision if he had been obeying the law.

Another case incorporating the *rescue doctrine* was *Solomon v. Shuell*.[72] Two plain clothes officers were in the process of arresting robbery suspects when the decedent came out of his house brandishing a gun. He thought the officers were attacking the suspects and he was thinking that he could rescue them. He was shot and killed in the confusion. The jury was instructed that the *rescue doctrine* could only apply if the victim was in actual danger. Because of this instruction, the jury found both parties were negligent. On appeal, the appellate court affirmed. On further appeal, the Michigan Supreme Court held that the contributory negligence doctrine would not apply so long as the rescuer had a reasonable belief that the victim was in actual danger. As such, the jury instruction was improper as it would not allow the jury to consider if the rescuer's actions were reasonable.[73] They reversed the lower court's decision and remanded the case back for a new trial.

In *Smithwick v. Hall & Upson Co.*,[74] Smithwick was told not to work on a platform but he was not told that a wall was about to collapse. He went up on the platform anyway, thinking that the only danger was falling. He was then injured by the collapsing wall. The trial court ruled for Smithwick and the appellate court affirmed, holding that the failure to heed the warning did not constitute *contributory negligence* because the injury was the result of a different source of risk caused by the defendant and Smithwick was not made aware of that risk.

While the *Contributory Negligence* doctrine is no longer used by most states, these cases are illustrative as to how courts think and come to decisions.

Comparative Fault Doctrine

In the pure *comparative* negligence model, the jury or the judge will assign a percentage of the fault to each responsible party. The damages awarded will then be apportioned based on the parties percentage of fault. Under this system, an injured plaintiff may still recover damages even if he is found to be 99% responsible for his injuries. He will be allowed to recover 1% of the damage award. The jurisdictions which follow this system will typically assign the damages between the parties using one of three variations of the model: (1) the pure comparative negligence model; (2) the modified comparative negligence model — 51% rule; and (3) the modified comparative negligence model — 50% rule. Make sure your attorney knows if your state uses this model or uses a modified comparative fault system. In this system, the plaintiff may be allowed to recover damages if he is found to be 49% responsible or less.

The states that use the *comparative fault doctrine* have it either written into their statutes or as the holding (the common law) of the courts. In Tennessee, the Supreme Court used the case of *McIntyre v. Balentine*[75] to make *modified comparative fault* the law of the State.

In *McIntyre*, the Plaintiff, Harry McIntyre and the Defendant, Clifford Balentine, were involved in a motor vehicle accident with severe injuries to the Plaintiff. McIntyre had pulled out of a truck stop and collided with the defendant's tractor. Both parties had consumed alcoholic beverages and Plaintiff's blood alcohol level was measured at 0.17.[76] Testimony showed that the Defendant was speeding.[77]

The jury found both Plaintiff and Defendant were equally at fault, so they ruled for the Defendant since, at that time, Tennessee followed the *contributory negligence* doctrine. Plaintiff appealed alleging that the trial court should have instructed the jury regarding the doctrine of *comparative negligence*. Even though the state was not using *comparative negligence*, the Plaintiff was making a good faith argument that the law of the State should be changed.

The Court of Appeals affirmed the lower court's ruling as they were not willing to change the State's law. The State's Supreme Court took the appeal as they were now willing to abandon contributory negligence, which they did. As a result, the case was sent back for a new trial using comparative fault as the law. Many believe the *comparative fault* doctrine is fairer to all concerned where negligence is involved. Each negligent party will be responsible only for their percentage of the fault.

Statute of Limitations

There is a general belief that civil actions must be brought within a reasonable time frame so that documents will not be lost, memories will be fresh as possible, and witnesses will still be available. In Tennessee, this belief is codified, written into the law, as a *statute of limitations* — a law which places a time limit for Plaintiff's to pursue their *cause of action*. For medical malpractice, the statute of limitations is one year in Tennessee. If Plaintiff does not file his case within one year of the alleged incident, then he will not be able to file in regards to that case or controversy ever again.

There are other reasons why this statute is so important. Without the *statute of limitations*, all physicians would have to keep paying premiums until their last patient died and then they would still need to keep paying in anticipation of being sued by the patient's estate. It would force physicians to never be able to retire as they would unlikely be able to afford the malpractice premiums with just their retirement income to rely on. Without a *statute of limitations* most physicians would probably end up bankrupt either from their never ending malpractice premiums or from successful lawsuits that are brought after the malpractice coverage had to be dropped for financial exigency. Check your state for the time-frame for the *statute of limitations*.

Now when a physician retires, he has to pay a *tail* to the insurance company which will allow him to remain covered until the *statute of limitations* on his last patient has ended. The law also allows the insurance companies some assurance that they will not be liable for events from the past so that they can better predict their potential liability in the future.

Not surprisingly, plaintiffs oppose *statutes of limitation* because they fear that these laws might prevent legitimate claims from being litigated. This would mean that an injured party would be left without a remedy. They also argue that the passage of time should only have a minimal effect on the quality of the evidence but even if it did, the plaintiff would be the party most at risk since the burden of persuasion is still their responsibility.

As with other laws, there are exceptions, the most notable of which is called the *Discovery Rule*. This protects the plaintiff who could not have reasonably known that he was a victim of malpractice until the one-year statute of limitations had passed. Under the *discovery rule*, the plaintiff is permitted to file a suit within a certain time frame after the injury is discovered. In Tennessee, the *discovery rule* tolls, meaning it stops the clock on the *statute of limitations* until the plaintiff knows, or reasonably should know, that he has been injured by medical malpractice and who it was that caused the injury.[78]

The *discovery rule* will not permit the patient to delay filing the suit until he becomes aware of all the possible injuries or persons involved in the alleged malpractice. He needs to know that the statute starts to run when they become aware of enough facts to put a reasonable person on notice that they have been injured as a result of medical malpractice and they know at least one of the health care providers who may be liable. If the law was otherwise, a plaintiff who misses filing before the statute has run out could claim that he still does not know what further injuries he may develop over time or who else might have been involved in his care. This would defeat the whole purpose of a *statute of limitations* which is to have the case litigated while the facts are still relatively fresh in the party's minds and the evidence is still readily obtainable.

In *Matz v. Quest Diagnostics Clinical Laboratories, Inc.*,[79] the defendants were awarded a summary judgment on the grounds that the *statute of limitations* had run before the plaintiff had filed the complaint. Mr. Matz went to see his physician, Dr. Hughes in April of 1999 for evaluation of a bleeding lesion on his head. Dr. Hughes did a biopsy that was sent to the defendant laboratory but no malignancy was found. When the tumor recurred in April 26, 2000, the diagnosis of melanoma was finally made. Mr. Matz alleged that the failure to make the diagnosis a year earlier had lessened his chances for survival.

During his deposition, Mr. Matz testified that he knew all along that the mass was probably a malignancy but the diagnosis had been missed in the 1999 biopsy. Mr. Matz's wife also testified that her husband knew "all along" that he had cancer but they had just failed to diagnose it. With this testimony, the defendants moved for a summary judgment based on the fact that the statute of limitations had run out. They won the motion at the trial court level.

On appeal, Plaintiff argued that Mr. Matz's subjective fear was not enough to let the statute continue running. After all, the rule requires that the plaintiff know "the occasion, the manner, and the means by which a breach of duty that caused his injuries occurred."[80] Sure enough, the appellate court overruled the summary judgment stating, "Matz' subjective belief or fear, however, had no factual basis, because the doctors' findings were that no cancer was present. The *discovery rule* requires that the plaintiff be aware of *facts sufficient* to put a reasonable person on notice that he or she has suffered an injury as a result of the defendant's wrongful conduct." Shadrick v. Coker, 963 S.W.2d 726, 733 (Tenn. 1998). The court further pointed out that the injury was not the diagnosis of cancer but the fact that the diagnosis was missed, allowing the cancer to progress until April 26, 2000. The court went on to say, "The question of when Matz's injury was reasonably discoverable given Mr. Matz's knowledge and circumstances is a question of fact inappropriate for determination by summary judgment."[81] The case was remanded back to the trial court for a new trial.

Shadrick is a great example of *tolling* under the discovery rule.[82] The patient, Mr. Shadrick, had several operations done on his spine which were not successful. Finally, in March of 1990, the surgeon did an operation where hardware was placed to stabilize the spine and fuse the vertebrae. Unfortunately, in November of 1990, one of the screws that had been placed in the spine broke and had to be removed and Mr. Shadrick's pain was not relieved.

While watching the TV show "20/20," Mr. Shadrick learned the screws used in his surgery were experimental and they were failing at a very high rate. These were facts brought out on the show's expose which were never discussed with Mr. Shadrick prior to his operation. The show also mentioned that the screws were not even approved by the Food and Drug Administration until December, 1993. One year after learning about the problem with the screws, Mr. Shadrick brought suit alleging malpractice, lack of informed consent, and battery.

The trial court granted the defendant's motion for summary judgment. The court of appeals reversed because they found there were disputed issues of material fact as to when Mr. Shadrick should have discovered his cause of action. The Supreme Court of Tennessee affirmed the Court of Appeals. The surgeon was not successful in claiming that the statute of limitations had run its course because there was evidence that he intentionally kept vital information from his patient, Mr. Shadrick, so the patient could not have reasonably discovered the alleged malpractice until he fortuitously got the information he needed by watching a television show. Juries and judges do not look favorably on physicians who are not honest and forthcoming.

It's important to know when a patient has sufficient information to be aware his injury was caused by a negligent act of a health care provider. This can be difficult question to ascertain so it's not surprising that it will be up to the jury to decide the issue.

In *McIntosh v. Blanton*,[83] Ms. McIntosh was a 77-year-old with an 11th grade education who had carpal tunnel syndrome. In 1995, Dr. Blanton did a successful operation on the patient's right wrist. In 1998, the operation was done on the left wrist but it wasn't successful. In fact, Ms. McIntosh lost the feeling of two of her fingers on the left hand after the operation. Ms. McIntosh brought suit claiming the ulnar and radial nerves were injured at the operation. She said she discovered the negligence during a conversation with Dr. Blanton on April 5, 1999 and with conversations with another surgeon, Dr. Muhlbauer, on April 20, 1999. She filed her complaint within the one-year requirement from these two conversations.

Dr. Blanton argued that he informed Ms. McIntosh of his cutting the palmar fascia instead of the transverse carpal ligament on a postoperative visit on February 12, 1999. Since the claim was filed over a year after that conversation, he moved for a judgment based on the fact that the statute of limitations had run out.[84]

Although the patient acknowledged the conversation of February 12, she claimed that there was no reason to believe that the act described by Dr. Blanton was negligent as he described it as a known risk and complication of the operation. She also claimed that Dr. Blanton had a "reassuring attitude" and also discussed the complications in terms of known risks. No issue of negligence was raised.[84]

So when did Ms. McIntosh have the necessary information to know that she had sustained the injury? Remember, the inquiry doesn't require the patient has knowledge a breach of the *standard of care* has occurred. All that is required is they know the injury is a result of *wrongful conduct* and they know the identity of the person who performed the act which led to the injury. The trial court decided Ms. McIntosh should have known after the conversations with Dr. Blanton and they awarded a summary judgment for the defendant based on the *statute of limitations*.

The appellate court reviewed the record and felt there was a genuine issue of material fact as to when Ms. McIntosh was reasonably put on notice that her injuries were the result of *wrongful conduct* and not just a consequence of a known complication of the procedure.[86] The court ruled that the jury should have been allowed to hear the case and make a judgment. The court reversed the summary judgment of the trial court and remanded the case back for trial.

In an interesting side note of the case, Dr. Muhlbauer, a neurosurgeon, was subpoenaed by plaintiffs. He did not believe that the injury was due to negligence but was actually due to brachial plexus involvement by metastatic breast cancer which the patient was known to have.[87] This information never made it into the opinion of the appellate court but it was clearly related to the issue of *causation*.

Besides the *Discovery Rule*, the statute of limitations may be tolled for other reasons. Mental incompetence, minority, and a defendant's bankruptcy are all circumstances that can toll the statue. For example, it would not be fair to have the statute run out on a minor or a person rendered mentally incompetent by injury. In Tennessee, *the statute of limitations does not begin to run until the minor's eighteenth birthday*. Whether the *statute of limitations* should be tolled can be a difficult question and may need to be litigated.

In *Sherrill v. Souder, M.D.* the plaintiff brought a medical malpractice suit alleging that the physician was negligent in prescribing a drug.[88] The drug, metoclopramide, is known to cause a tardive dyskinesia, a movement disorder, in some patients. The plaintiff developed the movement disorder and the defendant missed the possible connection of the drug to the disorder. The diagnosis was finally made by another physician but by then, the patient's neurologic state was such that she continued to take the drug although she was advised to stop it.

The defendants made a motion for summary judgment based on the fact the suit was brought after the one year statute of limitations had run out. The trial court granted the motion and the Court of Appeals affirmed. However, the Tennessee Supreme Court ruled there was a genuine issue of material fact regarding the plaintiff's mental state on the date that the *cause of action* happened. There was evidence presented which showed Ms. Sherril was not able to manage her daily affairs. The fact that she continued to take the drug although she had been advised to stop lends credence to the mental incapacity issue. This would raise the issue of tolling the statute of limitations which was not further investigated by the trial court.

Since the issue of the plaintiff's mental state had not been litigated, the Supreme Court remanded the case back to the trial court so that the jury could determine whether the plaintiff was of unsound mind on the date that the alleged malpractice occurred. If it were determined that she was not of sound mind, then the statute of limitations would be tolled and she could then be allowed to bring the suit to trial.

There is also an automatic stay on the statute when the defendant declares bankruptcy. The stay is lifted when the bankruptcy is resolved. This prevents the defendant from avoiding liability by declaring bankruptcy and then waiting for the statute of limitations to run out. Tolling, the discovery rule, and bankruptcy will all raise issues as to timing of the running of the statute of limitations so it is critical you hire a qualified, knowledgeable lawyer so that the *statute of limitations* as it applies to your specific fact pattern can be used to your advantage.

Statute of Repose

A *statute of repose* is a law which prevents a lawsuit from being filed after the passage of a time period specified by the law. For example, the statute of repose for a malpractice action in Tennessee is three years. This means that, by law, a malpractice claim cannot be filed if the filing would be over three years from the time of the event that led to the claim. This holds true even if the injury occurred long after the event.

Let's say a surgeon repaired an abdominal hernia by placing some mesh into the abdominal wall defect. The patient does well for over three years, but then has a recurrence because the mesh, allegedly, was not sutured in properly. A claim cannot be filed because, even though the injury occurred several years after the operation, the *statute of repose* had run on the operation. The surgeon can no longer be liable for negligence that may have occurred during the operation.

The purpose for a *statute of repose* is to eliminate the possibility of a claim which could arise years after the *tortious* act for which maintaining records and insurance is thought to be too great a burden for the defendant and thus, unfair. The same scenarios discussed for the *statute of limitations* could be used for this discussion on the *statute of repose*.

As with the *statute of limitations*, there is an exception to the *statute of repose*. This exception is called the "fraudulent concealment exception to the statute of repose." The defendant will not be allowed to actively prevent the plaintiff from learning about the possible cause of action in order to avoid a lawsuit that the plaintiff cannot file on time. In *Shadrick v. Coker*, an opinion of the Tennessee Supreme Court in 1998, the Court outlined what a defendant can't do in hopes of letting the *statute of repose* run out. The defendant will not be allowed to take affirmative action to conceal the cause of action or remain silent so as not to disclose important *material* facts even if he has a duty to do so. On the other hand, the plaintiff must not have been able to discover the *cause of action* if he were to exercise *reasonable care* and *diligence* — so even if the defendant were trying to conceal the facts, if the plaintiff could have found the facts with his own reasonable diligence, the exception to the *statute of repose* will not apply. Clearly, the burden is on the plaintiff to prove that he should be allowed the exception. This burden will not come into play unless the defendant first satisfies his own burden that the *statute of repose* has run out. This is an affirmative defense. The defendant will not be allowed the defense unless he claims it. This is done by bringing it to the court's attention.

Darryl Weiman

Vocabulary

contributory negligence
comparative negligence
Eckert v. Long Island Rail Road Co.
Baltimore & Ohio R. Co. v. Goodman
Alexander v. Kramer Bros. Freight Lines, Inc.
Brown v. Kendall
Martin v. Herzog
rescue doctrine
Solomon v. Shuell
Smithwick v. Hall & Upson Co.
McIntyre v. Balentine
modified comparative fault
comparative fault
statute of limitations
cause of action
tail
discovery rule
Matz v. Quest Diagnostics Clinical Laboratories, Inc.
McIntosh v. Blanton
wrongful conduct
Sherrill v. Souder, M.D.
statute of repose
reasonable care
diligence

Citations

[62] www.the-injury-lawyer-directory.com/negligence_chart.html
[63] Black's Law Dictionary, Bryan A. Garner, editor-in-chief, Seventh Edition.
[64] *Eckert v. Long Island R.R. Co.*, 43 N.Y. 502 (1871).
[65] *Baltimore & Ohio R. Co. v. Goodman*, 276 US 66 (1927).
[66] *Alexander v. Kramer Bros. Freight Lines, Inc.*, 273 F.2d 373 (1959).
[67] *Butterfield v. Forrester*, 11 East 60 (1809).
[68] Id.
[69] *Brown v. Kendall*, 60 Mass, (6 Cush) 292, (1850).
[70] Id.
[71] *Martin v. Herzog*, 126 N.E. 814 (1920).
[72] *Solomon v. Shuell*, 457 NW 2d 669 (1990).
[73] Id.
[74] *Smithwick v. Hall & Upson*, 59 Conn. 261 (1890).
[75] *McIntyre v. Balentine*, 833 S.W. 2d 52 (Tenn. 1992).
[76] Id.
[77] Id.
[78] Under the discovery rule, the statute of limitations for medical malpractice starts to run when the plaintiff discovers, or reasonably should have discovered the occasion, the manner, and the means by which a breach of the standard of care that caused the injuries occurred and the identity of the person who caused the injury. *Stanbury v. Bacardi*, 953 S.W.2d 671,677 (Tenn. 1997).
[79] *Matz v. Quest Diagnostics Clinical Laboratories, Inc.*, WL 22409452 (Tenn.Ct.App. 2003).
[80] *Stanbury v. Bacardi*, 953 S.W.2d at 677.
[81] *Matz v Quest Diagnostics Clinical Laboratories, Inc.*, WL 22409452 (Tenn.Ct.App. 2003).
[82] 963 S.W.2d 726 (Tenn. 1998).
[83] *McIntosh v. Blanton*, 2004 WL 1869977 (Tenn.Ct.App.). 164 S.W.3d 584, (Tenn.Ct.App. 2004).
[84] Id.
[85] Id.
[86] Id.
[87] Personal communication with Dr. Muhlbauer.
[88] *Lou Ella Sherrill et al. v. Bob T. Souder, M.D. et al.* No. W2008-00741-SC-R11-CV-Filed October 28, 2010.

Chapter 7: Damages

In order for laws to work, they must be reasonable and predictable. Unfortunately, damage awards for *pain and suffering* and *punitive* damages are often irrational and unpredictable which make them the topics of contentious debates.

According to Black's Law Dictionary, *damages* are "[m]oney claimed by or ordered to be paid to, a person as compensation for loss or injury."[89] In a malpractice case, there are generally two kinds of *damages* sought by the plaintiff. *Ordinary*, also called *compensatory*, damages is an amount, usually in dollars, that is awarded to the plaintiff to pay for the actual losses that are proven. These damages include such things as loss of earnings, which would also include the potential loss of future earnings, the costs of the medical care already rendered to the plaintiff, and the costs of future medical expenses related to the injury from the alleged malpractice. These types of *damages* can be readily proven by bills, history of previous earnings and projected earnings, and costs of future medical expenses based on known costs of today. Expert testimony may be needed to help the jury understand what these costs may be.

Damages for *pain and suffering* can also be asked for by the plaintiff. These types of damages are for the cost of past and future loss of enjoyment of life, past and future *pain and suffering*, permanent impairment or disfigurement, and loss of consortium. These types of costs can be difficult to prove and the jury is often faced with having to make a cost determination on which they have very little evidence and these damages can be very high.

The plaintiff may also make a claim for *punitive damages*. *Punitive damages* are aimed to deter blameworthy conduct alleged to have been done by the defendant. *Punitive damages* can be awarded if it is proven that the defendant acted with recklessness, malice, or deceit. In general, punitive damages should not be part of a pain and suffering award, but in practice, it seems that some juries will increase the size of the award in an effort to punish the defendant for causing some particularly egregious pain and suffering.

Punitive Damages

BMW of North America sold Mr. Gore a car that had been repainted because it had been left out in an acid rain storm and the original paint was damaged. Gore found out about the new paint job after he bought the car and decided to sue. The jury awarded Gore compensatory damages of $4,000. Surprisingly, the jury also awarded punitive damages of $4 million based on the theory that there were about one thousand other people that had bought cars that had also been repainted without the new owner being told.

The United States Supreme Court heard the case and held that certain guidelines should be used to ensure that *punitive damage* awards are not excessive, as they can be very high. In *BMW v, Gore,*[90] the Court held that three guidelines should be used to help determine whether a punitive damages award is excessive. They directed the lower courts to evaluate (1) the reprehensibility of the conduct being punished; (2) the reasonableness of the relationship between the harm and the award; and (3) the difference between the award and the civil penalties authorized in comparable cases.[91]

The issue the United States Supreme Court was asked to address was the constitutionality of the large *punitive damage* award. In its analysis, the Court found that BMW's behavior was not really that bad and, in some other states, cars with new paint jobs after similar types of damage were still considered to be *new*. The Court also noted that BMW's conduct had not hurt anyone nor did the new paint job affect anyone's safety. The Court also considered the fact that the maximum penalty for violation of that state's—Alabama—Deceptive Trade Practices Act was only $2,000. As such, the punitive damage award was 500 times higher than the compensatory award. In *BMW*, the Court ruled that there had to be some sort of limits on *punitive damages* so that the defendant would have some idea of the risk he was facing with his behavior. If a defendant were not able to calculate the risk, he would not have the notice required under the *due process* clause.[92]

In dissenting opinions, Justice Scalia and Justice Thomas came to the conclusion that the Court had established a substantive right of defendants to not be liable for *punitive damages* that would be considered *grossly excessive*.[93] They didn't believe the Constitution put any limits on the size of punitive damages.

Even though the holdings of *BMW* were only applicable to Federal courts, the Supreme Court went on to address state *punitive damages* in its decision in *Cooper Industries, Inc. v. Leatherman Tool Group (2001)*.[94] In *Leatherman*, the jury found that Cooper was liable for unfair competition and awarded Leatherman $50,000 in compensatory damages and $4.5 million in punitive damages. The District Court held that the punitive damages award was not so excessive as to violate the Federal Constitution. The Court of Appeals ruled the District Court had not abused its discretion in deciding to not lower the amount of *punitive damages*.

In *Leatherman*, the Supreme Court held that appellate courts may review *punitive damage* awards with a *de novo* standard as opposed to the usual abuse of discretion standard. This meant that the appellate courts could decide on the level of *punitive damages* based on their own review of the facts of the case. Prior to *Leatherman*, the appellate courts could only overturn the lower courts if they found the lower court had abused its discretion in coming to a value for punitive damages.

This time in a concurring opinion, Justice Thomas again stated that the holding in *BMW of North America v. Gore* should be overruled, but that wasn't the issue the Court was ruling on in this case. Once again, he stated the Constitution does not place limits on the size of punitive damages. Justice Scalia agreed with Justice Thomas saying that the *Due Process Clause* is not violated with excessive punitive damages, but he also agreed there are precedents for de novo reviews for the constitutionality of excessive fines[95] so he agreed with the overall decision. As a result, they sent the case back to the Court of Appeals for applying the wrong standard of review in deciding on the constitutionality of the punitive damages award.

In *State Farm Mutual Insurance v. Campbell (2003)*,[96] the Supreme Court further refined the limits of punitive damages when they stated that *punitive damage* awards that were higher than a single digit multiplier of the compensatory damages were not likely to comply with the *Due Process Clause*, especially in the case where the compensatory damages are high and there was no harm due to "physical assault or trauma."[97] In writing for the majority, Justice Kennedy said, "An application of the *Gore* guideposts to the facts of this case, especially in light of the substantial compensatory damages awarded (a portion of which contained a punitive element), likely would justify a punitive damages award at or near the amount of compensatory damages."[98] Although the Court declined to define a mathematical ratio of punitive to compensatory damages that would clarify the punitive damages that would be consistent with due process the Court did say "…that, in practice, few awards exceeding a single digit ratio between punitive and compensatory damages, to a significant degree, will satisfy due process."[99]

The wording of the decision does provide some wiggle room for plaintiffs. In fact, the Court went on to say that higher ratios may be justified in particularly egregious cases where the compensatory damages are small and the non-economic damages are difficult to determine. The wealth of the defendant should not be used to assess the *punitive damages*.

In a dissenting opinion, Justice Ginsburg argued that the Supreme Court was out of order in imposing on the States a single digit multiplier of the *compensatory damages* to cap the *punitive damages* under the auspices of the *Due Process Clause*. However, she felt it would be justified if a legislative body or the state high court itself made the decision as part of their own plan to limit punitive damages. Critics of these Supreme Court opinions state that the Court overstepped its authority by making a new form of *substantive due process* that diminishes state's rights and the right to a jury trial where the jury was supposed to have the right to decide on damages.

If the premise is true that the jury has the right to decide on damages, then wouldn't a legislative cap on damages for such things as pain and suffering be unconstitutional, violating the separation of powers? I don't have a good answer to this question.

Ordinary Damages

The states have made statutes which define the kind of damages that will be awarded in a malpractice action. In Tennessee, "[i]n a malpractice action in which liability is admitted or established, that damages awarded may include (in addition to other elements of damages authorized by law) actual economic losses suffered by the claimant by reason of personal injury including, but not limited to cost of reasonable and necessary medical care, rehabilitation services, and custodial care, loss of services and loss of earned income."[100] The plaintiff can also make a claim for *pain and suffering* and/or *punitive damages* and this is where the big money awards can occur.

In 2011, Tennessee placed a cap on *pain and suffering* at twice the amount of *compensatory damages* or $500,000, whichever is greater. The new law also capped non-economic damages at $750,000 but this may be raised to $1 million for catastrophic cases where a person is paralyzed, burned, blinded, suffered an amputation, or otherwise died and left behind minor children. The Tennessee Supreme Court has not yet ruled on the constitutionality of these new caps, so we really don't know if the caps are constitutional or not.

Pain and Suffering

How can you put a monetary value on pain and suffering? In medicine we can't quantitate pain very well and yet the courts are expected to come up with a dollar amount on each applicable case.

Paul Niemeyer, a United States Circuit Judge, has said that awards for pain *and suffering* are the "irrational centerpiece of our tort system."[101] Juries have very little experience upon which to base awards for *pain and suffering* and are often instructed to do what they think is best. How could they have any idea what the award for *pain and suffering* should be except to rely on their own experience which is likely to be based on emotion? Because the experience of each jury is likely to differ, it is not surprising that similar injuries may result in vastly different jury awards.

Caps on *pain and suffering* for medical malpractice cases are an effort to limit the amount of the award for the plaintiff. It is believed that these caps will bring down the costs of malpractice insurance since they would eliminate the chance of being sued for unlimited damages. Most states have these caps. In Mississippi, for example, if someone sues a physician or a hospital for medical malpractice, they can't recover more than the $500,000 cap for *pain and suffering*. The plaintiff can still recover the costs of the illness due to the malpractice, but this cost is generally much less than what they could get for the *pain and suffering*.

The benefit of having a liability cap is that it encourages people to enter into high risk professions that are needed in the state. Since the cost of the malpractice insurance premiums would go down, physicians would have a significantly lower overhead and would make a better living in the states that have the caps. States which face shortages of physicians are the ones more likely to adopt liability caps so as to encourage those specialists to set up practices in their state.

Of course plaintiff's attorneys are against the caps as they pretty much eliminate their chance for a huge payday. They argue that the patient who has suffered a grievous injury should be compensated to the highest level that the court decides. The Supreme Court has not yet weighed in on caps for *pain and suffering*, but its stance on *punitive damage* limits leads one to believe that some sort of rational analysis would be deemed necessary to allow for some predictability for these damages so the *Due Process Clause* would not be violated.

There may be conditions attached to the liability limits so you need to check with the laws of your state. For example, if a physician were to act recklessly, or broke the law and the patient suffered, the caps might not apply. There may be situations where a creative attorney may allege *gross negligence* so as to keep the caps out of play.

Just because a state legislature adopts caps on *pain and suffering* for their state doesn't mean the courts will allow it to take effect. For example, the Illinois Supreme Court has disallowed caps on non-economic damages—pain and suffering for medical malpractice cases—three times since the 1970s.[102] In Illinois, the latest reversal occurred in *Lebron v. Gottlieb Memorial Hospital*, where the court ruled, in a 4-2 vote, that the cap violated the state constitution's separation of powers, because it took away the court's power of *remittitur*.[103] *Remittitur* is a judicial tool which gives judges the power to reduce jury awards that they deem to be excessive. The power of *remittitur* would still be with the courts, but the awards that they would be exercising the power on would be less. That's obviously not the way the Illinois Supreme Court saw it.

In March, 2010, the Georgia Supreme Court unanimously struck down the state's medical malpractice limit of $350,000 but their argument was different from Illinois. The Georgia court held that the $350,000 on non-economic damages violated the plaintiff's right to a jury. This may seem like a stretch since the plaintiff still had the right to a jury trial, only the trial would have caps attached to the award.[104]

In essence, some states have the caps; some states don't because of what each state's Supreme Court allows. There is still the risk that states which allow the caps, can have them deemed to be unconstitutional by a simple vote of their judges who are elected to their posts and subject to the electorate for their jobs. Since the electorate decides on the judges, the judges may be inclined to do what the voters want. If the voters don't want caps, all they have to do is vote for judges who will overrule the legislature on this issue.

Illinois is one of 38 states that select judges through some form of election. It's only one of seven that holds partisan elections where the judge is deemed to be a candidate of a particular party. In the 2004 Supreme

Court race in Illinois, the Republican, Lloyd Karmer, was supported with $4.8 million from business interests and their lawyers. The Democrat, Gorden Maag, drew over $4 million from a core of plaintiff's attorneys. Karmer won the election and in a dissenting opinion in *Lebron*, he focused on the political issues of health care costs and improving quality of care. Karmer was scolded by the state's Chief Justice who stated the decision was based on the State's constitution and not on the political climate. Obviously, this was a contentious issue in Illinois.

So where is the law going on caps for *pain and suffering*? Nothing can be said with any certainty, but it doesn't look favorable for physicians and hospitals at this point in time.

Vocabulary

pain and suffering
punitive damages
BMW of North America v. Gore
due process
grossly excessive
Cooper Industries, Inc. v. Leatherman Tool Group (2001)
de novo standard
Due Process Clause
State Farm Mutual Insurance v. Campbell (2003)
substantive due process
gross negligence
Lebron v. Gottlieb Memorial Hospital
Remittitur

Citations

[89] Black's Law Dictionary. "Damages are the sum of money which a person wronged is entitled to receive from the wrongdoer as compensation for the wrong." Frank Gahan, *The Law of Damages 1 (1936)*.
[90] 517 U.S. 559, (1996).
[91] Id.
[92] Id.
[93] Id.
[94] 532 U.S. 424(2001).
[95] *United States v. Bajakajian,* 524 U.S. 321(1998).
[96] 538 U.S. 408(2003).
[97] Id.
[98] Id.
[99] Id.
[100] Tenn Code Ann. Section 29-26-119.
[101] Ola B. Smith Lecture at the University of Virginia School of Law, March 23, 2004.
[102] ABA Journal, May 2010, p. 16-17.
[103] Id.
[104] Id.

Section Two: The Trial

Chapter 8:
The Jury

Jury Selection

If you've had the opportunity to watch TV shows about lawyers, you can reasonably come to the conclusion that trials are won with superb closing arguments or with vicious cross-examination of an opposing witness. Of the many episodes of Boston Legal, it's amazing the perfect rhetoric on closing argument of actor James Spader whose character, Alan Shore, could speak quickly, perfectly and so convincingly there was never any doubt the jury would return a verdict in his client's favor.

This rarely happens to lawyers in real life. Think back to the saga of *Bush v. Gore* that was played out in real-time on TV. These lawyers were said to be among the best in the country and their fee structure at least confirmed they were among the most expensive, and yet neither side's counsel's ability to make clear, concise, convincing arguments was very impressive.

In trials, with discovery rules requiring all parties to have all of the information that is to be presented at trial, television-type surprises are not likely to occur. In actual practice, many trials are won or lost at the jury selection phase where much research has shown that jurors can be selected that already have a predilection to decide a case one way or the other.

How a jury comes to be selected depends on the statutes, rules of the court in which the trial is being held and, to some extent, on the judge involved in the case. These laws and rules control how jurors are initially called for questioning and what qualifications they must have. The number of jurors involved in the trial and whether or not alternate jurors should a juror not be able to fulfill his obligation will be used are in these rules and laws.

The jury pool consists of many more potential jurors than needed for the trial. From this pool, the jurors are selected in a process called *voir dire*,[105] a French legal term meaning *to speak the truth*. This process of questioning the potential juror is done to decide *whether the prospect is qualified and suitable to serve on a jury.*[106]

After potential jurors are brought in, each side is allowed to ask them questions usually relating to their backgrounds, life experiences and, if allowed by that particular court, questions of law. For example, a plaintiff would not want to have a juror who is a medical doctor who believes that there is no such thing as malpractice. A defendant might not want a juror that thinks all doctors are money hungry and uncaring, or a juror that believes he was a victim of malpractice himself. Your lawyer's questions are designed to unveil any bias the potential juror might have that would be contrary to your case.

Each party will try to guess which of the potential jurors are likely to be sympathetic to their cause and they will try to get those people seated on the jury. Each side has the right to ask that certain people not be allowed to sit on the jury for legal reasons—called *cause challenges*, and each side will be allowed a certain number of *peremptory challenges* which allow them to strike any juror for almost any reason they want. In the past, lawyers could use the *peremptory challenges* for any reason and they didn't have to explain their rationale. However, several Supreme Court cases have placed limits on this strategy.

In *Batson v. Kentucky*, the Supreme Court held that in criminal cases, the prosecutor could not enter *peremptory challenges* against members of the defendant's race based solely on account of their race.[107] In *Powers v. Ohio*, the holding in *Batson* was applied to white defendants who were objecting to a prosecutor's attempt to exclude black jurors.[108]

This line of reasoning was extended to civil cases in *Edmonson v. Leesville Concrete Co.* in 1991.[109] In *Georgia v. McCollum,* the Court applied the holding in *Batson* to Defendants in criminal cases.[110] Most recently, the Court applied *Batson* to gender in *J.E.B. v. Alabama.*[111] This group of Supreme Court cases basically made it illegal to use *peremptory challenges* based solely on race and/or gender.

So what happens if an opposing party objects to a *peremptory challenge* claiming it is based on race or gender? The Supreme Court dealt with this issue in *Purkett v. Elem.*[112] In *Purkett,* the Court said that the party making a *peremptory challenge* that is being objected to as being made on the basis of race or gender, need only come up with a race/gender neutral reason for the challenge. The reason doesn't need to be persuasive or even plausible. Once the explanation is made, the burden of persuasion shifts to the opposing party who must then prove purposeful racial or gender discrimination—which can be a difficult thing to do. The trial judge must make the final decision after both parties argue their side.

Although the Supreme Court has not yet applied the holding of *Batson* to other recognized constitutionally protected classes such as religion and ethnicity, some of the lower courts have. As previously stated—and it can't be overstated—it's vital your lawyer be familiar with the rules of your court.

In some courts, the lawyers are the ones doing the questioning of potential witnesses while in other cases only the judge does the questioning, and in some courts they both may do the questioning of potential jurors.

Some lawyers use Internet networking sites to learn as much as they can about potential jurors.[113] With the new computer tablets or other electronic smart devices and their ease of portability, this online look into a person's background can be done while the potential juror is being questioned. Researching their private lives online provides more information as to how the person is likely to decide the issue at hand. Since this computer vetting is divorced from court oversight, questions have been raised as to whether court rules are being violated. This is a new area of procedural law so it will be interesting to see how various jurisdictions will deal with these "searches."

Jury selection has become so important that a new group of professionals called *jury consultants* has emerged who make their living by studying juror's body language, backgrounds, and responses to the *voir dire* questions so that they can advise the attorneys on those who would likely be on their side or against them on a particular case.

In most cases, jury selection takes about half a day, but in complex cases it may take longer. After a jury is selected, they are then sworn in by the court clerk to be the jury that decides the case at hand.

Preliminary Instructions of Law

After the jury has been sworn in, the judge will usually give them *preliminary instructions* dealing with the law. The process of the trial will be part of these instructions so the jury will have some idea of what is about to transpire. Among these instructions will be the duties of the jury. These duties include following the law, determining the facts of the case—which means they will have to make a judgment on the credibility of the witnesses to decide who is telling the truth—and then applying the facts to the law so a judgment can be made.

During these instructions, the jury will be warned to not discuss the case with anyone except themselves, and when they do discuss the case they are to do so only when all members of the jury are present in the jury room. They are not to discuss the case during recesses except for recesses where all jurors are present in the jury room. They are not to visit the scenes in question by themselves nor are they to do any research on the case on their own.

The movie *12 Angry Men* does a terrific job dealing with the legal system, even though not very realistic as to real-life trials. The late actor Henry Fonda played a juror who went on his own to the neighborhood where the crime had been committed and he was able to buy a switchblade which was exactly like the one the prosecutor claimed was unique and had been found on the accused. This independent investigation led to a verdict in Defendant's favor.[114] By today's standards, this type of action by a juror would have resulted in a mistrial.

Some courts don't allow the jury to take notes. Some not only allow note-taking, they will even supply pads and pencils or pens. Some will even supply the jurors with notebooks which have pictures of the witnesses along with space to write their notes. It just depends on the rules established for that particular court.

In some trials, one or both parties may ask the judge to *invoke the rule*.[115] If the judge agrees, witnesses who will be called to testify will not be allowed to sit in the courtroom while other witnesses are testifying. This exclusion, of course, does not apply to the plaintiff or the defendant, or to someone the judge has deemed *essential*. Expert witnesses hate this rule because it often means sitting for hours in the hall or another room. There may be no televisions to watch, computers to play with, magazines or newspapers to read, or people to talk to while waiting to testify. They are allowed to use their own electronic devices while they are waiting for their turn to testify.

Darryl Weiman

Vocabulary

Bush v .Gore
voir dire - to speak the truth
cause challenges
peremptory challenges
Batson v. Kentucky
Powers v. Ohio
Edmonson v. Leesville Concrete Co.
Georgia v. McCollum
J.E.B. v. Alabama
Purkett v. Elem
jury consultants
preliminary instructions
12 Angry Men
invoke the rule

Citations

[105] Black's Law Dictionary, Seventh Edition, Bryan Garner, editor-in-chief.
[106] Black's Law Dictionary, Seventh Edition, Bryan Garner, editor-in-chief.
[107] *Batson v. Kentucky*, 476 U.S. 79 (1986).
[108] *Powers v. Ohio*, 499 U.S. 400 (1991).
[109] *Edmonson v. Leesville Concrete Co.*, 500 U.S. 614 (1991).
[110] *Georgia v. McCollum*, 505 U.S. 42 (1992).
[111] *J.E.B. v. Alabama*, 511 U.S. 127 (1994).
[112] *Purkett v. Elem*, 514 U.S. 765 (1995).

[113] Laala Al Jaber, Google Transforms Jury Selection Process, ABA Journal. www.abajournal.com/news/article/internet_transforms_jury_selection_process posted February 18, 2011.

[114] 12 Angry Men, the movie.

[115] Federal Rules of Evidence number 615.The Exclusion of Witnesses. This rule states, "[a]t the request of a party the court shall order witnesses excluded so that they cannot hear the testimony of other witnesses, and it may make the order of its own motion. This rule does not authorize exclusion of (1) a party who is a natural person, or (2) an officer or employee of a party which is not a natural person designated as its representative by its attorney, or (3) a person whose presence is shown by a party to be essential to the presentation of the party's cause, or (4) a person authorized by statute to be present."

Chapter 9:
Opening Statements

After the preliminary instructions, the court will be ready for opening statements. The opening statements are the first chance for the lawyers to tell the jury what they expect the evidence to show during the course of the trial and why they should win for their client. It is also the initial impression made on the jury in regard to the trial. As in most areas of life, the first impression is often the one that lasts and thus will go a long way to your winning or losing the case. The opening statement should be forceful and logical. It should establish the theme and present the facts that you plan to show which will entitle you to a verdict in your favor. Your opponent will try to accomplish the same thing for their side.

Your attorney will explain your version of the case— what really happened from your point of view. He should mention the facts that are uncontested and then move to the facts in dispute and explain your version of these contested facts. He should be logical, understandable, and be consistent with common sense. He should not twist the facts, mislead, or try to confuse. The jury will see right through this ill-advised strategy.

He should not be repetitious and he should not overstate your evidence. Some lawyers will disagree with this last statement. They believe you should present your main themes at least three times so that they will stick in the minds of the jury. It's a matter of personal choice, but many lawyers prefer "less is more." Don't bring up any evidence that you don't intend to prove in the course of the trial. This would be a disaster as the jury may think you have purposely tried to mislead them.

Make it so the jury will come to realize your case is even better than you laid out in the opening statement. You can do this by understating your evidence. Juries may feel empowered if they conclude that your case is even stronger than you have led them to expect. Studies have shown that most people can only maintain a high level of concentration for about 15 to 20 minutes. Therefore, it is advisable that the opening and the closing arguments be no longer than thirty minutes.

Juries are generally made up of laymen with no medical background. Your attorney should know this and should do his best to make the statement understandable and interesting. Keeping an eye on the jury's body language is important. If it looks like they are getting tired or bored, it usually means the statement was too long and/or they didn't understand some things said in the statement. It's very important to listen to the opposition's statement because it's not unusual for them to mention evidence that they may never present at the trial. If this happens, your attorney should point out this shortcoming during the closing arguments. Juries have a tendency to resent misrepresentation and the opponents will be sure to focus on these shortcomings of their adversaries in their closing statements.

The opening statement is usually presented in a storytelling form with themes of what the attorney believes are based on their client's viewpoint. It is not unusual for the judge to put a time limit on these statements. It is acceptable to use exhibits during the openings and they can be very important in clarifying some difficult issues. They can also be very effective in getting the jury's attention. However, if the jury is focusing on an exhibit, they may be distracted from what you are trying to tell them. As in all parts of the case, your attorney will be weighing the risks and benefits of how best to present your case. If you have a good attorney, you defer to his experience and judgment just as he should defer to you on the medical issues.

The opening statement is meant to state facts. Your lawyer will not present any argument during the opening statement because he wants to build into his arguments. The closing statement is for both facts and arguments. In the closing, the arguments can be for conclusions, credibility of witnesses, common sense experiences, and any other matter the lawyer deems to be important for your case.

Since the opening is reserved for a statement of facts, there should be no personal opinions. Facts alone should project the picture you want. For example, stating that a sponge was left inside the abdomen during a laparotomy would be proper. Stating that the surgeon was an incompetent idiot who recklessly left a sponge inside the plaintiff would not be proper and the person saying that would lose credibility with the judge and jury.

However, if your lawyer is trying to lay out a theme for the case which is technically an argument, the judge will usually give him some latitude since the themes are meant to help the jury better comprehend the stance of the two parties. In some courts, the defendant may reserve their opening statement until after the plaintiff has presented all of their evidence. This strategy is mainly used in criminal trials and is used to prevent the plaintiff from surmising some of the defendant's legal strategy.

Some courts require that the opening statement describes all of the elements which are required to make a *prima facie* case. Lawyers statements are taken as admissions so if their statement is lacking, they may lose their case very early. Perception is critical and without a strong opening statement, the jury may not pay attention to anything else the lawyer has to present in the trial. This requirement applies to both the plaintiff and the defendant. The defendant may have to present all of the elements required for a counterclaim or for an affirmative defense or they can lose very early, also.

If there are any weaknesses to the case, the attorney may decide to let the jury know about them right away. If you acknowledge your own weaknesses they will usually not be as damaging to you as they would be if they were first brought up by your opponent. For example, if you have neglected to ever become board certified in your specialty, your opponent can make it look like you were never really competent to practice what you do. If, however, you admit to not being board certified but hospitals will routinely allow physicians to have privileges so long as they went through the proper training, any damage your adversary will try to inflict will not be as severe.

At the conclusion of the opening your attorney will usually tell the jury exactly what he wants from them, a verdict in your favor.

Darryl Weiman

Vocabulary

prima facie

Chapter 10: Plaintiffs

Plaintiff's Case in Chief

Since the burden of proof—*burden of persuasion*—is on the plaintiff, they get to present their evidence first. If the evidence does not support every element required to win the action, the plaintiff will be at risk for a motion for a *directed verdict*. Although the burden of proof is initially with the plaintiff, it may shift during some portions of the case. These shifts will occur if the defendant presents an *affirmative defense* or if the defendant has a *counterclaim*. *Affirmative defenses* and *counterclaims* must be proven by the party claiming them; i.e., the defendant in this situation.

The plaintiff will call a witness to testify. The witness will be sworn in by the court clerk and then the witness will sit in the witness chair and will be asked questions by the plaintiff's attorney. These questions are usually open-ended so as to allow the witness to tell his story in his own words. This examination of the witness is called *direct examination* and is done by the party calling the witness. A "leading" question is one in which the questioner supplies information and the witness is then asked to agree or disagree. Usually this type of question is not allowed; however, they may be deemed proper if they supply background information or deal with matters that aren't in dispute.

There are special problems you might face when you put an expert witness on the stand. If you have an expert with superb credentials, don't be surprised if the opposing party tries to keep you from bringing those credentials to the attention of the jury. They will do this by trying to stipulate that while the expert is qualified to testify, for the sake of brevity it will not be necessary to legally establish his expert qualifications. Do not fall for this trap unless his credentials are really not that good. Remember, it's the jury who must decide which expert witness they will believe so it's important for them to have some idea of his knowledge, education, training, experience, and skill.

One issue that often comes up in regard to the credibility of the expert witness is the fee. If the expert is charging a reasonable fee for their work and appearance at trial, then the *offering side* may choose to not bring up the details. However, if the witness is charging an exorbitant amount, the *offering side* may want to bring this out on direct examination since it will likely have a lesser effect on the jury than if the information is explored on the cross-examination. Remember, if the expert is charging a high fee, then the jury may think that more than his expertise is being bought. High fees do not necessarily mean the witness is more qualified to be an expert witness.

On the issue of fees, courts have agreed that it's appropriate for the expert witness to be compensated for his time and expertise. However, the fee cannot be contingent on the outcome of the case. In fact, any plaintiff's attorney that agrees to compensate an expert on a contingency basis will be violating a rule of professional responsibility for which he can be sanctioned.[116]

One of the most important tasks facing the attorney is to convince the jury that the expert they are presenting is credible. They will do this by presenting the expert's formal education and then going into his actual work experience. Often, too much time is spent with the education which can be formidable. Many believe the jury is more inclined to listen to a practicing physician who has actually done the procedures in question and has taken care of similar types of patients. Juries will tend to believe that an expert who has done something hundreds of times with good results has probably gotten pretty good at doing it and knows what they are talking about.

It is important to discuss the education and training of the expert. It's just as important to portray your expert as modest and not arrogant. Perhaps the best way to accomplish both goals is to ask leading questions which will allow your expert to agree with the most impressive credentials you've brought up. This approach will give the impression your expert is humble.

Minimally, you will want the expert to describe his undergraduate and graduate education and the degrees he's earned, the certifications and licenses he has gotten, the articles he has authored especially those related to the case at hand, his teaching experience, his previous expert witness experience, and any other activity that may have a direct relationship to the case. To supplement the testimony, the expert's Curriculum Vitae (CV) should be offered as an exhibit which will allow the jury to go over other accomplishments without boring them with long drawn out testimony which may make the witness look like a show-off. As an exhibit, the jury will be allowed to have the CV when they are deliberating.

The expert witness will be asked to give an opinion as to whether or not the standard of care was met and they will generally be asked to give an opinion as to *causation*. Causation is a legal term meaning what caused the injury. The bases of their opinions—the information that they relied on in creating their opinion—will need to be revealed. When giving his opinion, the expert may try to sneak in information that may have been deemed to be inadmissible. If he succeeds, the jury will have the information even if your attorney makes a motion to strike the testimony and he wins the motion.[117] Often just hearing the information before it is stricken from the record is all the jury needs to have the seed planted.

It's routine practice for the opposing attorney to object whenever an expert is asked to testify on what he has based his opinion. This is another reason that it's prudent, although it may be expensive, to depose any of your opposition's experts so that you know beforehand what they are going to testify about and what they have based their opinions on. It is also important in the deposition to ask them if they are going to raise any other issues at trial that were not discussed at the deposition. This will lock them in and prevent them from bringing up new information at trial, unless your attorney opens the door by raising a new issue with his questions. If the witness starts to stray from his deposition testimony, your attorney should object and stop him before the new information gets to the jury.

If you are worried that your expert might raise some objectionable material during his testimony, it would be wise to raise these issues in a pre-trial motion and let the judge make a decision. The judge has a great deal of discretion under the rules, and if he thinks you are trying to bring in some "back door hearsay" he will probably sustain any objection and he, likely, will be upset with your side for not being forthright.

In medical malpractice cases, it's usually the medical records that supply the bulk of the material on which the opinions are based. If the expert obtained some opinions from their colleagues, this should be brought out in the testimony as it's common for physicians to obtain the opinions of others while taking care of patients, and the jury needs to know if these opinions tend to strengthen the testimony of the expert on the stand.

When the direct examination of the witness is completed, the attorney will let the court know by saying something like "nothing further on direct, your Honor." At this time, the defendant's attorney will now be given the opportunity to do a *cross-examination* of the witness.

Cross-examination is a risky business. The opposing lawyer gets to question a witness put on the stand by the other side. It's wise for the attorney about to embark on a cross-examination to have a reasonable expectation of what it is he wants to accomplish and what he is likely to accomplish. The best way for him to have this reasonable expectation is to have deposed the witness before the trial. Hopefully, the deposition will have elicited the same testimony that the witness will be giving at the trial and the final questions of the deposition will be designed to get the witness to agree that the total scope of the planned testimony will be limited to what was covered at the deposition. This should prevent the witness from pulling a surprise at the trial.

Many plaintiffs' attorneys do not depose all, or any, of the defendant's expert witnesses. They possibly do this to save money since they are responsible for paying the opposing expert's fees for the deposition. This may leave them open to potentially devastating testimony.

One of the strategies that lawyers are taught is to simply ignore it when a witness gives a damaging answer to one of their questions. By keeping a straight face and basically ignoring a devastating answer, the lawyer is trying to limit its impact on the jury. If the jury sees only a minimal reaction by the attorney, they may think that the answer is not as bad as they thought it might be. Just like on television, good lawyers are good actors.

There are two main goals to be accomplished on the cross-examination. The first is to get the witness to agree to the facts you know will support your case, which in turn will be consistent with your theory of what the case is all about. The second goal, if you decide to pursue it, is to discredit the witness or his testimony so that the jury will be more likely to disregard what he said. The second goal may need to be ignored if the witness has given you favorable testimony. It doesn't make much sense to try and discredit the witness after you have gotten him to testify favorably as to the facts and the theories.

The questions used on cross-examination are usually *leading,* meaning the questions are formed so as to suggest the answer. As such, these questions can be answered by a simple *"yes"* or *"no."* It's acceptable to ask non-leading questions when you know the witness has previously committed to an answer from prior testimony or you know that you can *impeach* him from an unexpected answer—such as an answer that is different from what is stated in a previous deposition or affidavit or from a previous article he has written.

Don't have the witness repeat what he said on the direct examination in hopes that he'll make a mistake in the second telling. The mistake is not likely to happen and will only serve to reinforce what he's already said to the jury. It's a mistake to argue with the witness. The lawyer who argues with the witness is acting unprofessionally and his credibility will be negatively affected. The jury will not look favorably upon a lawyer who is seen to be bullying a witness who is not familiar or comfortable with the courtroom environment.

Usually the *cross-examination* is limited to subject matter which was brought up on the *direct examination.* In some states, the *cross-examination* can go into any relevant matter. This could be useful if the witness said some things during the discovery process that would be helpful to your case, but were areas that were ignored by plaintiff's attorney on direct examination.

A recent case involved the plaintiff's expert witness claiming malpractice had occurred because the defendant heart surgeon had mismanaged the fluids of the patient in the post-operative period. On the expert's affidavit and during his deposition he went into the fluid shifts which usually occur in a patient who has had heart surgery with the use of the heart lung machine. There were issues raised about electrolyte shifts, falls in platelet counts, dilution of the red blood cells, and end organ dysfunction, all of which they attributed to the heart lung machine. The problem with the plaintiff's argument rested on the fact that the patient had an off-pump bypass for which the heart-lung machine wasn't used. Rather than get a new expert, the plaintiff chose to hope that the defendant's attorney had missed this obvious discrepancy and went ahead with the expert's testimony at trial; again using the theory that the fluids had been mismanaged, but never mentioning the shifts inherent with use of the heart-lung machine.

On *cross-examination,* it was very easy to question the statements in the affidavit and the deposition to show the expert had not done a very good job of reviewing the medical records since a competent heart surgeon would have seen from the operative note and the anesthesia record that the heart-lung machine had not been used.

This witness's credibility was successfully attacked and he was forced to admit it was more likely that the shifts were due to overwhelming sepsis—which was the theory espoused by the defendant. This was a huge step in the defendant's winning the case.

It is interesting to note that the witness, although a Board Certified thoracic surgeon, did not do cardiac surgery. He had limited his practice to thoracic, non-cardiac, and vascular surgery. Not surprisingly, the defendant won the case.

If you are a witness, as a defendant or expert, beware of the *cross-examination*. Your lawyer is now sitting down and in his place is the opposing attorney whose job it is to tear you and your testimony apart. This is often a time of high anxiety. However, keep in mind that the attorney can never know as much as the clinician who took care of the patient. The attorney may have read up on the case and been instructed by his own medical experts, but he did not examine the patient, form a treatment plan, and follow the clinical course like the clinician did.

However, don't underestimate the opposing attorney. Assume he has done his homework on the issues and he is probably aware of several articles which support his position. You must always treat opposing counsel with respect. Listen carefully to the questions and don't start to answer until you have given them some thought. This will give your attorney a chance to object if he feels it is necessary and it will also give you a chance to consider vague or misleading words that he may have used in the question. If the question is vague, it's appropriate to ask for a clarification. If the attorney tries to slip in a fact you don't agree with, it's alright to state you do not agree with the fact.

During a trial, an expert witness was asked, "Since we know that the tear in the aorta originated in the descending aorta, it could not be considered an ascending aortic dissection. As such, shouldn't the patient first have a trial of medical therapy?" This particular patient had an extension of the tear going proximally into the ascending aorta so the surgical option needed to be considered first. The expert witness, who was a thoracic surgeon, didn't let the attorney get away with the false statement.

Be especially careful with a cross-examiner who is overly polite. He is probably setting you up for some very difficult questions. Don't be surprised if the examiner asks if you have rehearsed your testimony with your attorney. Surely you have discussed your potential testimony with your attorney and he likely educated you on the legal aspects of the case. It is acceptable to say this in your answer.

If you have memorized your testimony, the cross-examiner will make this obvious with his questions; he will get you confused and you will forget where you are in your memorized statement. Always stick with the facts of the case. Keep the facts in mind, and your answers should come easily and remain consistent. Don't be surprised if the cross-examiner tries to get you angry. He may ask repetitive questions, keep you on the stand for a long time, and cast aspersions on your integrity. He may even give you a stack of medical records and ask you to look through it for the facts that you have relied on. Maintain your composure, do not respond in anger, and calmly start reviewing the chart. No matter how tired you are, don't lose control no matter how hard opposing council tries to get you angry. Being grilled on a cross-examination is exhausting; try to stay as calm as possible. If you lose your composure you will also lose your credibility.

The jury and the judge will recognize if the examiner is trying to bully you. It's alright to ask for a clarification or even have counsel repeat the question. If the question asks for a "yes" or a "no" answer, then just use those words. Anything you volunteer will only open you up for a new line of questioning. Your goal is to finish the cross-examination with your original testimony intact.

If you have been the witness and the two sides are done examining you, be careful how you leave the stand. The jury and the judge are still watching everything you do. It's wise to maintain your composure and walk off the stand in a dignified manner. Don't look sheepish or flustered. This will give the impression that you have lost the battle. On the other hand, do not look smug or even smile. You should never assume that you will be victorious as there is little certainty as to the eventual outcome of a lawsuit. Remember, body language is critical to how you are perceived.

After the cross-examination has been completed, the direct examiner is now given the opportunity to do a *re-direct*. The *re-direct* is usually used to *rebut* or explain issues that were raised on the cross-examination. Since the jury usually has a short attention span, it would be unwise to revisit matters that were already presented on the original direct examination.

If your witness has been *impeached* during the cross, it will be a chance for the direct examiner to try and *rehabilitate* the witness. It's also an opportunity to let the witness explain, in detail, any questions that he was forced to answer in a "yes" or "no" fashion by the cross-examiner. Any new matters that were brought out on cross would now be fair game to explore on re-direct.

Besides witnesses, the plaintiff will also present evidence in the form of exhibits, stipulations, and judicial notice. Exhibits come in the form of real objects like blood, drugs, and surgical instruments; writings like contracts and letters; demonstrative objects like models, charts, and diagrams; and records like medical records. The side seeking to have exhibits admitted as evidence needs to establish a foundation that the exhibit is what it claims to be. This foundation can come in the form of testimony from a witness, a certification from a keeper of the record, or some other method. If the court admits the exhibit as evidence, the jury will then be allowed to consider the exhibit in their deliberations just like any other evidence that is presented at the trial.

Because there are different kinds of exhibits, the law has broken them up into various categories. Exhibits are called *real evidence* if they are the actual, tangible objects involved in the case. For example, if a chest tube is unintentionally rammed into the heart during its intended placement into the pleural cavity, the actual chest tube can be brought in and shown to the jury.

Demonstrative evidence are exhibits used to represent the real thing. Photographs, diagrams, models, and maps are kinds of *demonstrative evidence* that will be admissible as *real evidence* so long as they accurately and fairly represent the real thing and they will help the *trier of fact* to understand what is going on. Computer graphics are a relatively new example of *demonstrative evidence* and many courts are new equipped with state of the art audiovisual equipment so that these graphics can be projected for the jury to see.

Writings are documents that have legal significance. These can be contracts, wills, and checks or other promissory notes. Since these are legal documents in and of themselves, they are not considered to be *hearsay*. However, the documents need to have been signed by the person who executed them and that signature must be shown to be genuine.

Business records such as medical records are actually *hearsay* but they are admissible as a *hearsay* exception so long as the legally required foundation is laid. This foundation usually requires that a custodian of the records or some other qualified witness is able to testify the documents were made under the requirements of the pertinent Rule of Evidence and that the record was accurately made and maintained by the business or hospital if it's a medical record.[118]

Laying the proper foundation for a particular kind of exhibit can be tricky, but if it is done properly, the reliability and the relevance of the exhibit will have been established. This goes a long way for the exhibit to be factually persuasive.

Stipulations are facts that have been agreed on by the parties and are not really in dispute. The *stipulation*s are usually in writing and are shown or read to the jury. For example, the physician's office location may be agreed to so that the jurisdiction of the court will not need to be argued. Also, the fact that the physician owed a duty to the plaintiff may be so obvious that it would be a waste of the court's time to argue the issue.

Judicial notice will allow certain facts to be presented to the jury when the fact is well known to the jurisdiction where the trial is being held. For example, the University of Tennessee Medical School is located in Memphis. Another example would be where the fact can be verified from a reliable source such as when the medical school graduated the defendant's class.

The order that the plaintiff uses to present the witnesses and the exhibits is totally strategic and he can choose whatever order he wants. However, the plaintiff's attorneys should have some idea how long each witness will be on the stand because they don't want to be in a position where they run out of witnesses before the day is done, nor do they want to run overtime so as to keep one of their witnesses in town an extra day and have to pay for another day of the witness' time.

After the plaintiff has presented all of his evidence, he *rests*. He will usually announce he is done by addressing the judge and jury and saying something along the lines of, "Your Honor, the Plaintiff rests." At this point of the trial, the judge will probably take a recess because it is likely the defendant will want to present motions which the judge will need to hear and make decisions about before the end of the trial.

Motions after Plaintiff Rests

After the plaintiff has presented his case, the jury is excused so the defendant can make a motion. This motion is usually for a *directed verdict*. In a Federal Court this is called a motion for *a judgment as a matter of law*. The purpose of the motion is to try and end the case because the plaintiff failed to present enough evidence to meet their burden on all of the elements they must prove in order to have a *prima facie case*. The judge needs to look at all of the evidence in a way that is most favorable to the *non-movant*, the plaintiff in this case, and it is up to the defendant to present evidence as to why the plaintiff has failed to meet his burden.

The judge may grant all or parts of the motion or he may deny the motion. For example, in a malpractice case, the judge may deny an allegation there was no informed consent but he may rule that the elements of a malpractice action have been met. If any part of the motion has been denied, the trial will continue.

Darryl Weiman

Vocabulary

burden of persuasion
directed verdict
affirmative defense
counterclaim
direct examination
offering side
causation
cross-examination
leading
impeach
re-direct
rehabilitate
demonstrative evidence
real evidence
trier of fact
hearsay
stipulations
judicial notice
directed verdict
a judgment as a matter of law
prima facie case
non-movant

Citations

[116] ABA Model Rules of Professional Conduct Rule 3.4(b) states "A lawyer shall not…offer an inducement to a witness that is prohibited by law." The comment to this provision explains, "With regard to paragraph (b), it is not improper to pay a witness's expenses or to compensate an expert witness on terms permitted by law. The common law rule in most jurisdictions is that it is improper to pay an occurrence witness any fee for testifying and it is improper to pay an expert witness a contingent fee."

[117] The Federal Rule of Evidence 703 says, "facts or data that are otherwise inadmissible shall not be disclosed to the jury by the proponent of the opinion or inference unless the court determines that their probative value in assisting the jury to evaluate the expert's opinion substantially outweighs their prejudicial effect."

[118] For example, the Federal Rule of Evidence 803(6); Records of regularly conducted activity. A memorandum, report, record, or data compilation, in any form, of acts, events, conditions, opinions, or diagnoses, made at or near the time by, a person with knowledge, if kept in the course of regularly conducted business activity, and if it was the regular practice of that business activity to make the memorandum, report, record, or data compilation, all as shown by the testimony of the custodian or other qualified witness, or by certification that complies [with other rules] or a statute permitting certification, unless the source of information or the method or circumstances of preparation indicate a lack of trustworthiness.

Chapter 11: Defendants

Defendant's Case-in-Chief

It will now be the defendant's turn to present evidence which is meant to disprove the evidence presented by the plaintiff. During this part of the trial, the defendant will also be allowed to present evidence to prove any *affirmative defenses* or any other claims they might have. The defense is given the opportunity to present witnesses, use exhibits, present stipulations and judicially noticed facts just like the plaintiff did. Just as in the plaintiff's case-in-chief, the plaintiff will be allowed to cross-examine any witness put on by the defendant.

After the defendant has presented his evidence, he will announce to the jury and the judge "the Defense rests." At this point of the trial, it is likely the judge will take a recess, again to hear motions that are sure to come from both sides.

Objections

During depositions or in court during a trial, formal protests can be raised to disallow the testimony of a witness or any other form of evidence that would violate a *rule of evidence* or a *rule of procedure*. These protests are called *objections* and they must be raised by the opposing party. Typically, the *objection* is raised after the question has been asked of the witness but before the witness has answered because counsel doesn't want the jury to hear the answer. If the answer has already been given, an objection can still be made and the jury can be instructed by the judge to disregard the answer, but the damage will have already been done.

After the *objection* has been raised, the judge must make a ruling. If the judge agrees with the objection, he will *sustain* the objection meaning the question, testimony, or other evidence will not be allowed to go to the jury. If the judge disagrees with the objection, he will say the objection is *overruled* and the evidence will be allowed in.

You can actually object to the judge's ruling. This *objection* will preserve your right to appeal the judge's ruling to the appellate court. If you do not raise this type of *objection,* you may lose your right to appeal on this particular ruling. Most courts have rendered this type of *objection* superfluous, meaning that the original *objection* would be enough to preserve your right to appeal the judge's ruling on the matter.

Lawyers make mistakes. Sometimes they make mistakes on purpose to try and get the jury to see or hear something they shouldn't be allowed to see or hear. Your attorney must be vigilant at all times so that he can object if one of these "mistakes" was to occur. Learning how and when to make an objection is very difficult.

Here are some samples of question types for which *objections* would be proper in American courts of law:

(1) Questions that are ambiguous or misleading, or confusing, such that it would be difficult for the witness to properly answer. These types of questions may have words which have more than one meaning so that the witness may have a misunderstanding of what the question is asking.

(2) Arguing the law instead of asking a question in an attempt to instruct the jury is improper. Questions that state a conclusion and then ask the witness to either agree or disagree are what your attorney is looking for here. These types of questions may be proper for the closing argument where the attorney is actually asking the jury to agree with his conclusions.

(3) Questions that make an argument instead of asking a question.
(4) Asking a question that's already been answered. The objecting attorney will object and then say something like, "asked and answered."
(5) Questions which assume facts that aren't in evidence won't be allowed. For example, if a physician has to take a patient back to the operating room to evacuate a clot from the chest and the plaintiff asks, "Isn't it true that the uncontrolled hemorrhage was due to your failure to do a proper suture?" This question assumes there was "uncontrolled hemorrhage" which would be a fact which is in dispute or not in evidence. If you weren't listening closely, this message may have made it to the jury's ears which would be harmful to your case.
(6) The lawyer doing the questioning isn't allowed to ask questions which are meant to antagonize the witness so as to evoke an emotional response. These types of questions are usually meant to make fun of the witness. Questions asked without giving the witness a chance to answer would fall into this category.
(7) *The Best Evidence Rule.* This rule requires that the original source of evidence is available if needed. A copy will be acceptable if the parties agree it's the same as the original. For example, asking the witness to recall a particular blood value result

would not be proper since the value would be in the medical records, or a copy of the medical records, which should be the actual document entered into evidence. If the questioner wants to know a particular lab value, he should refer to the medical records.

Sometimes the questioner is trying to embarrass the witness. He will try to convince the jury a good witness would remember the value without having to refer to the medical record. Most jurors would see through this ploy but it would be acceptable for you to admit that you don't remember and would like to refer to the chart.

However, if there is a genuine issue over the documents authenticity, such as a forged signature, then the original document, not a copy, must be produced.

(8) The rules state the questions asked on *cross-examination* have to be related to the points which have been brought out on the *direct exam*. Any attempt to ask a question that is beyond the scope of the *direct exam* can be objected to as being *beyond the scope* of the *direct exam*.

(9) Expert witnesses are allowed to give their opinions, but witnesses should not be asked for an opinion unless it is within the realm of their experience. For example, a nurse may not give an opinion as to how the aorta should be cannulated

in order to hook up to the heart-lung machine, but they may be allowed to comment they have never seen the cannula placed with the amount of force used by the surgeon during the case in question. Counsel can object if the question calls for an opinion rather than facts.

(10) If a question asks the witness to guess at an answer then counsel can object because the question calls for *speculation*. Cases are supposed to be decided on the facts and the law. Having a witness guess as to the facts or *speculate* on what might have happened is *irrelevant* so this objection really relates back to the *relevancy objection*. "Isn't it true that the patient would not have died from a heart attack if you had not operated in the first place?" This *objection* is similar to giving an *opinion objection*, and it may be hard to differentiate the two. The judge may have difficulty also, but he may allow the *objection* knowing that it is one or the other.

(11) Compound questions, where the questioner is asking several questions at once, are objectionable. You can have a good idea that the question is compound if the conjunctive "and" or the disjunctive "or" is used to join two or more questions. Imagine how stressful it would be to the witness if a compound question is asked – and no *objection* is raised – and the answers are different for the questions. "During the operation,

wouldn't it have been safer to use the heart-lung machine and perhaps even use deep hypothermia?" Which question should be answered? The one about the heart-lung machine or the one about deep hypothermia? Or does the witness have to answer both? It would be proper to have the questioner break things up into separate questions.

(12) *Hearsay* is objectionable. Asking the witness to relate what he heard from another person falls under the *hearsay* rule and is not allowed unless it falls under one of the *hearsay* exceptions.

(13) You may object to a question that the witness is not competent to answer. For example, a nurse would not be competent to answer if an operation is indicated for a particular patient as that procedure is usually beyond the scope of practice for a nurse.

(14) Questions that are intended to cause prejudice may be objected to, as well. This type of objection is usually related to exhibits, such as photographs, where the shock effect may be very *prejudicial* especially if the *probative* (tending to prove or disprove a fact) value of the exhibit is minimal. In a malpractice action, this *objection* may be raised if the injured party was asked to display their injuries to the jury. Lawyers who are objecting based on *prejudice* may object based on Rule 403 of the *Rules of Evidence*. This will let the judge

know why they are objecting, but will keep the jury in the dark. You would not want to arouse the curiosity of the jury by stating the evidence is *prejudicial*.

(15) During the direct examination, the questioner is not supposed to suggest the answer to the witness. If the questioner does ask a question that is *leading* this will lead to an *objection*. However, *leading questions* are allowed on *cross-examination* when the witness is generally deemed to be *hostile* — or if the attorney conducting the exam has gotten permission from the court to treat one of his own witnesses as *hostile*.

(16) A *narrative objection* could be raised if the witness starts to tell a story when the question did not ask for one.

(17) The witness may have a privilege granted by law which would allow him to not answer a question. For example, the marital spouse privilege would allow a wife to remain silent rather than answer a question that would be harmful to her husband.

(18) Irrelevant questions are objectionable. Questions should only be about the issues raised in the trial.

(19) The court has the discretion to stop *cumulative* evidence. For example, it would generally not be proper to have several witnesses say the same thing or have exhibits demonstrate the same

thing. A physician was once dismissed from a trial where he was called to be a *fact witness* to explain an email he had written. The opposing party had objected because the same email had been explained earlier in the trial by the person to whom it had been sent.

Objections are most commonly raised to the questions being asked by the examining attorney to the person on the witness stand; however, it may also be proper for the examining attorney to object to a witnesses answer or non-answer.

Objections are also commonly used during a deposition but, since the judge is not present, the witness will still need to answer the question. However, by raising the *objection*, the testimony may be excluded as evidence when asking the judge to rule on that objection at a later time. If the *objection* is not made, you may not be allowed to object at a later time since the attorney asking the question was not allowed the chance to rephrase the question to make it "unobjectionable."

When you are on the witness stand being examined by your adversary's lawyer, he will try to ask you questions in such a way that they can only be answered with a "yes" or a "no." Usually, the best strategy will be to do what he wants and use the one word answers. If you don't, he will ask the judge to strike your answer as being *narrative* — telling a story when the question didn't ask for one.

He will then ask the judge to instruct you to answer the question properly. By making this objection, he is trying to accomplish two things. First, he is trying to limit your testimony in a way that is favorable to his client. Second, he is trying to show the jury that he is smarter than you. How smart can you be if you cannot answer a simple "yes" or "no" question? If you try to dodge the question, he will try to convince the jury you have something you're trying to hide.

If the witness continues to try and dodge the questions, the lawyer may ask the court to admonish the witness. This admonishment will serve to notify the jury that the witness is not acting properly and, of course, this will affect the witness's credibility.

Sometimes, you may not be able to answer with a "yes" or a "no." For example:

> "Isn't it true, doctor, that a patient with symptomatic aortic insufficiency should have the valve repaired or replaced?"

Heart surgeons will generally agree a patient with aortic insufficiency who is symptomatic from the insufficiency should be operated on — so long as he is an operative candidate. Generally, the surgery will not be offered to a nanogenarian who has end-stage Alzheimer's disease or metastatic, untreatable cancer. So you may have to explain to the judge and jury that a one word answer is just not possible unless you have more information. By holding your ground you will actually show the jury that you are the one with the knowledge and, perhaps it is the opposing attorney who is trying to mislead.

There is another way to handle the questions you are prevented from expounding on and that is to have your attorney turn you loose when he has a chance on redirect after the opposing attorney is done. For example:

> "Dr. ABC, are there any questions that you were asked on cross-examination that you would like to expound on?"

At that time, it would be proper to explain how simple "yes" and "no" answers are just not reasonable for some of the questions that have been asked.

Another objection the opposing attorney might make while you are testifying to his questions is that you are "unresponsive." This may occur when he asks you one question and you answer a different question.

> "Dr. ABC, isn't it true that Dr. DEF is your friend?"

"Yes. I have worked with Dr. ABC for over ten years."

Notice that the second part of the answer was not in response to the question. Even though there would be a risk of annoying the jury by objecting to the unasked for response, it may be strategically necessary to keep the witness from adding commentary that is favorable to his side.

If a series of questions is being asked about some issue that counsel is objecting to and counsel is overruled, counsel may ask the court for a "continuing objection." By doing this, he will be preserving the right to appeal as it relates to the objection while at the same time he will not be aggravating the judge and/or the jury by objecting to every question being asked on the issue. The court has the discretion to allow the continuing objection and they will usually do this so the testimony can proceed with fewer interruptions. Stay alert, listen closely, and be prepared. Objections have a way of getting you off-guard and doing or saying something that could hurt your case.

Motions after Defendant Rests

After the defendant is finished with his witnesses, the judge will excuse the jury from the courtroom. The judge will then hear motions from the plaintiff. These motions usually are asking for a directed verdict on the defendant's affirmative defenses and any counterclaims that were raised during the trial. If the defendant has failed to prove any of the necessary elements required for an affirmative defense or a counterclaim, the judge will probably grant the motion as it pertains to that particular defense or counterclaim.[119]

Vocabulary

affirmative defenses
rule of evidence
rule of procedure
objections
sustain
overruled
The Best Evidence Rule
cross-examination
direct exam
beyond the scope
speculation
irrelevant
relevancy objection
opinion objection
hearsay
prejudicial
probative — tending to prove or disprove something
Rules of Evidence
leading questions
hostile
narrative objection

cumulative

fact witness

judgment

narrative (telling a story when the question didn't ask for one.)

Citation

[119] Thomas A. Mauet, <u>Trial Techniques</u>, Sixth Edition, p.9, 2002.

Chapter 12:
Plaintiff's Rebuttal and Defendant's Surrebuttal

After the defendant has presented his side of the case, the plaintiff will be allowed to present evidence that serves to rebut the defendant's evidence. This *rebuttal* evidence cannot go beyond what was presented by the defendant in his *case-in-chief*. This evidence may serve as a defense to any counterclaims or it may be evidence that contradicts any evidence presented by the defendant. After plaintiff's rebuttal, the defendant will then be given the opportunity to rebut any specific evidence that was raised during plaintiff's rebuttal. This is sometimes referred to as the defendant's *surrebutal*.

Any new evidence that was brought in during the *rebuttal* can be explored as to its credibility. This back and forth *rebuttal* is common and it usually doesn't take much time. As a result, there should never be a situation where evidence is presented to the jury that can't be scrutinized by the opposing party.

Vocabulary

rebuttal
case-in-chief
surrebutal

Chapter 13:
Instruction Conference

At some point during the case, the judge will need to decide on which jury instructions he will submit to the jury. The judge will meet with the plaintiffs and the defendants who will argue as to what instructions should be given, denied or modified. This conference may be held in court, without the jury being present, or in chambers. No matter the location, the court reporter needs to be present to record the requests and the objections so that a record will be available if an error is alleged in the instructions causing an appeal to take place.

In most jurisdictions, if a lawyer disagrees on a ruling made during the *instruction conference*, he must make a specific *objection* on the record if he is to raise the adverse ruling on appeal. Even if the *instruction conference* is made before all of the evidence has been submitted, the judge will usually not make any final decisions until he has heard all of the evidence. As such, the *instruction conference* usually occurs after both sides rest but before the closing arguments have been given.

Vocabulary

instruction conference
objection

Chapter 14: Closing Arguments

The *closing argument* is your last chance to communicate directly with the jury. It's essential the *closing argument* accurately presents your theory of the case along with your supporting evidence. It should also reflect your stance on the contested issues and the reasons why the jury should award you with a favorable verdict. The argument should be planned and organized in such a way that the jury can easily follow. Be persuasive and direct. Unfortunately, many lawyers are rambling, inarticulate, and inaccurate in their closing arguments. If you are worried about your attorney's oral skills, you should probably fire him.

Closing arguments are aptly named. You are expected to argue your side; this is no time for a dry summation of the events that have unfolded at trial. There's a role for emotion and you can be sure the plaintiff's attorney will use plenty of emotion to try and get the jury to feel for his client. It's not unusual for the plaintiff's attorney to even generate their own tears as they describe the unimaginable hardships their clients have endured due to the alleged medical malpractice. Former senator and presidential candidate, John Edwards, was even known to pretend to channel the thoughts of deceased babies during his closing arguments. An effective argument will drive the jury to do what you want and then feel good about doing it afterwards.

Like the opening statements, the closing should take from 20 to 30 minutes. Any more, and the jury may tune you out. Do not use too many details as that may overwhelm the jury because they can only remember so much and you want them to remember the key elements of your case. Revise the themes you had in the opening in your closing arguments. Your theory of the case should logically explain both the undisputed and disputed facts that have been admitted during the trial. Argue only the facts and avoid personal opinions. The jury has been instructed to decide the case based on the evidence. They should care less about your opinions and may even be put off if they perceive you are trying to tell them how to do their job.

Projection is a very useful tool in a *closing argument*. *Cathy Chapman, et al., v. James Lewis, M.D., et al.*[120] involved a motor vehicle accident where William Chapman II eventually died. The plaintiff brought a wrongful death action alleging malpractice on the part of the physicians. The plaintiff's expert as to the standard of care was a Dr. Witorsh who had a long history of testifying as a medical expert witness. During the trial, it was brought out that Dr. Witorsh had, in past trials, offered opinions relating to cardiology, neurosurgery, pathology, life-expectancy, and injuries related to SUV rollovers. In fact, Dr. Witorsh was a pulmonologist with no surgical training of any sort. At closing, defendant's counsel wanted to stress to the jury that Dr. Witorsh had a history of testifying on issues that were beyond his expertise so they projected some of the questions and answers from the transcript of the trial.

The plaintiffs objected to the *projection*, arguing there was no proper foundation of the projected testimony. The judge overruled the *objection* and allowed the *projection* to occur since they were the same questions used during the trial. Not surprisingly, the jury returned a verdict for the defendant.

The trial judge, after the verdict, had a change of heart and reversed the decision on the motion. The judge agreed that a proper foundation had not been laid on the *projected* material and the defendants had failed to give proper notice of their intention to use parts of the trial transcript that had not yet been verified. He then awarded the plaintiff a new trial.

The defendants appealed and the appellate court ruled for the defendants and reinstated the original verdict.

The appellate court said, "It is well established that there is nothing wrong with reminding the jury of testimony of various witnesses in closing argument."[121] Choosing to *project* portions of the testimony that were favorable for the defendant's theory of the case were deemed to be proper. Since both sides had agreed what had been projected had come directly from the trial transcript, there was no issue as to the accuracy of what had been projected. As such, the appellate court ruled there was no harm to the plaintiff as to the projection of portions of the transcript during the defendant's closing argument.[122]

This decision is consistent with Tennessee law which states, "In a trial of any civil suit, counsel for either party shall be permitted to use a blackboard, model, or similar device, also any picture, plat or exhibit introduced in evidence, in connection with counsel's argument to the jury for purposes of illustrating the counsel's contentions with respect to the issues that are to be decided by the jury, provided that counsel shall not, in writing, present any argument that could not be properly made orally."[123]

Some people are visual learners and some are auditory learners. Testimony can be *projected* onto a screen during *closing arguments*. Remember this as it can be very useful for your case. Those of the jury who are visual learners will be better able to understand your case if they can see it on a screen.

Just as you want to stress the strong points of your argument, you may want to point out the weaknesses of your opponent's argument to force him to explain these weaknesses. Of course, you don't want to be led into a trap where he has a great argument that has been held back to use in the rebuttal.

How the *closing argument* is delivered is really dependent on the individual style of the lawyer. It's important the jury feels your lawyer firmly and passionately believes in your side of the controversy, no matter what style is used. Near the end of the closing, it is important to again let the jury know what it is you want and why you are entitled to have what you want.

The plaintiffs have the added obligation of asking for damages and trying to explain the *intangibles*, like pain and suffering, which would justify the amount they are requesting. Defendants should probably avoid any conversation about damages in their closing. Why talk about an issue that would only be relevant if you were somehow liable? Since you are claiming no *liability*, a discussion of *damages* might indicate you may not be so sure of your position.

In states where *comparative fault doctrine* is used to apportion the amount of damages, it may be reasonable to discuss the issue with your attorney prior to the closing. One thing you do not want to have happen is to have the various defendants all pointing fingers at each other saying that one or the other is the negligent party.

If it's clear there are several parties, including the plaintiff, that might have liability, then it may be good strategy to present this issue to the jury. They may need to be reminded that they can apportion the liability not only on the defendant, but also on the plaintiff, others who may have settled, and even on non-parties who were never named in the suit to begin with. The issue of *comparative fault* can be complicated so be sure to have this discussion with your attorney so you do not lose out on this important opportunity to educate the jury.

Remember the jury instructions. Be sure your closing argument reminds the jury about what facts have been shown and how those facts either prove or fail to prove what the law requires them to establish. Since the *burden of persuasion* is on the plaintiff, the courts will generally allow him the opportunity to rebut issues which were raised by the defendant in the *closing argument*. If the plaintiff's *closing argument* is weak, he may be sandbagging whereby he is saving his best arguments for the *rebuttal* of the defendant's closing. If you and your attorney feel this is the strategy of the plaintiff, it is within your rights to waive your closing argument or, perhaps, limit the closing to one or two very specific issues. This could block any attempt by the plaintiff to bring up issues on *rebuttal* since you did not raise them during your closing. This is a strategic decision best left for your lawyer.

For example, if your closing only deals with liability, the plaintiff cannot bring up the issue of damages or causation in his rebuttal. In these types of strategic issues it is best to defer to the knowledge and experience of your lawyer who will have a better feel on how strict the court will be in sustaining scope of rebuttal objections. Remember, the courts have a great deal of discretion and they may allow issues to be brought up in rebuttal even if there was nothing in your closing to rebut. Again, this is a strategic issue best left for the lawyer.

Bring up *applicable law* as you argue the case. A good attorney will show how his interpretation of the facts is permitted by the law which will have been explained by the judge with his instructions prior to the closing arguments. Argue your strengths and point out your adversaries' weaknesses. It may be wise to address your weaknesses up front as the jury will then respect your honesty and candor. It will also do much to deflate any arguments your opponent will have on these issues. The closing arguments are the chance to solve any problems that have come up during the trial. Don't ignore them as the jury will then wonder why you did. Maintaining credibility is crucial.

Vocabulary

closing argument
Cathy Chapman, et al., v. James Lewis, M.D., et al
Liability
damages
comparative fault doctrine
burden of persuasion
rebuttal
applicable law

Citations

[120] *Cathy Chapman, et al., v. James Lewis, M.D., et al.* No. E2009-01496-COA-R9-CV (Tenn.Ct.App).
[121] Id.
[122] Id.
[123] Tenn. Code Annotated section 20-9-303.

Chapter 15:
Before the Jury Deliberates

Jury Instructions

After the closing arguments have been completed, the judge will need to instruct the jury on how the law needs to be applied to the case at hand. In a malpractice action, the judge will usually instruct on the elements which must be proven by a *preponderance* of the evidence. These include definitions on *a duty owed*, the *standard of care*, and *causation*. Of course, he will also need to instruct them on the legal definition of *preponderance of the evidence,* meaning "more likely than not."

Instructing the jury on the *standard of care*, the judge will usually tell the jury that the health care provider will be held to *the standard of care* and knowledge commonly possessed by members of his profession and specialty.

He will usually point out the provider doesn't need to be the best and the brightest with the best skills, but he should be at least minimally *competent*—the key word being *competent*. The judge will also explain that in situations where there are "two schools of thought," a good faith choice by the practitioner will not be considered to be malpractice just because another practitioner may have acted differently under the same or similar circumstances. If both schools of thought are accepted as "reasonable" within the profession, then one will not hold sway over the other, even if it is the majority opinion.

Listen very carefully to the judge's instructions to the jury. The standard of care is not necessarily what should have been done; hindsight is 20/20. It's what a qualified professional ordinarily and customarily does if faced with the same or similar circumstances. What if the practitioner makes an error in judgment which led to harm for the patient? An error in judgment will not be malpractice so long as the judgment was a reasonable one. Health care is an inexact science and the law recognizes this.

If a patient has a bad result, it's easy to look back and decide on what should have been done to minimize the risk of the bad result, but failing to do what possibly should have been done will not be malpractice so long as other reasonable, qualified professionals would have made the same mistake.

In Tennessee, which has a *locality rule*, the jury will also be told the standard must be the same standard found in the same or similar community. This limitation of the *standard of care* to the locality where the practitioner practices was originally put in place recognizing some practitioners don't have the resources that are usually present at major medical centers in big cities. It wouldn't be fair to expect a small town doctor to get the same results as the major academic centers with many subspecialists and advanced equipment.

The *locality rule* often made it difficult for the plaintiff to find an expert in the defendant's community since most practitioners would be reluctant to testify against a professional colleague. Today, with continuing medical education a requirement in most hospitals along with the wide-spread availability of top of the line medical equipment and specialists, the *locality rule* has been abandoned in many jurisdictions.

The *locality rule* in Tennessee is still in effect, but the Tennessee Supreme Court has written that perhaps it's time for the State legislature to do away with the rule. It looks like the courts are heading towards a national standard of care but until that occurs, be sure you know what the standards are in your state as they may prove helpful to your attorney and your case.

Remember, *negligence* by the practitioner is not enough to impose *legal liability*. The plaintiff must also prove, by a *preponderance of the evidence*, the *negligence* was the legal cause—the *proximate cause*—of the patient's injury. The *proximate cause* directly caused the patient harm. For example, if a patient received the wrong drug after suffering from a massive stroke, and that drug had nothing to do with the subsequent death, then the plaintiff cannot win by claiming the wrong drug prescription was malpractice. The *negligence* must have led to the harm. The judge will spend some time explaining this legal requirement to the jury.

The plaintiff may also name the employer of the health care provider as a party in the suit because the health care provider is an agent of the employer. As long as the employee was acting within his job description, the *law of agency* will make the employer liable for the acts of the employee.

It's not unusual for the spouse of the plaintiff to also claim an *actionable injury* for which money damages may be awarded. This *cause of action* is called *loss of consortium* and is based on the loss of sexual relations, love, and other services the spouse may have lost due to the injury to the plaintiff. The *loss of consortium* cause of action has an interesting history. It used to be only the husband had the right to bring the action based on the wife's household services and other general usefulness. In the late 1800s, the

Married Women's Property Acts were passed which gave women full legal status. With the Acts, some states decided a man could no longer sue for loss of consortium but other states interpreted the Act to allow women to sue for themselves. In 1950, the U.S. Court of Appeals for the District of Columbia in *Hitaffer v. Argonne Co.*, held a woman had the right to sue for loss of consortium.[124] Some states followed this ruling and some didn't. By the end of the 1970s, most of the states came around and decided to let women also sue for loss of consortium. Although the judge is unlikely to delve into this history during his jury instructions, it's common for them to instruct the jury to not award double damages or any excessive damages just because a loss of consortium is being claimed.

If the jury decides the defendant(s) is/are liable for the injuries of the patient, they will also be asked to consider how much compensation the plaintiff is entitled to and how that amount is to be divided among the various defendants, if more than one. The purpose of the monetary award—called *damages*—is to compensate the plaintiff for the injuries he suffered. Damages must be proven during the trial within a reasonable degree of probability and must not be speculative.

The jury will be instructed to consider the costs for medical expenses that have already occurred and the costs expected to occur in the future. The jury will be told the costs must be *reasonably probable*. These costs should have been brought up during the trial and they should have been quantified by expert testimony. Compensation for lost earnings and for future lost earnings will need to be considered. Economists are usually called to testify on these issues and their calculations must be explained to the jury.

If the jury decides to award damages for *pain and suffering*, they'll be instructed to be fair and reasonable. They are not to base the award on sentimental reasons. Any award for *pain and suffering* should be based on the evidence brought out at trial and should be deemed *reasonably sufficient* to compensate the patient *fully and adequately*. If an award is made for *pain and suffering*, the jury will be instructed to compensate for the *pain and suffering* that has already occurred and the *pain and suffering* that is reasonably expected to occur in the future. This award will necessarily be subjective as there are no hard and fast rules for calculating the amount needed for compensation.

In states which have other requirements like the *locality rule* these will also need to be defined.

The jury will be informed in a case where a unanimous verdict is required.

The jury will be told evidence that is evenly balanced between the two parties will require the decision on a particular issue must be against the party that has the burden of proof—usually the plaintiff. In most of the courts, the judge will read the instructions to the jury and then will supply them with a written copy so that they can refer to it during their deliberations. In some jurisdictions, only verbal instructions will be given.

Oftentimes, the jury will also be supplied with verdict forms they will need to fill out. There may be multiple forms if there are several parties involved and if there are multiple claims and counterclaims. There may be third parties that have been pulled into the case and claims against them will also require a verdict. In some complex cases with multiple parties, the jury instructions can take a great deal of time, but in most malpractice cases, they can be done in less than an hour.

Jury Deliberation and Verdict

After the jury has been given instructions as to the law, the judge will dismiss them to the jury room to begin their deliberations. Before they leave the courtroom, the alternate jurors will be dismissed as they are no longer needed. The bailiff will be responsible for maintaining the jury's privacy during the deliberations.

Exhibits that have been admitted into evidence and the jury instructions in written form will go with the jury to the deliberation room so they can be referred to as needed.

The jury is usually instructed to pick a foreman who will be presiding over the deliberations, but other than that, how the deliberations will be conducted will be up to the jurors.

If any questions arise during their deliberations, the jury will write them down and give them to the bailiff who will then deliver them to the judge. The judge and the opposing attorneys will meet to decide how to respond to the questions. After a response is prepared, the jury is brought back to the courtroom and given the response. They then go back to their room for further deliberations.

When the jury reaches a verdict, they sign the appropriate verdict forms and they let the judge know. The judge brings the parties back into the courtroom where the verdict forms are checked. If the forms are done properly, the judge will let the court clerk read the verdict. Usually, a unanimous verdict is required in a malpractice case, but sometimes a majority decision is allowed if the parties agree to this beforehand.

Occasionally, the jury can't agree to a verdict. They will notify the judge, who will then push them to try harder. The judge may even encourage them to listen more closely to each other's opinions and he may even give them the *dynamite charge* so they will be more inclined to come to a verdict. If the jury still is not able to come to a verdict, the judge is then forced to declare a mistrial.

If a mistrial is declared, the judge will dismiss the jury. Discussions are then started with the parties in regard to scheduling a new trial. It's not unusual for the parties to come to some sort of a settlement rather than go through the time and expense of another trial.

Vocabulary

duty owed
standard of care
causation
preponderance of the evidence–more likely than not.
locality rule
negligence
proximate cause
law of agency
cause of action
loss of consortium
Hitaffer v. Argonne Co.
damages
pain and suffering
dynamite charge

Citation

[124] *Hitaffer v. Argonne Co.*, 183 F.2d 811 (D.C. Cir. 1950).

Chapter 16:
Conduct of the Attorneys

Each lawyer has his own way of conducting himself during a trial. There are some generalizations which you might keep in mind while you're working with your own counsel because different lawyers have different styles. First and foremost, your lawyer must be truthful. A lawyer's reputation for integrity is probably his most important attribute. If he does something that brings his honesty and candor into question, his professional standing will be adversely affected as will his ability to serve as your legal counsel. Once this part of his reputation is called into question, it may be lost forever.

A lawyer should never get angry with the judge even if the judge has lost his cool. If there is a volatile situation developing where your attorney feels he is not being treated fairly by the court, don't be surprised if he asks for a recess. A recess gives everyone a chance to calm down, and it will give your lawyer some time to figure out how to get out of the hot water he may have gotten into.

The best lawyers know not every ruling is going to go their way. Most judges are really trying to make a fair ruling and attorneys who think every adverse ruling is a reason for them to act annoyed are not acting as your best advocates. If a judge has made an adverse ruling, the best attorneys accept it and go on. Attorneys who continue to argue with the judge make it seem the decision is still open for debate or, worse, the judge's decision doesn't really matter. This isn't a good idea as it shows absolutely no respect for the judge. Once the judge has made a decision, it is best to put your objection into the record as a reason for appeal, and then move on.

On a similar note, judges usually don't like to have their decisions reversed on appeal. For an advocate to tell the judge he has just committed an error will probably be looked on as an insult or a threat. It's not likely to change the judge's mind and will probably cause him to take steps to remind the attorney as to who is in charge. These steps may actually harm the client's case and put the attorney at risk for sanctions.

Good advocates will immediately stop talking when the judge has a question. Questions from the judge should be looked upon as a message as to what is bothering the Court (meaning the judge). The response should be tailored to focus on this issue and it should be persuasive. After answering the judge's question, it would then be appropriate to return to the argument you had been hoping to present earlier. It's wise to never interrupt the judge when he is speaking. The interruption is unlikely to lead the judge in the direction that you want him to go and he will get the message you are not interested in what is on his mind. Legal counsel always needs to show the judge the proper respect, whether he likes the judge or not or agrees with the judge's legal rulings.

An advocate who is courteous to opposing counsel will go a long way in getting the attention of the Court when it comes his time to speak. Always let the opponent have his say for whatever time the Court is willing to listen. The Court will note your patience and attentiveness and will be more willing to listen to what you have to say in response. The jury will also pay more attention to the courteous lawyer as opposed to one who is always interrupting. After all, both sides have a right to be heard and this is really what the trial is all about.

The best lawyers will be careful to state the facts accurately. This includes the facts that are not helpful to their case. If they don't at least acknowledge the contrary facts, the Court will suspect they are intentionally trying to mislead. The lawyer must be equally accurate on his statements of the law. He needs to cite the law correctly and his interpretations of prior case law similar to your situation had better be precise. It would be a mistake to think that the Court will not check up on the cases cited because they will check.

It all comes down to preparation. The best lawyers are prepared for anything. Their documents and exhibits are organized and easily accessible. They must have the facts and the law at their fingertips and, if they are using electronic tools, like PowerPoint, to make a point, they had better know how to use it. If they fumble, they will leave the judge and the jury confused and distracted. Not being prepared is another way counsel can hurt their credibility.

> It all comes down to preparation.

Chapter 17:
After the Trial

Post-Trial Motions and Appeal

After a verdict is reached, the parties are given a certain number of days in which to file post-trial motions. The losing party is likely to file a motion for a judgment *non obstante veredicto* which means they are asking the judge to set aside the jury's verdict and award the verdict to them.[125] They are basically telling the judge that the jury made a mistake and he, the judge, should fix that mistake.

Another common motion after a malpractice verdict deals with the amount of damages that have been awarded by the jury. If the plaintiff isn't happy with the award, they can make a motion to have the judge increase the amount of the award. This is called *additur*[126] whereby they are asking the court to increase the award. The defendant may ask the court to decrease the amount of the verdict—this is called *remittitur*.[127] Again, these motions imply that the jury made a mistake which should be corrected by the Court.

After the motions are presented, the judge will set a date for a hearing on the motions. At the time of the hearing, oral arguments will be made. The judge will eventually rule on the motions and the answer will be in the form of a written order. A final judgment will be entered after the verdict is in and the post-trial motions have been ruled on by the judge. This will end the case at the trial court level. At this point, if a party wishes to appeal the verdict, they must file their intentions to appeal with the trial court within a time frame dictated by law. This filing with the Clerk of the Court will start the appellate process through which a higher level court will be asked to look at the objections made and the overall process to be sure the trial court did not make a mistake.

The appellate court is not a trial court. They will only review parts of the trial court's records and the appellate briefs submitted by the attorneys. There will be no further jury trial unless the appellate court decides the trial court made a mistake. They will uphold the verdict if the mistake is minor. They will probably send the case back to the trial court for a new trial if they deem the mistake(s) to be significant.

Conclusion of the Trial

The courtroom process is often long and complicated. The federal and state courts have developed variations of how they conduct various stages of a trial and, in fact, courts are continuing to experiment with new changes all the time. It's important for the lawyers to keep up with all of these changes so they don't make a mistake and get their case thrown out because of some procedural error. Even lawyers can be subject to professional malpractice if they screw up.

If you want to become more familiar with the trial court environment before your own case, you might want to go to court and watch a case from beginning to end. This may allay many of the fears you might have knowing you are entering into a very stressful and foreign environment. Ask your attorney when cases are coming before the court which could be beneficial for you to observe.

Darryl Weiman

Vocabulary

non obstante veredicto
additur
remittitur

Citations

[125] Judgment notwithstanding the verdict, also called judgment non obstante veredicto (JNOV for short) is a judgment entered for one party even though the verdict was originally given to the opposing party. Black's Law Dictionary, Seventh Edition, Bryan Garner, editor-in-chief.
[126] Additur—"a trial court order, issued usu. with the defendant's consent, that increases the damages awarded by the jury to avoid a new trial on grounds of inadequate damages; the term may also refer to the increase itself, the procedure, or the court's power to make the order." Black's Law Dictionary, Bryan Garner, editor-in-chief.
[127] Remittitur—"the process by which a court reduces the damages awarded by a jury verdict; a court's order reducing an award of damages." Black's Law Dictionary, Bryan Garner, editor-in-chief.

Section Three:
Other Legal Issues Pertaining to Medical Malpractice

Chapter 18:
Fault, Liability, Strict Liability

Fault

If you are found at fault in a malpractice action, it usually means you have breached the *standard of care*, which is a legal concept defined in your case by expert medical testimony. It could also mean you were so negligent — *gross negligence* — that the *trier of fact* can reasonably conclude you were at fault. For gross negligence, expert testimony is not required to establish the standard of care because the trier-of-fact should be able to figure it out on their own.

The legal definition of *fault* is "an error or defect of judgment or of conduct; any deviation from prudence or duty resulting from inattention, incapacity, perversity, bad faith, or mismanagement."[128] While the terms are often interchanged, this is not the same as *negligence*.

Liability

Liability is "the quality or state of being legally obligated or accountable; legal responsibility to another or society, enforceable by civil remedy or criminal punishment."[129] In a malpractice action, you may become *liable* for the *civil remedy* decided on by the Court. This is usually damages measured in money but there are cases that have been deemed so egregious that the Court has assessed criminal punishment. "Liability or responsibility is the bond of necessity that exists between the wrongdoer and the remedy of the wrong."[130] If you are found at *fault* in a malpractice action, you will probably be *liable* for damages. Your insurance carrier should get ready to write a check.

Strict Liability

The Institute of Medicine (IOM) conducted a study which concluded that between 44,000 and 98,000 patients die each year in the United States as a result of medical errors.[131] Granted, there were debatable issues with the study including the fact that the statistics were extrapolated from reviews of records from the states of New York and Wyoming. It is far from certain that these two states are representative of the other forty-eight states in America. Further criticism of the IOM study is that it's not known how many of the patients went on to die from their disease process. In other words, the medical error was not the *proximate cause* of the death. Did the medical errors lead to the death or were they just incidental findings in a patient who was going to die anyway? The findings of the study may have been given more significance than they deserved. Be that as it may, it has been claimed that a reduction of these errors should reduce the number of patients injured as a result of medical errors every year. If physicians are to be effective participants in the debate on medical malpractice reform, they must have some working knowledge of the IOM report. It would be worth reading on your own.

It's also argued most patients who are injured by medical errors never receive compensation because they never bring suit and even in those who bring suits, few are able to meet the requirements necessary to win. Because of these alleged problems with the current negligence system, some have been advocating a change to a *strict liability* model so that more injured patients can receive their deserved compensation.

Under a *strict liability* model, the medical care organization providing the medical care, whether it is an HMO, hospital, or other organization, will be required to buy insurance which will then be used to pay a patient for a bad outcome. Under this system, the health care provider would be relieved of the negative consequences accruing from negligent care and the injured patient would be compensated without having to use the courts to seek redress under a negligence system.

A variation of this model would require the patients to buy insurance to protect themselves from an untoward result during medical care. In this proposal, the risk of free-riding where many patients would not buy the insurance is significant. It's unlikely this model will ever be put in place.

Noam Sher, a noted opponent of *strict liability*, writes, "While a strict liability regime increases the number of claims compared to a negligence regime, the latter entails higher costs per claim, since it requires an investigation of the liability issue in addition to the issues of causality and damage assessment."[132]

Will a strict liability system lead to a decrease in health care spending? Nobody really knows. Theoretically, physicians will order fewer tests as they will no longer need to practice defensive medicine. The costs of litigating through the courts will also be removed. However, more patients will seek compensation since proving negligence will no longer be required.

There are several disadvantages of a *strict liability* system. Physicians and hospitals will no longer need to study their outcomes and adjust their care to come into compliance with the standard. In other words, there will no longer be a motivation for the physician to continue with his medical education or for hospitals to invest in quality management as there is no longer the risk of being attacked for negligence. The costs of quality management are high. The costs of continuing medical education are also high. The costs of continuing education will be weighed against the benefits and possibly less education would result. Remember, the time spent in continuing education is time away from the practice or with the family and these also have value separate from the meetings attended and the payments made for the educational activity.

Under a negligence system, the courts can be used to study the information on which the *standard of care* should be based. This is information which comes out in the process of the litigation; this information has the potential of being disseminated to society since the appellate decision is written and is a matter of public knowledge. As a result, patients can learn more about the care that affects them. The dissemination of this critical information may not occur in a *strict liability* system.

No one seems to know how a *strict liability* system would be used to assess the quality of care being provided by the individual practitioners. Under the current system, physicians who have liability payments made on their behalf get listed in the National Practitioner Data Bank. All payments are predicated on a *negligent act* by the physician. Although this data is not available to the public, it is available to hospitals so they can use it to make decisions on credentialing and privileging. There is an incentive for the physician to try to do what is best for each of his patients. No one wants to be listed in the National Practitioner Data Bank.

Under a *strict liability* system, would all payments made on behalf of a physician be listed and available for the public? This information would be helpful if the patients were to use it to decide which doctors to choose for their care. It most likely would not be fair if the payments were made and no negligence was involved. The physicians who are willing to take on the sickest patients would be linked to many payments resulting from the disease process itself where no negligence was involved. The public may conclude that these physicians—who may very well be the best ones out there—are not very good because of the many payments made to their patients. How will this inherent unfairness be sorted out by the marketplace? The answer is not known, but it is worth keeping in mind during the malpractice reform debate.

The lawyer's role would be significantly lessened in a *strict liability system* and that would lead to less cost. However, it is doubtful that lawyers will support a strict liability system as it would decrease their caseload and, as a result, they would not make as much money.

Darryl Weiman

Vocabulary

standard of care
gross negligence
trier of fact
fault
negligence
liability
liable
civil remedy
proximate cause
strict liability
negligent act
strict liability system

Citations

[128] Black's Law Dictionary, Seventh Edition, Bryan A. Garner, editor in chief. "An error or defect of judgment or of conduct; any deviation from prudence or duty resulting from inattention, incapacity, perversity, bad faith, or mismanagement."
[129] Black's Law Dictionary, Seventh Edition, Bryan A. Garner, editor in chief.
[130] John Salmond, *Jurisprudence* 364 (Glanville L. Williams ed. 10th ed. 1947) in Black's Law Dictionary, Seventh Edition, Bryan A. Garner, editor in chief.
[131] Institute of Medicine, To Err is Human: Building a Safer Health System 1 (Linda T. Kohn et al. eds., National Academy Press 2000).
[132] Noam Sher, New Differences Between Negligence and Strict Liability and Their Implications On Medical Malpractice Reform, *Southern California Interdisciplinary Law Journal*, Vol. 16:335 (2007).

Chapter 19: Commentary on the American College of Surgeons Expert Witness Affirmation

In 2004 the American College of Surgeons formulated and published an Expert Witness Affirmation ("Affirmation").[133] By signing the pledge, a surgeon who plans to perform as an expert witness, agrees to provide testimony that is "fair and accurate."[134] The pledge, while voluntary, is believed by the College to "assist in the promulgation of credible and appropriate testimony."[135]

While the goal of the pledge appears to be to improve the quality and scope of expert witness testimony, safeguards already present in the legal system through *discovery rules*,

rules *of evidence,* and *rules of professional conduct* for lawyers, appear to make the pledge unnecessary. Although legally unnecessary, the action taken by the College will probably be looked upon favorably by the judicial system which needs help in policing expert testimony.

A critical look at the components of the pledge shows they may not be necessary to insure the quality of the expert witness testimony.

1. I will always be truthful.[136]

The expert is under oath during depositions and at trial. A good cross-examination of the expert by opposing counsel should ruin the credibility of a non-truthful witness. Also, by not being truthful, the expert puts himself at risk of punishment for perjury.

2. I will conduct a thorough, fair, and impartial review of the facts and medical care provided, not excluding any relevant information.[137]

Under the Rules of Evidence, the basis upon which the expert drew his opinions must be revealed.[138] If the expert were not "thorough, fair, and impartial," this should become evident with effective cross-examination by opposing counsel. The "Affirmation" would do nothing to prevent this cross-examination and would do little to help the credibility of the discredited witness.

3. I will provide evidence or testify only in matters which I have relevant clinical experience and knowledge in the areas of medicine that are the subject of the proceeding.[139]

The expert will only be allowed to testify as to the areas in which the Court has deemed him to be an expert. Under the legal definition, an "expert" is "a person who, through education or experience, has developed knowledge of a particular subject, so that he or she may form an opinion that one without such knowledge could not provide."[140]

Before the expert is allowed to testify, his knowledge, education, training, and experience will be put before the Court, which will then decide if he has the "relevant clinical experience and knowledge." The "Affirmation" will not be enough to keep the Court from making its own informed decision in this regard.

4. I will evaluate the medical care provided in light of generally accepted standards; neither condemning performance that falls within generally accepted practice standards nor endorsing or condoning performance that falls below these standards.[141]

The *standard of care* is an issue of fact that will be decided by the *trier-of-fact* — jury or judge if it is a non-jury trial. In general, the jury must weigh the opinions of opposing expert witnesses and come to its own decision as to what the *standard of care* was at the time of the alleged injury. An expert's pledge in this regard does nothing to remove or lessen this obligation of the trier-of-fact.

5. I will evaluate the medical care provided in light of the generally accepted standards that prevailed at the time of the occurrence.[142]

As previously mentioned, this is a fact issue the jury must decide. The "Affirmation" will not help the jury in making this decision since the opposing expert witnesses are both under oath at deposition or in court when they make their opinions known, and, of course, their opinions will be at odds.

6. I will provide evidence or testimony that is complete, objective, scientifically based, and helpful to a just resolution of the proceeding.[143]

The Rules of Evidence would preclude the expert from testifying unless he is basing, the testimony, on knowledge, generally accepted by those in the relevant community.[144] If the expert is not being complete and objective, this should come out in effective cross-examination by opposing counsel. The jury will decide if the testimony is complete and objective and the "Affirmation" would not be helpful in this regard.

7. I will make a clear distinction between a departure from accepted practice standards and an untoward outcome.[145]

The main issue in most malpractice cases hinges on this *distinction*. *Negligence* in a medical malpractice setting is a failure to exercise the standard of care a reasonably prudent person, physician in this case, would have exercised in the same or similar circumstances. The jury has the duty to decide if the injury to the patient was due to negligence or was just an untoward outcome which could have occurred with other reasonable physicians in the same or similar circumstances. The jury cannot use the "Affirmation" as a means to decide on this issue.

8. I will make every effort to determine whether there is a causal relationship between the alleged substandard practice and the medical outcome.[146]

In any malpractice case, the burden is on the plaintiff to show he was injured and the injury was a result of substandard care. This is what is known as the *proximate - legal - cause* in the tort of *medical malpractice negligence*. If the patient's injury was not the result of the physician's breach of the *standard of care*, the plaintiff will lose his case. This is the *causation issue* and the "Affirmation" does nothing to help jurors make up their minds.

9. I will submit my testimony to peer review, if requested by a professional organization to which I belong.[147]

This pledge, on its face, makes sense to curb the "guns for hire" in a medical malpractice case. However, having the expert witness subject to a peer review of his testimony, especially if the organization can levy sanctions against the witness, may be viewed by the courts as a form of *obstruction of justice*. In a malpractice action, plaintiffs must show *negligence* and, in most cases, this is done through expert testimony. If the courts decide the potential experts are being intimidated to not testify for fear they may be punished by a professional organization, the courts may hold the organization in contempt. "Because such conduct interferes with the administration of justice, it is punishable, usually by fine or imprisonment."[148] In actuality, it is unlikely that the courts will look upon the College as tampering with witnesses. In fact, it is likely that the action of the College will be looked upon as lawful since it is intended to "encourage, induce, or cause the other person to testify truthfully."[149]

The fear that a professional organization may be at risk for witness tampering prosecution has not been born out. In *Austin v. American Association of Neurological Surgeons*, 253 F. 3d 967 (7th Cir. 2001), the Seventh Circuit held that an expert witness had no right to challenge his suspension from a professional organization for giving *irresponsible* testimony. Judge Richard Posner, the author of the opinion, made it very clear professional societies have the right and the duty, to monitor their members who are functioning as expert witnesses. Judge Posner concluded judges would welcome the help of professional societies in screening experts and this function would serve a valuable public interest. Based on Judge Posner's opinion, it's unlikely that the American College of Surgeons would be at risk of contempt proceedings if they make legal testimony subject to peer review so long as the surgeon in question is afforded due process, notice and a hearing before peers that do not have a stake in the proceedings.

10. I will not accept compensation that is contingent upon the outcome of the litigation.[150]

Under the Model Rules of Professional Conduct, which most states have adopted in some form or another, the medical expert witness may not have a stake in the outcome of the case.[151] This goes to the credibility of the witness. The lawyer who allows a *contingent fee* to be paid to the expert witness would be subject to disciplinary measures of that states controlling legal authority.[152]

The United States has an adversary system for legal justice. Safeguards are already in place for lawyers via the Rules of Civil Procedure, Rules of Evidence, and Rules of Professional Conduct to help insure the truthfulness and credibility of the medical expert witness. The American

College of Surgeons Expert Witness Affirmation may be helpful to our legal system by having a mechanism to punish *irresponsible* testimony that the courts are ill-equipped to do. To be able to review the testimony of the so-called *hired guns*, professional societies would be performing an important public service which, so far, has been looked upon favorably by the courts. The "Affirmation" will only enhance the truthful, non-frivolous, testimony of potential expert witnesses in the medical malpractice setting. The medical expert witness should be willing to face a true *jury of his peers* in this situation.

Vocabulary

discovery rules
rules of evidence
rules of professional conduct
standard of care
trier-of-fact
Affirmation
proximate – legal – cause
medical malpractice negligence
causation issue
obstruction of justice
Austin v. American Association of Neurological Surgeons
contingent fee
hired guns
jury of his peers

Citations

[133] American College of Surgeons. Expert Witness Affirmation, 2004.
[134] Id.
[135] Id.
[136] Id.
[137] Id.
[138] Federal Rules of Evidence Rule 703 states in part, "The facts or data in the particular case upon which an expert bases an opinion or inference may be those perceived by or made known to the expert at or before a hearing. If of a type reasonably relied upon by experts in the particular field in forming opinions or inferences upon the subject, the facts or data need not be admissible in evidence in order for the opinion or inference to be admitted." Most, if not all states have a similar rule for their courts.
[139] American College of Surgeons Expert Witness Affirmation, 2004.
[140] Blacks Law Dictionary Pocket Edition, 1996, p. 244.
[141] American College of Surgeons Expert Witness Affirmation, 2004.
[142] Id.
[143] Id.
[144] Federal Rules of Evidence Rule 703 as above.
[145] American College of Surgeons Expert Witness Affirmation, 2004
[146] Id.
[147] Id.
[148] Blacks Law Dictionary Pocket Edition, 1996, p.131
[149] Under U.S.C. section 1512(e) which states "In a prosecution for an offense under this section [witness tampering], it as an affirmative defense. . . that the conduct consisted solely of lawful conduct and that the defendant's sole intention was to encourage, induce, or cause the other person to testify truthfully."
[150] American College of Surgeons Expert Witness Affirmation, 2004
[151] ABA Model Rules of Professional Conduct comment to Rule 3.4.
[152] Usually the state's highest appellate court.

Chapter 20:

Daubert v. Merrell Dow Pharmaceuticals, Inc.

The *Daubert* decision is extremely important in understanding what an expert witness is allowed to testify to in a malpractice action. In *Daubert,* the Supreme Court of the United States weighed in to explain the role of the medical expert in Federal Courts. Subsequently, the states have adopted the holdings of *Daubert* for their state courts.

In Tennessee, testimony by experts is defined by Rule 702 in the Rules of Evidence for the state which is basically putting the holding of *Daubert* into statutory law. Rule 702 states, "If scientific, technical, or other specialized knowledge will substantially assist the trier of fact to understand the evidence or to determine a fact in issue, a witness qualified by knowledge, skill, experience, training, or education may testify in the form of an opinion or otherwise."[153] An advisory commission comment to Rule 702 lists five factors which the court should take into consideration when determining whether the testimony will *substantially assist* the jury. These factors are taken directly from the *Daubert* opinion, but they are not exclusive. The five factors are "(1) whether scientific evidence has been tested and the methodology with which it has been tested; (2) whether the evidence has been subjected to peer review and publication; (3) whether a potential rate of error is known; (4) whether, as formerly required by *Frye*[154], the evidence is generally accepted in the scientific community; and (5) whether the expert's research in the field has been conducted independent of the litigation."[155]

Prior to this 2001 advisory opinion, testimony by experts had to undergo the "Frye test" but in *McDaniel v. CSX Transportation, Inc.*,[156] the Tennessee Supreme Court adopted the factors listed in *Daubert*.

Opposing attorneys will try their best to discredit the expert witness on cross-examination and they have many weapons in their arsenal. The most common strategy is to let the jury know how much has already been paid to review the medical records, study deposition testimony and answers to the interrogatories, and how much is being charged per hour to do the reviews, give testimony at depositions, and testify at trial. The amounts can be substantial, and it's clear that there are many professionals who make a very nice income performing as an expert witness. If it can be shown a lot of money has been paid to a particular witness, the jury may conclude the opinion is being bought and thus, the credibility of the witness will suffer accordingly.

Another common strategy is to imply that the expert is a friend of the defendant and is not being truthful. Dr. Phil Schoettle was the chief of Cardiothoracic Surgery at one of the hospitals in Memphis. He was known as an outstanding clinical surgeon and a surgical innovator. He was often the first to learn a new technique in the lab and then bring it to the clinical practice. He would then teach it to others in the community.

Dr. Schoettle had treated a patient with non-bypassble coronary artery disease with a transmyocardial laser revascularization. The operation used a special laser to drill holes in the patient's left ventricle, which would often decrease the pain of myocardial ischemia. The patient did well after the operation in that his anginal pain was relieved but, the phrenic nerve was found to be injured after the operation. Phrenic nerve injury can occur from an unintended burn from the laser, a cut from a knife or scissor, or from a stretch injury when the pericardium is opened and retracted so that the laser probe can be directly applied to the myocardium under direct vision. A patient can have trouble breathing if the phrenic nerve is not able to stimulate the diaphragm to contract so clearly the patient had a legitimate injury. The question was whether the injury was caused by *negligence* or was a known complication of the procedure and wasn't due to *negligence*.

Dr. Schoettle's operative note, which was dictated on the day of the operation, clearly stated the phrenic nerve was identified and kept free from injury. Since the note was dictated on the day of the operation and the phrenic nerve injury was not identified until several days later, it was very unlikely the note was used as a means to minimize the risk of liability. This makes the note more credible than if there had been a delay in the dictation. The note was evidence that he did what a reasonable surgeon would do to protect the nerve, and if the nerve was injured as it was then, it was just one of those unfortunate things that happen on occasion when taking care of patients. There was no breach of the *standard of care*.

A physician asked to be an expert witness for the defense side reviewed all of the medical records and looked at the films. Relying on the operative note, the expert believed the phrenic nerve injury was not due to malpractice and he testified to that effect at the trial. However, the plaintiff's attorney never deposed this physician prior to the trial because his strategy was to discredit the physician based on his friendship with Dr. Schoettle.

On cross-examination, the questions immediately focused on the friendship.

> "Dr. X," he asked. "Isn't it true that the defendant is a friend of yours?"

> "He is," Dr. X responded.

> "You've socialized on occasions?"

> "Yes."

> "Gone out to dinner on occasion?"

> "Yes."

> "Isn't it true that you are now lying to help Dr. Schoettle in this proceeding?"

The expert witness was taken aback by the question but quickly recovered.

> "I am under oath and I am testifying as truthfully as I can. In my opinion, there was no breach of the standard of care which led to the phrenic nerve injury."

Notice how the expert witness/physician took the opportunity to restate his opinion to the jury. A more artfully asked question by the attorney would have prevented him from doing this. It was really a question that could have been answered with a "yes" or "no" and the attorney could have objected to the answer, but he didn't.

The physician was certain the cross-examination would soon end as it was not in the plaintiff's interest to have him repeat his opinions, but he was wrong. For the next hour and a half, the expert witness had to repeat his answers on numerous queries. He found it very uncomfortable to have the attorney insinuate—and even state in the form of a question—that he was lying under oath.

The expert witness knew the defendant's attorney could have objected to this line of questioning as being repetitious or badgering, but he was surprised to find they were silent. He was afraid to look over to the defendant's counsel as the jury might construe that as a plea for help and thus a sign of weakness on his part. He never wavered in his testimony. He kept his cool and was always respectful to the questioning attorney. In fact, he even apologized for not being clear with his answers since the questions kept being repeated.

After the expert witness's testimony was completed, the jury was dismissed for the day and the court was adjourned. He went over to the defendant's attorneys and asked them why they were letting him be grilled when they could have easily objected on numerous questions. They looked at him and the lead attorney said, "Dr. X, you were doing a great job and the jury appeared to trust you. It also was very obvious that the jury was getting aggravated by the badgering and the mean spirited demeanor of plaintiff's attorney. Under the circumstances, it made sense to let the plaintiff's attorney bury himself." The defendant's attorneys were making a strategic decision and they turned out to be correct. The jury returned a verdict for the defendant after only 30 minutes of deliberation.

The moral of this story is to be truthful, keep your cool, and always be respectful even if the attorney questioning you is badgering you. The jury is watching you very closely; they are also scrutinizing the attorney at the same time. No attorney can ever match the stress that most surgeons face on a daily basis. Use this experience to your advantage. Remember, a patient's life is *not* on the line based on how you choose to answer.

During the pre-trial discovery process, the expert witness which a party will be using must be disclosed if it is a federal court. Most state courts have a variation of the same rule.[157]

The disclosures required by the rules are called Rule 26 *disclosures*. Not only must the expert be identified, but the opinions he will be expressing must also be disclosed as well as the basis of those opinions. Courts have gotten away from the surprises that used to occur during a trial since both parties should have all the information that is going to be presented to the *trier of fact* beforehand. The Rule 26 *disclosures* are often written by the attorneys and it isn't unusual for the witness to back off of some of the *disclosures* during a deposition or at trial during testimony. Good lawyers make sure their witnesses are in agreement with the *disclosure* prior to submitting it to the court and to opposing counsel. As a defendant, it's worth deposing all adverse witnesses to lock them in to what they are planning to say at trial. If they then try to blind-side you with new testimony in court, you can object that the testimony is outside of the Rule 26 *disclosure*. The judge is likely to disallow any testimony that was previously not disclosed and this is likely to be to your advantage.

In a further effort to keep any of the parties from being blind-sided at trial, the Federal Rules also allow any party to *depose* any person who has been identified as an expert and whose opinions are likely to be presented at trial. If a party has retained an expert to help them on a case, but they aren't going to use that expert to testify at the trial, in most instances they can protect that person's identity and opinions. However, if the opposing party can show they need those opinions and they have no other way of getting them, the court may allow them to obtain that information by interrogatories or by deposition.[158]

One of the things to keep in mind about the Rule 26 disclosures is the opinions expressed by the expert will be the only opinions he can express at the trial unless the opposing party were to *open the door* by asking him for other opinions. The following is an example of a situation where a medical expert was allowed to testify about a medical matter that was not in his Rule 26 disclosure.

The physician served as an expert witness on a case where a lung mass was ignored in a patient until it had become unresectable for cure. The mass turned out to be a lung cancer and the patient died shortly thereafter. The expert was asked to come to an opinion as to whether or not a surgeon could have resected the mass when it was first seen on the radiograph. After reviewing the medical records and seeing all of the radiographs, the expert/physician opined that the tumor could have been removed at an early stage with a reasonable expectation of a *cure* meaning five-year survival with no evidence of recurrent disease.

This patient also had emphysema with decreased lung function. Some patients with this disease can have an improvement of lung function by doing a *lung volume reduction* whereby a portion of the diseased lung is removed which then allows some of the better lung to expand more fully. This allows for an overall improvement in gas exchange. The expert made no mention of *lung volume reduction* for patients with emphysema in his disclosure as that was not the question he was asked to address.

After the expert had given his opinion, the opposing attorney got up and asked the following question:

"Isn't it true, Dr. X, that even if a surgeon had been able to remove the tumor at the earlier stage, it is unlikely that she would have been able to tolerate the lung resection since her lung function was so poor?"

Dr. X: "Actually, I think that her lung function may have improved since the uninvolved lung could then have expanded better."

Opposing attorney: "How could lung function improve if you are actually removing lung tissue?"

The expert then proceeded to explain the *lung volume reduction* operation for patients with emphysema. After he finished, the attorney moved to have the testimony stricken since the expert had nothing about this *lung volume reduction procedure* in the disclosure. The judge did not allow the motion as the opposing attorney had opened the door to let this testimony in. Dr. X was only answering the questions that the attorney had asked. Once the door is opened, the expert can answer the question even if it is beyond the Rule 26 disclosure.

Experts can charge for their time and their work product and there are now many so-called expert witnesses that make a substantial income doing this kind of work. The courts recognize these experts should be paid and they put in the rules that "the court shall require that the party seeking discovery pay the expert a reasonable fee for the time spent in responding to discovery."[159] Of course, if the expert witness charges an exorbitant amount for his work, then the jury may conclude that more than his expertise is being paid for.

The expert is also allowed to charge a reasonable fee to the party that has hired him to formulate an opinion.

Darryl Weiman

Vocabulary

Daubert
substantially assist
Frye
McDaniel v. CSX Transportation, Inc.
disclosures
depose
open the door
lung volume reduction

Citations

[153] Rule 702, Tennessee Rules of Evidence.
[154] *Frye v. United States*, 293 F. 1013 (D.C. Cir.1923)
[155] 2001 Advisory Commission Comment to Rule 702 of the Tennessee Rules of Evidence.
[156] 955 S.W.2d 257 (1997).
[157] Rule 26 in the Federal Rules of Civil Procedure.
[158] Rule 26(b)(4)(B) of the Federal Rules of Civil Procedure.
[159] Rule 26(b)(4)(C) of the Federal Rules of Civil Procedure.

Chapter 21: Federal or State Court

There are 51 court systems in the United States; these are the 50 state court systems and the Federal system. The lower courts within a system are only obligated to follow the higher legal authority in their states and, of course, the United States Supreme Court. One of the Supreme Court justices has started to use decisions of some foreign courts to justify his positions and he has taken a great deal of criticism for doing so. However, he is not obligated to follow the holdings of those courts; he only uses their reasoning if they agree with his opinion. Although most medical malpractice cases use the common law of the state where the alleged malpractice occurred, some cases get filed in, or removed to, the Federal system.

The reason to choose one system over the other is because a particular court may use laws favorable to your *cause of action*. Remember, the laws, both *procedural* and *substantive*, are not the same in all of the state courts. The plaintiff will initially choose a court that he believes will be favorable for his side, either because of rules of the court or from previous rulings of the court in similar circumstances.

If a case gets filed in or *removed* to a Federal court, what law will the Federal court use? Prior to the case of *Erie R.R. v.* Tompkins,[160] the Federal court could decide using its own *general law*. In the landmark case *Erie v. Tompkins*, the Court decided to require federal courts to follow state court decisions on the matters that dealt with state, not federal, law.

Tompkins, a citizen of Pennsylvania, was walking by the tracks of the Erie Railroad when he was struck by the swinging door of one of the cars of a passing train. He was knocked down and his arm fell across the tracks where it was severed by the train.

Under Pennsylvania law, Tompkins was a trespasser and under the law he would have to prove that the negligence of the Erie Railroad was willful or wanton. It would be difficult to prove *willful* or *wanton* under the facts presented. Because of this, Tompkins chose to sue in the New York Federal court using the *diversity of citizenship* claim. He chose New York because that is where the Erie Railroad had its headquarters and with this choice of courts, he would be allowed to sue for *ordinary negligence* — a general common law issue for the federal system. There would be no requirement to prove *willful* or *wanton* behavior.

The trial court ruled in Tomkins' favor. On the first appeal, the Second Circuit held the railroad could be held *liable* for *ordinary negligence*. On the next appeal, the Supreme Court of the United States reversed, holding the law to be applied will be the law of the state where the injury occurred which in this case, was Pennsylvania. The Court said *common law* is the purview of the states and the Constitution has no clause which would give power to the federal courts to make up their own law. At that time, the Court said that "there is no federal general common law." This was *dicta* so it is not really the law. Dicta are the parts of the written opinion that are not part of the "holding"; only the "holding" becomes the law.

Martha Field wrote, "Judges are to make federal common law only when important federal interests require it. There is uneasiness with such an open-ended approach, yet no workable alternative has been found. Because state law may apply if judges do not make a federal rule, the exercise of restraint in developing federal common law contributes to a healthy federalism."[161] The power of the states to make their own laws was preserved.

Tompkins' case got sent back to the trial court which then had to apply Pennsylvania law since that is where the alleged tort occurred. Since Tompkins was a trespasser under Pennsylvania law, he lost the case.

The main thing learned from *Erie v. Tompkins* is that the federal courts will generally use the state's laws in deciding common law issues, such as malpractice. This decision served to discourage *forum shopping*. However, subsequent decisions show that federal judges have discretion to decide if state laws apply or if they would be better served to devise a federal common law to rule on a particular case.

Vocabulary

cause of action
procedural
substantive
removed
Erie R.R. v. Tompkins
general law
willful or *wanton*
diversity of citizenship
ordinary negligence
liable
common law
dicta
forum shopping

Citations

[160] *Erie Rail Road Co. v. Tompkins,* 304 U.S. 64 (1938).
[161] Martha A. Field, Federal Common Law, <u>The Oxford Companion to the Supreme Court of the United States</u>, 2nd edition, p. 321, 2005.

Chapter 22: Locality Rule

The state of Tennessee has what is called the *locality rule* which requires expert witnesses to come from Tennessee or a *contiguous* state and they must be familiar with the *standard of care* in the community, or a similar community, where the alleged negligence occurred. The courts have ruled a contiguous state is a state that shares a border with Tennessee. States that meet this requirement are Mississippi, Arkansas, Kentucky, North Carolina, Missouri, Alabama, Georgia, and Virginia. The court may waive this requirement if it determines the appropriate witness(es) would otherwise not be available.

Here is an example of a situation where the locality rule may be waived. Dr. Arthur Herbst, Chairman of the Gynecology Department at the University of Chicago, was the first to find the association of diethylstilbesterol given during a woman's pregnancy with the development of clear cell adenocarcinoma of the vagina in off-spring. The development of this carcinoma could occur up to 30 years after the drug had been taken. Dr. Herbst was the first to show estrogen therapy could be cancer producing in humans. These findings were published in the *New England Journal of Medicine* in 1971 and the galleys of the article were immediately sent to the Food and Drug Administration so quick action to take the drug off the market could be taken. Because Dr. Herbst was the only expert on this subject, and millions of women were at risk of the cancer causing potential of this estrogen therapy, he became subject to subpoena by many courts. Dr. Herbst would most likely fit the criteria for being an allowed expert from a *non-contiguous* state.

Issues have arisen in regard to what constitutes *adequate familiarity* of the community. By law, it is the responsibility of the judge to decide if the expert testimony will be admissible. In proffering an expert witness, the party must show the expert is familiar with the same or similar community involved in the malpractice action. This offer of proof usually consists of numerous questions relating to the similarities of the two medical communities. For example, are there any medical schools in the communities? Are medical specialties similar in the communities? Is there a similar number of hospitals and is the population they are serving similar? In *Johnson v. Richardson*[162] the court said, "[e]stablishing the similarities in communities is as much a part of the burden of proof under the locality rule as is establishing the witness practices in a contiguous state." *Carpenter v. Klepper*, 205 S.W.3d 474,483 (Tenn.Ct.App 2006) (citing *Bravo v. Sumner Reg'l Health Sys., Inc.*, 148 S.W.3d 357, 368-69 (Tenn.Ct. App. 2003)). "This burden may be met by comparing factors between the similar community and the community where the alleged malpractice occurred; such as the populations of the communities, the proximity to a teaching hospital, medical facilities, medical specialties, and the literature and training available."[163]

Although the medical expert does not need to know everything about the medical community in question, it is clear that vague assertions about perceived similarities will not be enough to meet the locality rule requirements, at least in Tennessee.[164] Usually, the expert has been prepared for these types of questions by the attorney so it is unusual to have the expert dismissed because of lack of familiarity of the community where the alleged tort occurred. But if the expert is unprepared or he forgets what he's told, he may not be allowed to testify.

In *Tina Johnson v. David Richardson, M.D.*[165] the plaintiff's expert witness gave testimony which was very inaccurate about his community of Springfield, Missouri, and his knowledge of Memphis as to *standard of care* was also suspect. In fact, he tried to claim a national standard of care which the Supreme Court of Tennessee has refused to recognize as being acceptable for the *locality rule*. The testimony given at deposition was not challenged until the video deposition was attempted to be presented at trial. At that time, the defendant moved to disqualify the expert as not being knowledgeable about the medical community of Memphis. The Court agreed with the motion and disqualified the expert. Without the expert, the plaintiff lacked expert proof. As a result the trial court entered a directed verdict for the defendant. The Court of Appeals agreed with the trial court.

In its Affirmation, the appellate court wrote, "After thoroughly reviewing the record, we find that [plaintiff's expert] has not demonstrated that the trial court abused its discretion in disqualifying [the expert]. While [the expert] did present information about the medical community in Memphis, he failed to sufficiently compare Memphis to the community in which he was familiar, Springfield. The only comparisons [the expert] provided to the trial court were the population of the two communities, that both had the same medical specialties, and that both had outlying hospitals. As to population, it was demonstrated that [the expert] was simply incorrect and that the population of the two communities was anything but similar."[166]

It is interesting from a strategic standpoint that the defendant did not move to have the plaintiff's expert disallowed until the time of the trial since they could have done it at any time after the deposition. Perhaps they didn't want the plaintiff to have time to add to the testimony with an affidavit or to try to obtain another expert who could have answered the *locality* questions more artfully. Either way, it worked in the defendant's favor.

The court did address this issue of timing in writing the following, "Whether [the defendant] delayed in challenging [plaintiff's expert], is irrelevant to the trial court's decision on the motion for a directed verdict. We have not been presented with a scheduling order that required [the defendant] to challenge [the plaintiff's expert's] qualifications prior to his testimony at trial."[167] For strategic reasons, the defendants did not challenge the witness's locality knowledge until it was too late for the plaintiff to remedy the situation.

Vocabulary

locality rule
contiguous
standard of care
non-contiguous
adequate familiarity
Johnson v. Richardson
Carpenter v. Klepper
Bravo v. Sumner Reg'l Health Sys., Inc.
Tina Johnson v. David Richardson, M.D.
Affirmation

Citations

[162] *Johnson v. Richardson*, No.W2009-02626-COA-R3-CV-filed August 12, 2010.
[163] Id.
[164] Id.
[165] *Johnson v. Richardson* No. W2009-02626-COA-R3-CV –filed August 12, 2010.
[166] Id.
[167] Id.

Chapter 23:
Doctrine of Informed Consent

In *Canterbury v. Spence*,[168] Dr. Spence performed surgery on Mr. Canterbury's back. However, Dr. Spence failed to tell Mr. Canterbury potential risks involved with the operation. During the operation, Dr. Spence noticed that there was swelling of the spinal cord and he took steps to relieve the swelling. While Canterbury was recovering, he fell and was almost paralyzed. Dr. Spence performed another back surgery and Mr. Canterbury improved.

Mr. Canterbury brought a suit alleging the defendant, Dr. Spence, didn't inform him of the potential risks associated with this procedure. He also sued the hospital for not having a side rail on his bed and not having a nurse present to help him at the time of his fall. The trial court ordered a directed verdict for the defendant based on the fact the plaintiff had failed to produce any evidence of *negligence*. The court didn't address the issue of a *breach of duty* to inform the patient of potential risks associated with the operation.

On appeal, the appellate court reversed the decision and *remanded* for a new trial. The appellate court held a physician should discuss the risks of an operation so a *reasonable* patient would have enough information so he could then decide whether or not to undergo the operation. The court said there would be two exceptions to this rule. If the patient was unconscious and the harm from a failure to treat was greater than the harm of the proposed procedure, then the physician did not have to get the patient's consent.[169] The other exception would be where disclosing the risks to the patient would be a threat to the patient's well-being.[170]

The issue of *informed consent* is one of the theories that the plaintiff's attorneys use in pursuing a *malpractice action*. The legal dimensions of this theory find their origins in the Law of Battery whereby any unpermitted contact or offensive touching is considered to be a personal indignity. This personal indignity is not allowed. It relates back to a right of privacy that, although not explicitly stated in the United States Constitution, the Justices believe to be in there somewhere.

The *right to privacy* in a *malpractice action* is usually thought of as a right to refuse lifesaving treatment. The

Supreme Court has said this right was evident from the *penumbra*, meaning the shadowed regions, formed by *emanations* from the Bill of Rights. The specific Amendments often referred to include the 1st, 3rd, 4th, 5th, and 9th. The 14th Amendment applied these privacy implying amendments to the States. This right to privacy forces the clinician to obtain an informed consent from the patient before any procedure can be done.

A brief look at these amendments is useful to see where the justices might be getting the idea that privacy is an important right, although not explicitly stated in the Constitution. The 1st Amendment mentions the free exercise of religion, free speech, free press, the right to peaceably assemble, and the right to petition the government for redress of grievances. These issues all can be used to argue for a privacy right as they are all privacy issues.

The 3rd Amendment says citizens do not have to quarter soldiers in times of peace. Who you allow into your home is clearly a privacy issue so this is further evidence that there is a right to privacy. Of course, the Amendment implies you may have to quarter soldiers in a time of war, but the manner must be prescribed by law.

The 4th Amendment deals with the right of the people to be secure in their persons, houses, papers, and effects, against unreasonable searches and seizures. This amendment is meant to protect against searches and seizures by the government and it is difficult to see how this would apply in a patient-physician relationship but it does imply that your body is a private thing.

The 5th Amendment says you may not be deprived of life, liberty, or property, without due process of law. Again, this amendment was meant to restrict the State but again, it implies there is some inherent privacy issue that may even be invoked when a physician may be asking to do something to you that may affect your life, liberty, or property.

Under its police power, the state may make laws that are meant to ensure the general welfare. This allows the states to have a body of *common law* or *statutory law* which will define what constitutes *informed consent*. This has been done in Tennessee where *informed consent* has been deemed to be the process where the practitioner who is doing the procedure on a patient has discussed the risks and hoped for benefits of the procedure along with alternative forms of therapy, including doing nothing. It would be in the practitioner's best interest to document that this conversation has occurred, and outline what was discussed. It would also be prudent to document the date and time the discussion took place. This documentation is evidence that the informed consent process did occur.

Plaintiff's attorneys sometimes have said, "If it's not documented in the chart then it never happened." This saying may be applicable to many things such as following up on ordered tests, steps taken during various procedures, phone conversations with nurses or patients and their families, the conversations done during the *informed consent* process, and many other things that may have occurred with a particular patient that were not documented in the medical records. *Informed consent* is a little bit tricky in this regard because the opposite may be true—there may be a consent form signed by the patient in the chart, but that form does not in and of itself, constitute *informed consent*. So what constitutes *informed consent*?

In Tennessee, *informed consent* depends on what a *reasonable patient* would need to know to come to a *reasonable decision*. The *appropriate information* is a question for the jury and does not require expert testimony. The jury should be able to decide on its own if the patient was given the *appropriate information* to come to a reasonable decision. It's easy for the juror to put himself in the shoes of the plaintiff in order to decide if enough information was provided so that an *informed consent* could be given by the patient for the proposed procedure. However, the question of what should have been discussed with the patient *does* require expert testimony on the subject. In this regard, the expert witness will need to illuminate what a *reasonable practitioner* would need to discuss with a *reasonable patient* so the patient would have the appropriate information to come to an *informed decision*.

Case law has clarified this issue. The practitioner must discuss the diagnosis and the nature of the condition, the reasons for the proposed treatment or procedure, risks involved and prospects for success, alternative methods of treatment along with the risks and benefits of such treatment. The practitioner must also tell the patient if the treatment or procedure is experimental. Whether the information given is sufficient "depends on the nature of the treatment, the extent of the risks involved, and the standard of care [applicable to the health care provider]."[171]

The plaintiff must prove, by expert testimony, the defendant did not provide the appropriate information to the patient in obtaining his *informed consent*. In Tennessee, this testimony must educate the jury as to what constitutes acceptable professional practice in the profession and in the specialty, and in the community, or a similar community, so the jury can decide if the appropriate information was conveyed to the patient.

In 1992, the American Medical Association wrote in its Code of Ethics that the physician's duty was to provide sufficient information to the patient so the patient could make an informed decision as to their treatment plan. The Code specifies the physician must disclose what a *reasonable patient* would need to know in order to give an *informed consent*. This requirement is now referred to as the *patient-centered standard* and this is the law in the state of Tennessee. However, most states do not use this *patient-centered standard* and have instead opted for what is called the *professional disclosure standard*.

Using the *professional disclosure standard*, the physician must disclose what a *reasonably prudent* physician would disclose under the same or similar circumstances. Note that this standard may not provide the patient with the information he might need to make an *intelligent* decision. Also, this standard would require a medical expert witness to educate the jury as to what information the reasonable practitioner would need to provide under the circumstances of the case. In the *patient-centered standard*, the jury decides what is reasonable without the help of an expert witness.

Most hospitals require the patient to sign a document signifying that consent has been given for the planned procedure. Is this document consent in and of itself? By law, consent still lies in the conclusion of the discussion between the patient, or his legal representative if the patient is unable to give consent himself, and the health care practitioner. However, the document is evidence the consent process did occur.

In many hospitals, the nurses are assigned the responsibility of having the patient sign the operative consent form. It seems this assignment by the hospital may be construed as the hospital assuming the duty of obtaining the consent, but this isn't the case. The court cases that have looked at this issue have decided the consent forms were not designed to replace the *informed consent* process required of the practitioner who is doing the procedure. In other words, the hospital was not gratuitously assuming the practitioner's duty to obtain consent. Telling your nurse to have the patient sign the consent form is not enough for *informed consent* to occur. The discussion with the patient must still be done and the patient should have an opportunity to ask questions. It would be in the physician's best interest to document this discussion in the chart outlining the risks and the goals of the procedure along with the options of other forms of therapy, including no therapy, along with their associated risks and benefits.

In general, the courts do not want hospitals to get involved in issues that lie at the heart of the doctor-patient relationship. The hospital may perform the *ministerial act* of documenting such consent, but the practitioner must still do the process of obtaining the consent himself. Absent the assumption, the hospital will not be liable for lack of *informed consent* because the hospital cannot assume this *non-delegable* duty. This serves as a warning to the practitioner that having someone other than himself go to the patient to get the consent forms signed may come back to haunt him if he does not in some way document he, himself, went through the process with the patient.

What if there is no consent form in the chart signed by the patient? Most plaintiffs' attorneys will say, "If there is no consent form, then there was no informed consent." The form will be evidence the consent process did occur. Without the form, the practitioner may have to prove consent occurred by oral testimony of witnesses or his own oral testimony under oath at a deposition or in trial or a written statement via an affidavit.

In a *malpractice action* where the plaintiff complains he did not have the information needed to make an *informed consent*, the practitioner has several defenses which might be applicable to defeat the action. In an emergency where the plaintiff is in no condition to undergo the consent process, no consent is necessary to save life or limb.

The patient may have waived his right to an *informed consent* by giving the practitioner carte blanche to do *whatever he thinks is right*. This waiver can be a valid defense, but only if the patient entered into the waiver *knowingly*. The *knowing* requirement implies some *duty of disclosure* on the physician's part. How much *disclosure* is required is uncertain. Also, it's not clear if the waiver must be in writing. For safety's sake, if patient doesn't want to know the risks, benefits, and alternative forms of therapy, document all of this and have the patient sign a waiver.

There is a therapeutic privilege where the physician may use his judgment to not get consent if he thinks the process will be too stressful and might actually cause harm to the patient. This can be a dangerous defense especially if the patient is credible. The jury may come away thinking that the physician is playing "god" and they will rule accordingly.

There are religious, cultural, or ethnic issues that come into play which may make getting an *informed consent* very difficult, but it would be wise to at least give it a try and document in the medical records what was done to communicate the options to the patient. These issues may come into play if death and dying are taboo subjects for the patient. Some religious groups favor physician beneficence over patient autonomy, but this is a rare situation.

There are also rare occurrences where the physician knows something the patient wants to keep secret e.g., the patient is HIV positive. If this patient were to present as an unconscious trauma victim, what information should the physician tell the surrogate decision maker so he can make an informed decision for the care of the patient? In this type of situation, the surrogate's right to know trumps the physician's obligation to patient confidentiality.

The hospital doesn't have an independent duty to obtain *informed consent*. The courts recognize only the practitioner is competent to explain the procedure or the planned course of therapy to the patient. However, the hospital may be liable for a physician's breach of the duty to obtain informed consent. This would occur in the situation where the physician is an employee of the hospital or the hospital controls the physician's practice in some way. The hospital may be liable if they know the physician did not fulfill the duty to obtain *informed consent*. The hospital should protect itself by having an informed consent policy which would have some sort of mechanism, possibly in the form of sanctions, to ensure the physicians have an incentive to go through the consent process in a reasonable way.

There will be *implied consent* in the situation where the surgeon discovers a different problem from the one the consent was given to treat. This might occur where a cancer is found during an abdominal operation for another reason. This type of defense is different from the *waiver* defense where some duty of disclosure still exists.

In states where *comparative negligence* is used to assess blame, the patient may have some liability if he does not provide his doctor with complete information which may be material to the problem. An example of this would be a cocaine-using patient who needs open heart surgery. If the surgeon does not know cocaine is an issue, he will not be able to convey the added risks the patient will have if he is to undergo the procedure. In some states, if the patient's liability is 50% or greater, then the surgeon will have no liability at all.

Darryl Weiman

Informed consent is a process whereby the health care practitioner discusses with the patient information a *reasonable* patient needs to know in order to make a decision as to consent. In Tennessee, the practitioner will be held to *a reasonable practitioner* standard for like or similar circumstances in the same or similar community.

Vocabulary

Canterbury v. Spence
Negligence
breach of duty
remanded
reasonable
informed consent
malpractice action
right to privacy
penumbra
emanations
common law
statutory law
reasonable patient
reasonable decision
appropriate information
reasonable practitioner
patient-centered standard
professional disclosure standard
ministerial act
non-delegable
duty of disclosure
implied consent
comparative negligence

Citations

[168] *Canterbury v. Spence,* 464 F.2d 772 (D.C. Cir. 1972).
[169] Id.
[170] Id.
[171] *Cardwell,* 724 S.W.2d at 749.

Chapter 24:
Emergency Medical Treatment and Active Labor Act (EMTALA)

In 1986, Congress passed the Emergency Medical Treatment and Active Labor Act (EMTALA) in an effort to prevent hospitals from refusing to treat patients who were either unable to pay for their care or were covered under the Medicaid and Medicare programs. The Act was designed to prevent *patient dumping* where hospitals would refuse to take care of the uninsured patients and would, instead, transfer them to other facilities who would take them, often in unstable condition. The ostensible reason that hospitals could deny patients access to their facility was there were no state laws which mandated the hospital had a duty to treat patients just because they had presented to the hospital and, of course, since no patient-doctor relationship had been entered into, there was not yet a duty placed on the physician.

Since the non-paying patients were often a financial drain on the hospitals, it made financial sense to transfer these patients to the *charity* hospitals which were already receiving funds from the state and local governments to care for these patients. Based on a perception, which may have been fueled by the *charity* hospitals, that critically ill patients were being transferred before they had been stabilized, Congress decided to mandate care to prevent this *dumping* of patients who were unstable due to an emergency medical condition.

Shortly after EMTALA was passed into law, plaintiff's attorneys started to claim EMTALA violations along with some malpractice causes of action. The reason to raise the issue of an EMTALA violation in a malpractice case is strategic. It provides leverage for the plaintiff to push for a settlement. Although the monetary damages of an EMTALA violation are relatively low, $50,000 per incident, none of which would go to the plaintiff, the possible loss of the hospital's ability to participate in Medicare/Medicaid would, in many instances, be a lethal blow to the hospital's ability to even stay in business. Under these circumstances, the hospital may decide it is better to settle than to take the risk of losing the ability to participate in Medicare and Medicaid. If the hospital were to settle, it would put more pressure on the health care provider to also settle on the malpractice claims.

EMTALA defines the hospital's obligation to a patient who "comes to the emergency department" requesting an "examination or treatment for a medical condition." For these patients, EMTALA requires first, that an appropriate medical screening examination be done to see if the patient has an "emergency medical condition."[172] If the screening examination determines that the patient does not have an emergency medical condition, then there is no further obligation under EMTALA placed on the hospital. However, *common law negligence* under the laws of the state still may be applicable, so the hospital and medical care providers still need to do what a reasonable health care provider would do under the same or similar circumstances or they may be liable *for medical negligence.*

If the medical screening exam finds a person had an *emergency medical condition*, then the second requirement of EMTALA kicks in. This requirement is to institute the care needed to stabilize the condition as best the hospital can within its capabilities. The question arises as to when this *stabilization* requirement ends. EMTALA recognizes that a hospital may not have the capabilities to *stabilize* a certain condition and, when this occurs, a process is described in the law where an *unstable* patient may be transferred to a facility which does have the capability of stabilizing the condition.

This is the type of situation which may occur in a community hospital that is not equipped to do certain procedures, such as open-heart operations. A patient with, for example, an aortic dissection, may not be stabilized under the requirements of the statute without an operation. Since the hospital does not have the capabilities of doing this procedure, there is a mechanism in the law whereby a transfer of this unstable patient is allowed.

As is true with most legislation, the words used in the statute are open to interpretation even when the words themselves have been defined in the statute. Under EMTALA, "to stabilize" is defined as "…to provide such medical treatment of the condition as may be necessary to assure, within reasonable medical probability that no material deterioration of the condition is likely to occur during the transfer of the individual from a facility, or, with respect to [a pregnant woman having contractions], to deliver…"[173] On its face, it seems a patient will be *stabilized* under the requirements of the Act if the condition is not likely to worsen after leaving the facility. But what if the patient is being *admitted* to the facility? Unfortunately, different courts have interpreted the words differently in trying to determine when the hospital's duty to *stabilize* the patient has been met.

In 1990, the Sixth U.S. Circuit Court gave its interpretation of the *stabilization* requirement in *Thorton v. Southwest Detroit Hospital*.[174] Ms. Thorton had suffered a stroke and had been in the hospital for 21 days. She was then discharged to a nursing home where her condition worsened. She brought suit claiming the hospital had discharged her in an unstable condition and thus, had violated the requirements of EMTALA. The District Court heard the case and ruled the hospital had *stabilized* the patient but, even if she was *unstable* at discharge, the EMTALA *stabilization requirement* had ended when she left the emergency room and had been admitted into the hospital.

On appeal, the Appellate Court agreed with the district court that the patient had been *stabilized* prior to the discharge, but then disagreed that the EMTALA requirements had ended when the patient was admitted. The Appellate Court interpreted the words *emergency room care* to mean *emergency care* and thus, the hospital still had a duty to *stabilize* even if the patient had been moved out of the emergency room to be admitted to the hospital. The Sixth Circuit did not want hospitals circumventing the *stabilization* requirement by admitting the patient to another unit and then discharging the patient, or *dumping*, shortly thereafter.

In 2002, the Ninth Circuit Court of Appeals came to a very different interpretation of the *stabilization requirement*. In *Bryant v. Adventist Health System*,[175] the Court of Appeals held that the *stabilization requirement* was not intended to apply to patients who had been admitted to the hospital.

As such, EMTALA requirements ended when the patient was admitted to the hospital.

In *Bryant*, the patient had been treated for pneumonia and was then discharged. A check of the chest radiograph revealed a lung abscess so the patient was called back in and placed into the Intensive Care Unit (ICU). He was later transferred to another hospital, had surgery, and was eventually released. However, he soon died. The Ninth Circuit did not believe that EMTALA was meant to be a federal malpractice law for a failure to treat cause of action which they felt could be better addressed by state malpractice law. As such, the Court felt that the requirements of EMTALA did not apply to this case.

In *Bryan v. Rectors and Visitors of the University of Virginia*,[176] the Court stated that "[EMTALA's] core purpose is to get patients into the system who might otherwise go untreated and be left without a remedy because traditional medical malpractice law affords no claim for failure to treat."

In *Bryan*, the patient had been admitted for respiratory distress. She was treated for twelve days in the ICU and then a *do not resuscitate* order was placed against the family's wishes. The patient died eight days later from a myocardial infarction. The Court held, and the Appellate Court agreed, that stabilizing treatment had been provided for twelve days. When the patient had the myocardial infarction eight days later, EMTALA did not apply as that would mean the statute would require the hospital to provide treatment indefinitely, perhaps for years. The Court's reading of EMTALA was that it applied only to the emergency treatment required to stabilize the patient while the doctors considered whether they needed to admit the patient or transfer the patient for further care.

In *Harry v. Marchant*,[177] the Eleventh Circuit agreed with the Fourth and Ninth. In *Marchant*, the patient presented with pneumonia, possible sepsis, and a possible pulmonary embolus. She was admitted after being in the ER for more than seven hours during which time she did not get antibiotics or a lung scan. After she was admitted to the ICU, she arrested and died. The Court held the duty to stabilize an emergency medical condition applies whether a patient is going to be transferred *or admitted to the hospital*. However, once admitted, state law kicks in and the requirements of EMTALA end. In other words, the stabilization requirement "continues until the patient is stabilized for transfer, release, or admission."

The Fourth, Ninth, and Eleventh Circuits are in agreement. They all hold that the EMTALA stabilization requirement ends when the patient is admitted into the hospital.

Based on the *Marchant* decision, the Bush administration decided to clarify the issue as to when the stabilization requirement ends. According to a Centers for Medicare and Medicaid Services (CMS) letter, the decision to admit the patient into the hospital will not be enough to end the stabilization requirement of the statute; the patient will have to actually be admitted "…with the expectation that the patient will remain in the hospital at least overnight." Also, "…a hospital's EMTALA obligation toward an individual ends when the individual has been admitted for inpatient hospital services whether or not the individual has been stabilized." However, "[i]f it is determined that the hospital admitted the patient for the purpose of avoiding its EMTALA obligation, then the hospital is liable under EMTALA and may be subject to further enforcement action."[178]

There is some discomfort with the CMS interpretation of this requirement. As claimed by Sara Rosenbaum writing in The Nation, a periodical, "…the landmark, 2002 case *Harry v. Marchant*, which was quickly codified as a system wide rule by the Bush administration in 2003, held that EMTALA obligations end at inpatient admission; hospitals can now admit—and then dump—unstable patients, unless caught in a *subterfuge*, a virtually impossible act to prove."[179]

When different circuits interpret the law differently, and the Administration takes a position which is open to question, the Supreme Court may decide to look at a similar case to clarify the murky legal situation. It's difficult to guess on which side of the issue the Supreme Court will fall.

What about the patient who is deemed to be stable? Is it enough for the emergency room physician to certify in writing that the patient has been stabilized to a reasonable degree of medical certainty to end EMTALA liability as is required in the statute? Probably not.

In 2007, the U.S. District Court of the Northern District of Iowa held that the jury must determine if the physician weighed the medical risks and adequately deliberated when he made the decision that the patient was stable. In *Heimlicher v. Steele and Dickson County Memorial Hospital,* an emergency room physician had certified that Heimlicher was stable for transfer. She was transferred to another hospital where she was found to have a ruptured uterus. She survived the emergency operation, but the baby was stillborn. The Court denied the hospital's motion for summary judgment and sent the case back for a trial.[180]

Is there a futile care exception to the stabilization requirement? The Fourth Circuit Court addressed this issue in *In re Baby K*.[181] In this case the parents of an anencephalic child kept bringing the baby to the emergency room for episodes of respiratory distress. The hospital, believing that it was futile to keep treating this child, sought judicial permission to withhold ventilator care the next time the child presented to the emergency department. The Court rejected the hospital's request holding that there was no exception for *futile* care under the statute. The Court felt that Congress was free to add this exception to the law if they so desired, but it was not the Court's role to do so.

In conclusion, each hospital which is subject to the EMTALA statute should have their legal counsel study what the courts in their jurisdiction have concluded in regard to the stabilization requirement of the statute. The practice of admitting the patient to the hospital may not be enough to end the stabilization requirement of the statute which could make the hospital subject to severe penalties. There is also a risk that the written certification of a physician that the patient has been stabilized may be second-guessed in a court of law. Again, the hospital could be on the hook for a violation.

Lastly, stabilizing treatment should be started even if the physician recognizes that he may be providing futile care. Federal law trumps state law in this regard.

Medical Malpractice: A Physician's Guide

Vocabulary

patient dumping
charity hospitals
common law negligence
medical negligence.
emergency medical condition
stabilization
Thorton v. Southwest Detroit Hospital
stabilization requirement
emergency room care
emergency care
Bryant v. Adventist Health System
Bryan v. Rectors and Visitors of the University of Virginia
do not resuscitate
Harry v. Marchant
admitted to the hospital
subterfuge
Heimlicher v. Steele and Dickson County Memorial Hospital
In re Baby K.

Citations

[172] EMTALA Statute: 42 USC 1395 dd.
[173] EMTALA Statute: 42 USC 1395 dd.
[174] 895 F.2d 1131 (6th Cir. 1990).
[175] 289 F.3d 1162 (9th Cir. 2002).
[176] 95 F.3d 349, 351 (4th Cir. 1996).
[177] 291 F.3d 757 (11th Cir. 2002).
[178] CMS letter to State Survey Agency Directors to explain enforcement policies published in the Federal Register/Vol. 68, No. 174, pg. 53222 on September 9, 2003, effective November 10, 2003.
[179] Sara Rosenbaum, The Nation, October, 16, 2008.
[180] *Heimlicher v. Steele and Dickson County Memorial Hospital.* www.iand.uscourts.gov/e-web/decisions
[181] 16 F.3d 590 (4th Cir. 1994)

Chapter 25:
Borrowed Servant Doctrine

Most surgeons are aware of the *Captain of the Ship* doctrine which basically makes them responsible for all of the events that happen to their patient in the operating room. Surgeons have been advised since early in their training that this philosophy can make them a target for any adverse event which happens to their patient whether or not they are even there when the event occurred. However, in many states, this doctrine does not have legal standing.

A patient at a university hospital had recently undergone a liver transplant. The operation went well and he was recovering nicely when he started complaining of shortness of breath. The transplant team was concerned and rightly so. They ordered a chest film which showed a large cardiac silhouette and this led the team to get an echocardiogram of the heart. The echo showed a large pericardial effusion[182] and there were signs the fluid was causing pericardial tamponade.

A cardiothoracic surgeon was consulted to perform a pericardial window to drain the fluid. He went to the operating room where the patient had already been prepped and draped by the nurses. The anesthesiologist put the patient to sleep with the surgeon standing by ready to do a pericardiocentesis in case there was a sudden hemodynamic collapse which could occur if the patient lost his vascular tone from the anesthesia. The patient remained stable so the surgeon did the pericardial window and the operation went well.

As the doctors were removing the drapes, they noticed the patient had a partial thickness burn injury where the grounding pad for the electrocautery had been placed on the thigh. It was not clear if the pad was defective or if it had not been properly placed by the nurse. The surgeon cleaned the wound, which measured about 2 inches by 2 inches, placed antibiotic ointment, and put on a dressing.

In the Intensive Care Unit (ICU), the doctors consulted the Plastic Surgery service to evaluate the burn injury and institute any further therapy they felt was indicated. The surgeon spoke to the family about the operation and informed them about the burn injury along with the steps staff had taken to treat the problem. The family appeared to understand, and were pleased the cardiac problem had been resolved. When the patient had recovered from the anesthetic, the surgeon spoke to him and informed him of the burn injury along with the team's plan to treat it. The patient appeared understanding regarding the burn.

The fact that a patient and his family *appear* to be understanding does not mean you are out of the woods in regards to a malpractice suit. Even though the wound healed well and did not even require a skin graft, the surgeon was served with a lawsuit about two months later. Plaintiff's theory was the surgeon was responsible for all that had transpired in the operating room which included the placement of the grounding pad. This theory is what is known as the *Captain of the Ship* doctrine which, in this case, makes the surgeon ultimately responsible for all occurrences in the Operating Room (OR).

Luckily for the surgeon, the State of Tennessee doesn't work with the *Captain of the Ship* doctrine in this situation. Instead, Tennessee uses the *Borrowed Servant* doctrine. Under the *Borrowed Servant* doctrine, even though the court recognizes the surgeon is in complete charge of the operating room and the people who are assisting him with the procedure, there are certain duties of others, such as the nurses and anesthesiologists, which do not involve the professional skill and decision-making of the surgeon. These types of duties include prepping and draping the patient and performing sponge and instrument counts.

The surgeon relies on these professionals to perform these duties and will often inquire as to where they are in the process prior to the commencement of the operation. The surgeon can thus be assured the patient has been prepped properly and also be assured he is not leaving any sponges or instruments in a body cavity of the patient at the conclusion of the operation.

When the nurse is doing the types of activities the surgeon relies on, and these activities are within the nurse's scope of practice, then the court recognizes that any negligence in performing these activities will no longer rest with the surgeon under the *Captain of the Ship* doctrine. However, there will be liability created for the nurse and the hospital where the nurse is employed. The surgeon, in states which recognize the *Borrowed Servant* doctrine, is not held liable because these activities are not medical in nature and they do not require his knowledge, education, training, experience, and skill to accomplish them.

Here are two cases on point to serve as examples: In *Danks v. Maher*,[183] 177 So.2d at 417-418, the Louisiana court said, "In our opinion the counting of laparatomy squares in the instant case was not an act requiring the exercise of a particular skill or discretion acquired or developed by special training. It was an act which could have been done by an unskilled or untrained employee and it did not involve the exercise of any professional judgment. We conclude that the incorrect count was not a medical mistake; it was an administrative or non-professional mistake from which liability on the part of the hospital can result."[184]

In *Rural Education Association v. Bush*,[185] 298 S.W. 2d 761,767, the court again ruled that the surgeon had no liability for a foreign body left in the patient. In the words of the court, "[w]hen a nurse acts under the orders of a private physician in matters involving professional skill and decision; she is absolved from liability for her acts. Many acts of a nurse, however, do not result from orders of the physician. Furnishing proper personnel and equipment for an operation are duties of a hospital. The selection of proper sponges was the duty of the hospital. Counting the sponges so as to see that no sponge was left in the body of the patient required no special skill or decision of the surgeon. Indeed, [the surgeon] relied upon sponge count of the nurse."[186]

Based on the Borrowed Servant Doctrine, the surgeon was not liable for the burn injury from the grounding pad. The surgeon had no role in placing the grounding pad and, in fact, had relied on the nurses to do it properly. The surgeon had made no orders in regards to its placement nor did its placement require his knowledge, education, training, experience, or skill. It's no surprise, in regard to the *Captain of the Ship* versus *Borrowed Servant*, plaintiff's attorneys prefer the former and argue that the latter should be removed from the law. They prefer suing everyone in the room and letting the jury sort things out. Plaintiffs love to sit back and let the defendants point the finger at each other in assessing blame.

Vocabulary

Captain of the Ship
Borrowed Servant
Danks v. Maher
Rural Education Association v. Bush

Citations

[182] A pericardial effusion is fluid in the space between the pericardium and the heart.
[183] *Danks v. Maher*, 177 So.2d at 417-418 (La. App. 1965)
[184] Id.
[185] 298 S.W. 2d 761, 767 (Tenn. App. 1956).
[186] Id.

Chapter 26: Good Samaritan Rule

Black's Law Dictionary defines the Good Samaritan Doctrine as, "In tort law, the principle that a person who aids another in imminent danger will not be charged with contributory negligence unless the rescuer worsens the position of the person in distress."[187] Physicians often come across auto accidents with injuries or patients who have suffered some cardiac event in the non-hospital setting. What should they do in those situations? If they render care in emergencies, will they be at risk for being sued for malpractice? In order to address this situation, all states have instituted some form of a *Good Samaritan* law so as to give some protection to the health care professional willing to provide care in an out-of-hospital emergency.

So if you make an error that worsens the patient's position from where you found him, will you be liable for negligence? This could be foreseeable. For example, if you move a patient who has a spinal fracture and he becomes a paraplegic after the move or if you try to intubate a patient at the scene and you end up getting into the esophagus instead of the trachea, you may be liable for the injury. It would be a good idea to read the particular law of your state to see how much protection you are given. If you are sued for this type of situation, make sure your lawyer is well versed in the Good Samaritan law for your state.

Usually, the Good Samaritan law will grant the health care provider some form of immunity so long as he is not *grossly negligent* which would imply he was not trying to hurt the patient. In most states, plaintiffs must show clear and convincing evidence that the provider was grossly negligent. "Clear and convincing" is a difficult burden of proof, but it can be done.

Most state laws have two conditions that must be met in order to qualify for the immunity provided by the Good Samaritan doctrine. First, the aid must be given at the scene of the emergency. The second requirement is that the provider must not be motivated by the hope of being paid for his services. In other words, don't plan on billing the patient for the services you provided during this emergency situation that occurred out of this hospital setting. The only duty you owe to the person is to be *reasonably careful*. This is a different standard than what is required for medical malpractice.[188] Remember, in a malpractice action, the defendant will be held to the standard of a reasonable practitioner faced with the same or similar circumstances.

The reason for having the Good Samaritan doctrine is because it is good public policy to have people with the requisite knowledge and training to provide emergency care to a victim in distress. This care can be life-saving. The purpose of the doctrine is to take the fear of legal repercussions off the shoulders of caregivers who are fearful of making a mistake in the often chaotic environment of the accident or medical emergency site. There is no duty to stop and provide help unless it is part of your job description. Assisting at an emergency may even put you at risk. You can be injured by traffic flowing around the accident site or may even contract an infectious disease from the victim's blood or bodily fluids which is especially a concern if you don't have on any protective coverings.

What about the situation where a person, not your patient, has an emergency situation in the hospital or office where you are working? Be careful, the doctrine may not protect the physician providing the emergency care in the course of his regular employment—which is exactly what a physician would be doing to the patient in his health care facility.

Even though the law will provide the care-giver with some protection, it will not be total protection. Remember, if the patient claims that you made his condition worse because you acted negligently, the doctrine may not protect you and you will still end up having to defend yourself with all the costs of time, money, and energy the suit will entail. Although most states do not require you to stop and give first aid, they may consider it to be an act of negligence if you don't call the accident in to 9-1-1.

If you do decide to stop and render aid, then you must continue to do so until the victim either recovers, another trained person—an emergency medical technician, for example—takes over, or you become too exhausted to continue, such as doing CPR by yourself for a prolonged period of time. If you stop for any other reason, it could be interpreted as you *acting unreasonably* and the protection of the Good Samaritan law would disappear.

The *emergency* doctrine, which is closely related to the Good Samaritan doctrine, is a legal principle which implies that consent to medical treatment is *inferred* when the patient or some other responsible party is in no condition to do so. The doctrine applies when a reasonable patient would give consent if faced with the same or similar circumstances. But be careful; if the victim is conscious and can respond to your questions, it would be best to ask him for permission before you start any care. Also, bear in mind if you do decide to render care in an emergency, you will be held to the standard of a professional in performing the first aid. The law makes a distinction in this regard between a lay person and a person with training.

Under the Good Samaritan Doctrine, you must not leave the victim once you begin to render aid unless you need to call for help or someone arrives and has equal or greater expertise to provide the care. Most physicians, emergency medical technicians, or paramedics who are first responders will be considered to have greater expertise at a trauma scene but it can be argued that some trauma surgeons, for example, will have greater expertise in some situations.

Under the law, you are not expected to endanger yourself or others in treating the victim. For example, if the patient has AIDs and is bleeding, you are not expected to put yourself at risk without the needed protective clothing and gloves. Also, you will not be expected to stay with the victim if the car is about to go up in flames or a train is about to destroy everything at the scene.

Even if you think you are covered under the doctrine, there is nothing to prevent the patient from naming you in a lawsuit. Medical malpractice insurance policies should cover any liability. If you are named in a suit after providing emergency care, the defense attorney will probably file a motion to have you dismissed from the suit or will argue at trial that you should be dropped from the case on the basis of the *standard of gross negligence*. It would be extremely difficult—but not impossible—for the plaintiff to find an expert that would be willing to testify that you were *grossly negligent* in providing emergency care.

The information provided on the Good Samaritan Doctrine is most applicable for patients with life-threatening emergencies e.g., bleeding, no pulse, no respirations, shock. If you decide to treat non-life-threatening emergencies, you will be entering a legal gray zone where you may not have much protection. In these situations it may be best to back off and wait for the specialists to get involved in the hospital environment.

If faced with an emergency situation, you will be protected under the Good Samaritan Doctrine if you act in good faith, the emergency is outside of the medical facility where you work, you do not expect to be compensated for the care you provide, and you are not *grossly negligent* in providing the care.

Vocabulary

Good Samaritan
grossly negligent
reasonably careful
acting unreasonably
inferred
standard of gross negligence

Citations

[187] Black's Law Dictionary. 1996
[188] The standard of care for medical malpractice is what a reasonable practitioner of the same specialty would do if faced with the same or similar circumstances. In Tennessee, the locality rule would also apply.

Chapter 27:
Dynamite Charge

If a malpractice case does finally make it to trial, the costs associated with the trial can be very high and trials can last for weeks. There are often several attorneys associated with both sides and there is the added cost for the court's time. This includes such things as the judge's salary, the cost of the court reporter, and the cost of the guards and clerks. Other costs are harder to define but they include the time away from work for the plaintiffs and defendants, the costs of the witnesses and the costs of the experts. Because of these costs, it is not surprising that judges are not happy if a jury is unable to come to a verdict.

In those situations where a jury does claim to be deadlocked, some states allow their judges to instruct the jury to go back to their *deliberations* to try harder to come to a verdict. This instruction is known as the *dynamite* charge or sometimes referred to as the *shotgun* instruction, the *Allen* charge, or *third-degree* instruction. In giving the deadlocked jury this instruction, the judge may remind the jury to respectfully consider the opinions of others on the jury and he may caution them that another jury may not do any better of a job with the case than they are doing. Because of the inherent coercive nature of this instruction from the judge, some states prohibit its use claiming it is a violation of that state's constitution.

Allen v. United States,[189] involved a murder trial where Phillip Henson was shot and killed by the defendant, Allen. This case was tried in the Circuit Court of the United States for the Western District of Arkansas because the incident occurred in the Cherokee Nation of the Indian Territory. The jury was having a difficult time in deciding if there was the necessary element of *malice aforethought* so as to make the conviction for first degree murder. Even though *Allen* was a criminal case, the instruction was deemed to be applicable to both criminal and civil actions, at least in the Federal Courts where the case was tried.

In an effort to get the case resolved, the judge in *Allen* gave the jury further instructions as to how to come to a verdict by instructing in part, "…in a large proportion of cases absolute certainty could not be expected; that although the verdict must be the verdict of each individual juror, and not a mere acquiescence in the conclusion of his fellows, yet they should examine the question submitted with candor and with a proper regard and deference to the opinions of each other; that it was their duty to decide the case if they could conscientiously do so; that they should listen, with a disposition to be convinced, to each other's arguments; that, if much the larger number were for conviction, a dissenting juror should consider whether his doubt was a reasonable one which made no impression upon the minds of so many men, equally honest, equally intelligent with himself. If upon the other hand, the majority was for acquittal, the minority ought to ask themselves whether they might not reasonably doubt the correctness of a judgment which was not concurred in by the majority."[190] The Supreme Court held this type of instruction was allowed. Each juror should be willing to listen to the arguments of the others on the jury and not just doggedly fight for his opinion. A juror should listen with deference to the arguments of others who may very well be equally honest and as intelligent as himself.

The *Allen* opinion made clear that the dynamite instruction, although potentially coercive, would be allowed in the Federal courts.[191] However, some of the state courts have decided it to be a violation of their own constitutions which require a unanimous verdict of the jury. In California, for example, the state Supreme Court in *The People v. Robert Gainer, Jr.* decided that the *dynamite charge* should never be given, at least for a criminal trial. In its opinion, the California Supreme Court wrote, "The

Allen charge, to the extent it still survives, has been preserved because it is deemed to be an effective device for producing verdicts from otherwise deadlocked juries. However, it achieves such efficacy as it may have through a subtle mixture of inaccuracy and impropriety, in a manner which can dramatically distort the fact-finding function of the jury in a criminal case. Ultimately, even the saving of judicial resources, which has been the main justification for its continued existence, is outweighed by the burden the charge imposes on the appellate courts."[192] The California court refused to extend the abolition of the *Allen* charge for civil trials when, in a footnote of the opinion, it wrote, "Since the use of *Allen*-type instructions in civil cases may be subject to different considerations, we do not decide whether such use is also error."[193]

Other states are wrestling with the constitutionality of the *dynamite charge* feeling that it puts a burden on jurors to give in to majority opinions. In a malpractice case from Tennessee, a judge faced with a deadlocked jury gave the following version of the *dynamite charge,* "If a substantial majority of your number are in favor of finding a verdict, those of you who disagree should reconsider whether or not your doubt is a reasonable one, since it appears to make no impression upon the minds of the others."[194]

It seems obvious that this type of instruction, coming from the judge, has the potential of putting pressure on jurors to give up on their own opinion and side with the majority. This could be construed as the judge infringing on the constitutional role of the jury to be fact finders for the trial. No juror should have to give up on their opinion of the truth just because the court is looking for verdict.

Perhaps a hung jury is not a bad thing. It may give both parties in a civil suit a good reason to come to some sort of a settlement to avoid another trial. Or, if the parties choose, they may want to try the case again and perhaps do a better job of it the next time around. Either way, it would take away from the impression that the judge is more intent on getting a unanimous decision rather than pursuing justice.

Darryl Weiman

Vocabulary

Deliberations
Allen
Allen v. United States
malice aforethought
The People v. Robert Gainer, Jr.
dynamite charge

Citations

[189] *Allen v. United States,* 164 US 492 (1896).
[190] Id.
[191] *The People v. Robert Gainer, Jr.,* 566 P. 2d 997 (1977).
[192] Id.
[193] Id. Footnote 22.
[194] http://juryboxblog.blogspot.com/2009/06/dynamite-charge-might-blow-up-in-judges.html Edward Schwartz, June 16, 2009.

Chapter 28:
Lying Under Oath

Ben Franklin said, "Honesty is the best policy." When under oath, it is the only policy. Do not lie under oath—ever. Not for any reason.

"Perjury" is "[t]he act or an instance of a person's deliberately making material false or misleading statements while under oath."[195] Opposing attorneys will do their best to catch you in some sort of discrepancy so they can claim you are not being truthful. They will focus on any discrepancy to impeach your credibility to the jury and that will go a long way in having you lose your case. Any apparent change in what was claimed in the interrogatories, written in affidavits, said during depositions, or testified to in trial can be pointed out to the jury which then has the responsibility of judging on credibility.

If you are accused of lying under oath and can prove you aren't, the accusation can backfire in the face of the attorney who made the accusation.

It's possible that something you testify to isn't the truth but it doesn't necessarily mean you've committed perjury. For example, a physician was asked to review an office note that described an operation which had occurred in 2007, but was mistakenly noted to have occurred in 2006. The physician testified the office note was correct. He was wrong, but he wasn't *deliberately* making a false statement. Also, the year of the operation was not *material* to the case so there was no *perjury*. Remember, the legal definition of *perjury* requires that the person had to make the false statement *deliberately* and it had to be *material*; *material* meaning that the issue had some logical connection with the consequential facts.[196]

You stand to lose much more than your credibility if you decide to commit *perjury* because you think it may help you win your case. There can be criminal penalties which may result in jail time. As a physician, you stand to lose your license as well. The crime of *perjury* can be committed in both criminal and civil trials but a *perjury* prosecution is unusual for a civil suit possibly because it's difficult to prove that a witness is *intentionally* lying when all the defendant needs to do is claim that the testimony was honest, but perhaps based on a faulty memory. It can be pretty easy to convince the jury that you were not *intentionally* trying to mislead or misstate an issue of material fact for events that happened years ago.

Some attorneys will use the threat of a *perjury* prosecution as a means to coerce a witness to provide them with more favorable information. This strategy is well recognized and accepted by the legal profession. Never be intimidated when telling the truth.

Vocabulary

material
perjury
intentionally

Citations

[195] Black's Law Dictionary, seventh edition.
[196] Id.

Chapter 29: Conflict of Laws

In most legal disputes, the court hearing the case will apply the laws and procedures of the jurisdiction in which it sits. There are, however, certain situations which may arise that will require the court to apply the law of some other jurisdiction, such as the case earlier discussed: *Erie v. Tompkins.* In *Erie,* the Supreme Court held that each federal court must apply the laws of the state in which the conflict arose. The same court went on to rule that where a *conflict of laws* occurs, each federal court must use the *conflict of laws* rules of the state in which it sits.

Under Article 4, section 1 of the United States Constitution, "Full Faith and Credit shall be given in each State to the Public Acts, Records, and judicial Proceedings of every other State." The U.S. Supreme Court has interpreted this clause to mean that each state must accept a *judgment* rendered by the state which had *jurisdiction* over a matter and must use its powers to enforce that judgment. *Jurisdiction* is the capacity of the state to impose its authority over an action because of its connection with the parties and/or the subject matter of the litigation. The issue of which court gets to decide the case comes up when more than one state has an interest in the parties and/or the litigation.

The plaintiff makes the first choice because he is the one who started the action by filing in his court of choice. The defendant will, of course, try to have the jurisdiction changed if another venue would be to his advantage. These conflicts are not uncommon and the issues are complex and far from certain. Because of this, a significant *jurisprudence* has been produced in an effort to answer how best to decide whose laws will be used to decide a case or controversy.

Why would a *conflict of laws* occur? In the United States, each of the states has their own legal rules which often are different on the subject of a conflict. The court hearing a case must decide whether to use its own law or the law of another jurisdiction in deciding a case. Each court would prefer to use its own laws but that would encourage *forum shopping* by the parties and may even lead to different results from forum to forum. This wouldn't help a legal system that is looking for *uniformity*, *predictability,* and *advancement of public policy.* Contract law is the classic example taught in law schools. What should the court do with a contract signed in one state and mailed to another? What law will apply if one state's law says that a contract is effective when mailed and the other state says the contract is not valid until received? Rules have been set up whereby the case will be decided by the *law of the jurisdiction* which has the closest connection to the transaction. It would be ideal if the legal decision were to be the same regardless of where the case is brought, but that may not happen.

In the medical malpractice setting, the conflicts are usually due to the differences in the *statute of limitations, the notice requirements,* the *rules of contributory negligence* or *comparative fault,* and caps on *pain and suffering.* Say, for example, a patient who lives in State A is operated on in State B, he wants to sue, but he has missed filing before the *statute of limitations* has run out in State B. He will need to file in State A. The physician who practices in A and B would prefer to have the case in B where it would likely be dismissed. He may choose to have the case removed to federal court under a diversity of citizenship claim and then try to persuade the court to use state B's law; this would be reasonable if he lives in B, but what if he lives in State C?

You may think this is an unlikely scenario but in Memphis, for example, it can happen. Many physicians who practice in Memphis live in Arkansas which is just across the Mississippi River, some live in Mississippi, just a few miles south and some live in Tennessee. The patient can come from any of these states, or even other states.

Lex Loci Delecti is the legal doctrine which states that, in general, for a *torts action*, the *law of the place of the wrong* will govern. Seems reasonable; but the *place of the wrong* is defined as "where the last event necessary to make an actor liable for the alleged tort takes place." It is where the injury occurred—not where the negligence occurred—that will determine which law will be used in deciding the case. In *Alabama Great Southern Railroad v. Caroll*, 97 Ala. 126 (1892), the court ruled that Mississippi law applied where the plaintiff's injury happened in Mississippi from a negligent act which occurred in Alabama. Sort of like the unlatched train door from *Erie v. Tompkins*.

There are sound reasons for using the *lex loci rule*. *Uniformity* in the law is a desired quality of any legal system; the *lex loci rule* makes very clear what law will apply which helps in attaining *uniformity*. It also allows for *predictability* in that comparable cases will be treated similarly. It will prevent forum shopping which should prevent duplicate litigation and it should prevent judges from choosing which laws they want to use.

Although *lex loci* seems to be a good rule, the law has evolved over the years such that the more modern method of choosing the applicable law is done using the *center of gravity approach*. The law of the state with the most *significant contacts* will control the action. Again, the rationale is to attain *uniformity, predictability*, prevent *forum shopping*, keep judges from choosing the laws they want to use, and advance public policy of the states.

A variation of the *center of gravity* approach is the *compelling interest* analysis whereby the laws of the state with the *most compelling interest* should apply. If the parties are from the same state, apply that state's law. If they are from different states, then an analysis should be done by the court to determine which state's laws should be used. The analysis should keep in mind that any forum will have an *interest* in applying its own laws to the controversy. Each state has an *interest* in ensuring that residents of the state should be compensated for any wrong—as such the plaintiff must be a resident of the state. On the other hand, each state has an *interest* in protecting its own residents. With this in mind, it's not surprising that the states will want to have the defendant as a resident of the state.

The next step in the *modern analysis* acknowledges the state's desire to prevent any future harm within its borders. This analysis looks to see if the harm occurred within the borders of the state. If it has, then that state's laws should be considered. Anytime an *analysis* is used to decide a legal issue, the parties of the conflict will argue the *analysis* in such a way as to get their preferred *forum*. It will be up to the judge to make a decision so as to resolve the *conflict of laws* and, of course, that decision can be used as a basis of *appeal* by the losing party.

This is a complicated area of jurisprudence that is still being debated by some of the sharpest legal minds in the country. It is not easily understood.

The goals of *conflict of laws* jurisprudence are to prevent *forum shopping,* allow for *uniformity* in decisions, constrain judges in their decision making as to what law will apply, and *effectuate* the policies of the states involved. The courts are still experimenting how best to attain these goals. It would be wise to defer to your attorney in these strategic decisions so as to best meet your needs. However, you need to be aware of the potential conflicts so as to not be totally overwhelmed when your attorney tries to explain the strategy to you.

Vocabulary

Erie v. Tompkins
conflict of law
judgment
jurisdiction
jurisprudenc
forum shopping
uniformity
predictability
advancement of public policy
law of the jurisdiction
statute of limitations
the notice requirements
rules of contributory negligence
comparative fault
pain and suffering
Lex Loci Delecti
law of the place of the wrong
Alabama Great Southern Railroad v. Caroll
center of gravity approach
compelling interest
modern analysis
forum
appeal
effectuate

Chapter 30: Provider Regulation under Medicare and Medicaid

Intimidation is a well-recognized and accepted strategy in the legal profession. In the malpractice arena, it's not unusual for the plaintiff to allege that the defendant was not only liable for malpractice, but also guilty of health care fraud. The health care fraud allegation would put the defendant at risk for very high financial and even criminal penalties which would be separate and distinct from the alleged *malpractice liability*. These added risks make it more likely for the defendant to agree to a settlement on the malpractice issues so long as the alleged fraud allegations are dropped. This, of course, is the goal of the fraud allegations in the first place.

Medicare and Medicaid were enacted in 1965 as part of the Great Society envisioned by President Lyndon Johnson. At that time, the legislation had only one provision which prohibited making false statements in the billing process. Now there are numerous health care related *criminal, civil,* and *administrative anti-fraud laws* and *regulations* both at the federal and state level.

In 2004, it was estimated Americans spent nearly $1.9 trillion to purchase health care goods and services. This was 16% of the *gross domestic product* and, *per capita,* was $6,280 per person. It's predicted that these costs will reach $4 trillion by 2015 which will be about 20% of the *gross domestic product*. Of these costs, Medicare is projected to cost $800 billion in 2015 which will be 56% of federal health outlays. Medicare (Part A) covers inpatient hospitalizations including prescription medications while in the hospital. Medicare (Part B) covers payments for physician services and some outpatient services not covered under Part A. Medicare is financed by payroll taxes and monthly premiums for voluntary supplemental coverage.

With the new *Affordable Care Act* (ACA), it is apparent there is a perception that much money can be saved by cracking down on *health care fraud*. It begs the question as to how common *health care fraud* is. There is a political estimate that *fraud* is responsible for about 10% of health care costs. The Government Accounting Office (GAO) came up with the number based on an unscientific survey of unidentified individuals who were asked to estimate losses from *fraud and abuse*. These individuals guessed that *fraud and abuse* accounted for about 10% of the total costs for Medicare and Medicaid. Not very scientific, but the number has caught on and is used in most studies looking for solutions for Medicare and Medicaid fraud.

Many *statutes* have been written in an effort to curb *fraud*. On a federal level, the *criminal statutes* that have been applied to the problem include the following: (1) conspiracy to defraud the United States;[197] (2) false statements;[198] (3) mail fraud;[199] (4) wire fraud;[200] (5) money laundering.[201] There are also health care specific statutes such as: (1) anti-kickbacks;[202] (2) health care fraud;[203] (3) theft or embezzlement;[204] (4) false statements;[205] (5) obstruction;[206] (6) money laundering[207]. Several *statutes* have been written to *regulate provider conduct* so as to minimize costs. These include the False Claims Act, Stark I and II, the Medicare/Medicaid fraud and abuse statute, state laws criminalizing referral fees, and state medical practice acts.

The False Claims Act appears to have the most chilling effect on health care providers. It was enacted in 1863, in response to rampant fraud being perpetrated on the Union army during the Civil War. Over 140 years, multiple *amendments* have expanded the law to encompass virtually any entity that transacts business with the federal government. Under the False Claims Act, violators are liable for civil penalties of $5,500 to $11,000 per claim, plus three times government damages. The penalties can be astronomical which can lead to tremendous pressure on the defendant to settle. For example, just one hundred false claims can lead to a penalty of $1.1 million.

In *United States v. Krizek*,[208] the defendant was accused of receiving an overpayment of $245,392. This case involved a psychiatrist who was billing for 45-50 minute sessions when he was only spending 20-30 minutes with each patient. Each bill he submitted after the overpayment was considered to be fraudulent under the law so he was liable for a statutory penalty of $81 million. The District Court imposed a substantially lower sanction but you can see how the risk of losing everything is very high.

The Office of the Inspector General (OIG) had an initiative called "Physicians at Teaching Hospitals" (PATH) which looked at resident supervision. If the supervision was deemed to be inadequate then the bills generated were considered fraudulent. The University of Pennsylvania was investigated and during the audit period there were 1.4 million claims submitted. The audit of a sample found that there was inadequate documentation of resident supervision in 2% of the charts. The law allowed the OIG to extrapolate the sample to the total number of charts. The University found itself at risk for penalties for $280 million which did not include the triple damages for overpayments. Because of the huge risks, the University entered into a settlement for $30 million. It seemed that settling was the only viable option.

The University of Washington faced a similar situation and they entered into a $35 million settlement. In that case, an attending neurosurgeon was accused of *suborning* perjury which only added to the problems facing the University.

The Dartmouth Hitchcock Medical Center was investigated and they were eventually found liable for an overpayment of only $778. They were involved in a 10-month audit for which they paid $1.7 million. As you can see, even if a teaching hospital is significantly in compliance with the laws, the cost of defending an attack by the OIG under PATH can be substantial. Because of their successes, the OIG planned to audit all university and other teaching hospitals. A successful lobbying campaign by hospital representatives led to a moratorium of the OIG PATH investigations, but these investigations can be restarted at any time. Health care providers have had to spend resources to be sure that they are in compliance with the several laws because of the significant risks inherent with billing for health care services.

One of the concerns with the anti-fraud billing statutes is that they permit Qui Tam suits which allow for private whistle blowers who sue on the government's behalf to retain 15-20% of the proceeds of the suit. This is a powerful incentive for public policing in the health care market. Not only will a provider be at risk for malpractice allegations, but fraud allegations will be on the table, also. Because of the Qui Tam statutes, disgruntled employees and competitors can join patients and their families as those who have standing to bring suit against health care providers. Grounds for suit include mischarges—where the patient is billed for items or services that were not delivered, false negotiations and fraud in the *inducement* of a contract—whereby all claims submitted under the negotiated contract are false, and false certifications—where *certification* is a prerequisite to obtaining a government benefit.

Other grounds for suit are for delivery of substandard products and services and *reverse false claims* where the defendant used a false record to decrease or avoid a financial obligation that he owed the government. In *United States v. Pani*,[209] the government sued a neurosurgeon who submitted 157 claims for operations that he never performed. Pani was convicted on charges of mail fraud, false claims, and conversion. Pani tried to claim that the statute of limitations had run out on the United States since the limitation was three years for tort violations; the Court ruled that the violations were centered on contract law which had a statute of limitations of six years. Pani lost big!

In *United States v. Lorenzo*,[210] the government sued a dentist who fraudulently billed for oral surgery "consultations" when he was actually just doing routine dental check-ups which were not covered under Medicare. The United States was awarded a recovery of $392,157 in damages and over $18 million in penalties for 3,683 false claims.

It is also illegal for a licensed physician to allow another person who is ineligible to bill for reimbursement to bill in the physician's name. In *Peterson v. Weinberger*,[211] a physical therapy company billed in the name of an independent physician who did not perform the services. The appellate court affirmed a money judgment by the district court against Peterson for submitting false claims against the government.

In an effort to circumvent a state's anti-kickback statutes, a radiology center in Illinois paid physicians $400 to lease an MRI and CT scan. The physicians would then charge the patient's insurance $800 for the scans. The physicians were pocketing $400 for doing nothing except for referring the patients to the radiology group. This was deemed to be a violation by the Illinois Attorney General, Lisa Madigan, who brought suit. She had alleged that the payments were kick-backs for patient referrals. The defendants finally agreed to pay a $1.2 million settlement and there was an explicit requirement for the defendants to stop paying illegal kickbacks to the referring physicians in Illinois.

It's not unusual for a university practice group to contract out for services that they do not provide. Often, these contracts are entered into with a private group in town. The private group gets the Medicare A dollars for resident supervision. The private group will then pay the University practice group a percentage of their net collection. Some believe this is a violation of the anti-kick-back statutes. This issue has not yet been litigated.

It's also possible for the government to bring suit under the *theory of medical necessity* — where the government disagrees with the provider as to the necessity of the treatment. This is a difficult area for the government to win because all they can do is review the medical records and the issue is fact intensive. It's a *standard of care* issue and the defendant is likely to win. However, because the risk is so high under the False Claims Act, settlement may be the most reasonable option.

There are several things health care providers and hospitals can do to protect themselves from *fraud allegations*. First, know the law and follow it. Second, read the Medicare advisories and manuals and seek clarifications from the Centers for Medicare and Medicaid Services (CMS). Keep clear medical and billing records and never destroy anything. Before entering into any contracts for billing or for providing health care services, be sure to obtain competent legal advice. Be sure to have a compliance program in place and be sure your employees abide by the program. These steps will all be helpful if you are faced with allegations of fraud either separately or as part of a malpractice action. Remember, there is *prosecutorial discretion* under the fraud statutes and the government is less likely to come after those who have a robust compliance program as to those who do not.

False Claims Act violations, upcoding, wire fraud, mail fraud, racketeering, anti-kick-back laws, Stark 1 and Stark 2, and HIPAA all provide potential grounds the plaintiffs can raise in a malpractice action. You need to at least be aware of these laws and be prepared to defend yourself against any potential allegations.

Darryl Weiman

Vocabulary

malpractice liability
administrative anti-fraud laws
gross domestic product
per capita
health care fraud
regulate provider conduct
United States v. Krizek
suborning perjury
inducement
certification
reverse false claims
United States v. Pani
United States v. Lorenzo
Peterson v. Weinberger
theory of medical necessity
prosecutorial discretion

Citations

[197] 18 USC sec. 286, 371.
[198] 18 USC sec. 101.
[199] 18 USC sec. 1341.
[200] 18 USC sec. 1343.
[201] 18 USC sec 1956, 1957.
[202] 42 USC sec 1320(a)-7b(b).
[203] 18 USC sec 1347.
[204] 18 USC sec 669.
[205] 18 USC sec 1035 and 42 USC sec 1320a-7b(a).
[206] 18 USC sec 1518.
[207] 18 USC sec 1956(a)(1).
[208] 111 F.3d 934 (D.C. Cir. 1997).
[209] *United States v. Pani*, 717 F.Supp 1013 (S.D.N.Y. 1989).
[210] *United States v. Lorenzo*, 768 F.Supp 1127 (E.D. Pa 1991).
[211] *Peterson v. Weinberger*, 508 F.2d 45 (5th Cir. 1975).

Chapter 31: Confidentiality of Peer Review

It has long been believed that doctors could learn from their mistakes by performing critical self-evaluations in the presence of their peers where frank discussions could be held without fear of reprisal. Their quality of care could be improved by all involved in the process and the ultimate benefactor would be the patient. Unfortunately, some providers and hospitals are reluctant to participate in this process for fear that the records could be *discovered* by plaintiff's attorneys and the findings could be used against the physicians.

Morbidity and mortality conferences, which include *peer review*, can become very heated. It isn't unusual for one physician to accuse another of not meeting the *standard of care* or to make even worse accusations. Can you imagine the ammunition this kind of information could be in the hands of a plaintiff's attorney? In an effort to encourage a *good faith peer review* where candid discussions and evaluations could be done, all of the states have passed *statutes* designed to protect those who are participating in the *peer review* process by making them *immune* from suit. The *statutes* also allow the records made during the proceedings to be *immune* from *discovery*. Not surprisingly, the *statutes* vary in how much protection they provide.

First, the *statutes* provide protection of the peers who are doing the reviewing by making them *immune* from *liability* for participating in the process.[212] If a physician criticizes another physician during the conference, the physician giving the criticism shouldn't have to fear that the doctor he is trying to help will come after him with a *defamation* suit.

The *statutes* are also designed to protect the records generated from the *peer review* process. The discussions would probably not be very candid if there was a fear that what was said could be later read back in a court of law during a malpractice proceeding.

In the Tennessee law, subsection (e) states "[a]ll information, interviews, incident or other reports, statements, memoranda or other data furnished to any committee as defined in this section, and any findings, conclusions or recommendations resulting from the proceedings of such committee are declared to be privileged. All such information, in any form whatsoever, so furnished to, or generated by, a medical peer review committee, shall be privileged. The records and proceedings of any such committees are confidential and shall be used by such committee, and the members thereof only in the exercise of the proper functions of the committee, and shall not be public records nor be available for court subpoena or for discovery proceedings."[213]

With the *Peer Review* statutes on the books, many hospitals and other health care providers assumed that the protections set forth in the law could be applied to other committees that dealt with quality improvement such as for a *root cause analysis* after an adverse patient outcome. This belief came to a halt in Tennessee with the case of *Lee Medical Inc. v. Beecher*.[214]

In *Lee Medical*, the court held that documents generated by a *peer review* committee will only be privileged if they deal with a review of a physician's conduct, competence, or abilities. If a physician was not the focus of the review, the documents would not be privileged. The *majority opinion* was based on the premise that the state's discovery and evidence rules favored the policy that all relevant evidence was discoverable.[215] Before *Lee Medical*, the Tennessee courts had not addressed the scope of the Peer Review privilege so it was unknown if it applied to any peer review activities that did not involve physicians. However there was one unpublished opinion from the Court of Appeals that held that the post incident investigation of an Infection Control committee was privileged under the law.[216]

Why would a hospital want to do an investigation if the records generated in the investigation could be harmful if the case were to go to trial? Why would anyone on such a committee speak candidly if they were afraid that their words and conclusions could someday be read back to them at a trial?

In *Lee Medical*, the court's narrow definition of a *peer review proceeding* means that documents generated for all other *quality assurance* activities including *root cause analyses, morbidity and mortality* conferences—which are for teaching purposes as opposed to focusing on a particular physician's competence—, *utilization management*, and *infection control*, will not be protected by the *peer review privilege*. While it is true that the wording in the *statute* may have been ambiguous, the bright line definition drawn by the Tennessee Supreme Court means that several sensitive documents generated to help cut down on medical errors and improve the *quality of care* will now be *discoverable*. These documents would be the minutes of the meeting or findings and recommendations of the committee. Although *peer review* of physicians will be privileged, any investigations involving nurses, physicians assistants, and other non-physicians will not be. I believe this will have a chilling effect on any investigations of these groups of health care providers. This will have a detrimental effect on the goal of improving health care.

With the ruling in *Lee Medical*, it is possible that hospitals in Tennessee may even do away with some of their *quality assurance* activities. However, it would be more likely that they will try to reclaim the *privilege* of the documents under federal law such as the Patient Safety and Quality Improvement Act of 2005. There are more requirements under the federal law and hospitals may have to spend more money to be eligible for the protection, but these costs may be worth the effort if they lead to fewer malpractice suits.[217]

Before generating any records with your *peer review* and other *quality assurance* activities, be sure to check on the law in your state to see if you might have some of the same problems that are now present in Tennessee.

The *peer review* process has generally been considered to be confidential. This issue of confidentiality is very important because it prevents the proceedings from being *discoverable* by plaintiff's counsel in the event of a malpractice action being brought against a particular physician.

Darryl Weiman

Confidentiality and the Personnel File of Residents

During a recent malpractice action, a subpoena requesting a resident's evaluation file was delivered to the Department of Surgery at the University of Tennessee in Memphis. Unfortunately, the files were surrendered, effectively losing any claims the Department might have had for a *peer review privilege* in the case. As medical malpractice actions become more common and more contentious, any plaintiff's attorney who can show weaknesses in a physician's past performance may try to use such information to bolster his claims for *negligence*. Thus, the request by the plaintiff made strategic sense.

What can be done to deflect any future subpoena which requests a resident's file? The answer may be found in the Tennessee law of the *peer review* privilege. Different states may or may not recognize this privilege, but one doctor's review may allow other facilities involved in graduate medical education, i.e., departments which train future physicians, to develop a strategy to fight this very serious attack on the physician's ability to candidly evaluate the residents in training.

Under Article V of the Tennessee Rules of Evidence, privileges are described by which a person may refuse to produce an object or writing when requested to do so by the Court.[218] The privilege that the department of surgery should claim is the *Medical Review Committee – Informant*

Privilege, which is part of what is known as the Tennessee Peer Review Statute. The Tennessee Peer Review Statute defines a *peer review committee* as "any committee of a state or local professional association or society... the function of which, or one of the functions of which, is to evaluate and improve the quality of health care rendered by providers of health care service to provide intervention, support, or rehabilitative referrals or services, or to determine that health care services rendered were professionally indicated, or were performed in compliance with the applicable standard of care..."[219]

In a recent Tennessee case, *Alexander A. Stratienko, M.D. v. Chattanooga-Hamilton County Hospital Authority et al.*, the Supreme Court of Tennessee held that "information, documents, or records otherwise available from original sources are subject to discovery pursuant to Tennessee Code Annotated section 63-6-219(e), but only to the extent that they are not requested from the peer review committee and are not otherwise privileged."[220] In *Stratienko*, *appellee* Stratienko was trying to discover the *peripheral vascular credentials* of another physician with whom he had had a physical altercation causing Stratienko's hospital privileges to be suspended. Stratienko was able to get a temporary restraining order prohibiting the suspension and he was looking to support his claim to have the suspension reversed. The Court held that Stratienko could not get the requested information from the peer review committee but he was free to obtain the information from other sources so long as other privileges did not apply. Strategically, getting the information from other sources would be difficult as this would incur the legal costs of *deposing* witnesses or formulating *interrogatories* which would have to be answered under oath.

It is in the defendant's best interest to have the plaintiff incur costs in both time and money to get the information he is looking for. However, your lawyer, who is an officer of the court, is obligated to try and expedite the *cause of justice* and minimize the costs involved. As your advocate he must zealously work for your cause and in this situation, it will probably be proper for him to keep this protected information from the plaintiff and force the plaintiff to get the information in some other way.

Although the facts in *Stratienko* did not deal with a resident's performance file, the issue is on point. In *Stratienko*, the Tennessee Supreme Court recognized that the purpose of the Peer Review Law is "to encourage committees made up of Tennessee's licensed physicians to candidly, conscientiously, and objectively evaluate and review their peers' professional conduct, competence, and ability to practice medicine." These are the same activities that surgical faculty do during their meetings to evaluate their resident's progress during their training. There is a strong public interest that the surgical training programs train competent surgeons who can operate and take care of patients safely and independently. This training would clearly be impaired if residents could not be evaluated in confidence which would occur if the records of the meeting were subject to discovery.

A case out of Texas is pertinent to the resident files in question. In *Garza v. Scott and White Memorial Hospital*,[221] a federal district court held that resident evaluations were privileged under the Texas Peer Review Statute.[222] In *Garza*, a surgical resident was being sued for malpractice. As an employee of the hospital, the plaintiff was hoping to establish that the hospital was negligent for credentialing—hiring—this particular resident and they needed the files to support that claim. The Court held these documents fell under the *statute* and were privileged. As a result, the Residency Program Director did not have to release the file.

Plaintiff's attorneys may still try to get the information in the files but they will have to do it in a different way, such as by questioning the attendings and the resident during a *deposition* or by presenting *interrogatories* that must be answered in writing. They can do this because the facts that may have been used by the committee in their resident evaluation are discoverable. Facts are always discoverable. You cannot hide the facts of a case by presenting them to a peer-review committee and then claim that they are privileged.

Artfully asked questions as to the experience and training of a resident may be asked during the *deposition* and they must be honestly answered, but this may be less hazardous than revealing the cryptic minutes of the faculty meeting for resident evaluations.

Of course, claiming that the resident's evaluation file is privileged is only the first step in deciding this legal issue. Under the Tennessee Rules of Civil Procedure, Rule 26.02 section (5), the opposing party in the action will have to be informed that you are withholding the asked for information and you must provide him with enough information so that he can assess the applicability of the privilege. If opposing counsel disagrees with the claim, the Court will have to hear arguments and then make a decision as to whether or not the privilege applies.

In short, many believe that a resident's evaluation file is privileged and should not be made available even if subpoenaed for discovery. Only through candid discussions can the clinical faculty critically evaluate their residents so that, ultimately, the quality of care can be improved for the community. The courts will need to decide on this issue. If the trial court rules that the files are not privileged, an appeal to a higher legal authority, the court of appeals, for example, should be done. It is important the clinical faculty be able to evaluate their residents in confidence so that they can fulfill their obligations in training future physicians for the United States and the world.

A lobbying effort by the medical schools in our state led to the passage of a new law which makes the resident evaluation committee's documents privileged.

Peer Review and Privileging

Recently, the Joint Commission on the Accreditation of Healthcare Organizations (JCAHO) made a new requirement on medical staff organizations to assure there is a process to evaluate the performance of health care practitioners so that the quality of patient care is enhanced. Now, after granting initial privileges to a physician or other health care provider, a *Focus Professional Practice Evaluation* ("FPPE") must be done to show that the practitioner provides safe, high quality patient care. A clear *conflict of interest* may arise if a member of the committee doing the evaluation is biased either for financial, professional, or other reasons. This bias may give rise to *liability* to the hospital and the staff and, under these circumstances, the privilege may not apply. Federal immunity is contingent on the peer review process being fair.[223]

In order to prevent the appearance of bias, there are several things the health care organization can do so that the privilege of the committee can be invoked if the issue is raised. First, any financial relationship of the committee member with the facility must be disclosed and considered. Contracts, employment arrangements, leases, joint ventures, or any other financial arrangement between the member and the facility must be disclosed. *Disclosure* leads to *transparency* and this is a good first step in assuring an impartial peer review. Opening up the membership of the peer review committee to all members of the medical staff is another step in assuring fairness.

If there is still a question of fairness, it may be prudent for the facility to have a process where the professional review is done by external reviewers with no ties to the facility at all. This may be necessary if conclusions of an internal review could adversely affect a practitioner's privileges or if there is no one on the staff with the expertise to evaluate the procedure or areas under review. Of course, the facility may still be accused of *opinion shopping* if the ruling of the outside peer review is adverse to the practitioner but, at least, the facility can claim that they made a good faith effort to attain fairness in the evaluation. This good faith claim can go a long way in convincing a judge that the *privilege of the committee* should apply.

What happens if a plaintiff requests the results of an investigation that were used by a peer review committee in performing its peer review function? The Tennessee Supreme Court recently decided this type of case in *Powell v. Community Health Systems, Inc.*[224] In *Powell*, a former employee filed a suit against a hospital and an orthopedic surgeon. During discovery, the former employee wanted to depose the director of the hospital's infection control service who had the results of an investigation of post-operative nosocomial infections. Another sought-after piece of information was whether the orthopedic surgeon had tested positive as a carrier for a certain bacteria that may have been showing up in the wounds of patients. The hospital moved to protect the results of the infectious disease investigation claiming that it was privileged under the Tennessee Peer Review Statute.[225] The legal issue was whether or not the information sought by the plaintiff employee had been created in the regular course of the hospital's business, in which case the Infectious Disease Director would be the original source of the information—the information would thus not be privileged; or if the documents were prepared by or at the request of the Peer Review Committee exercising its peer review function, in which case the privilege would hold.

In this case, the Tennessee Supreme Court held that the underlying investigation was a part of the peer review process and was thus protected. In its opinion, the Tennessee Supreme Court stated, "The proper functioning of the peer review process hinges on the assurance to all persons participating in it—the members of the peer review committees, the persons under review, and the persons who provide information and opinions during the peer review process—that the information and opinions provided and discussed during the proceeding will remain confidential. Any breach of this confidentiality undermines the process."[226]

Darryl Weiman

Vocabulary

Morbidity and mortality
peer review
standard of care
good faith peer review
immune
liability
defamation
root cause analysis
Lee Medical Inc. v. Beecher
peer review proceeding
quality assurance
utilization management
infection control
peer review privilege
negligence
Medical Review Committee – Informant Privilege
peer review committee
Alexander A. Stratienko, M.D. v. Chattanooga-Hamilton County Hospital Authority et al.
interrogatories
cause of justice
Garza v. Scott and White Memorial Hospital
Focused Professional Practice Evaluation (FPPE)
Disclosure
transparency
opinion shopping
Powell v. Community Health Systems, Inc

Citations

[212] Tenn. Code Ann. Section 63-6-219 (TPRL). Subsection (d) grants immunity to participants in the peer review process.
[213] Id. Subsection (e).
[214] *Lee Medical Inc. v. Beecher,* No. M2008-02496-SC-S09-CV filed May 24, 2010.
[215] *Lee Medical* at 525.
[216] *Groller v. Methodist Medical Ctr. Of Oak Ridge,* 1989 5 WL 151498, (Tenn. Ct. App. Dec. 13, 1989).
[217] Under the federal law, the hospital will need to meet the requirements of a patient safety organization which is designed to improve quality of care and patient safety by compiling and analyzing medical data. If they meet the requirements, the records generated will be privileged under the federal law.
[218] Tennessee Rules of Evidence Rule 501.
[219] Tennessee Code Ann. Section 63-6-219(c).
[220] No. E2005-01043-SC-S09-CV — Filed May 14, 2007.
[221] 234 F.R.D. 617 (2005)
[222] Tex. Health & Safety Code section 161.032
[223] 42 U.S.C. sections 11101 et seq. For a more complete discussion see American Medical Association, Physicians Guide to Medical Staff Organization Bylaws (2008).
[224] No. E2008-00535-SC-R11-CV-filed May 24, 2010 In the Supreme Court of Tennessee at Knoxville, Sept. 3 2009 Session
[225] Tennessee Code Ann. Section 63-6-219(e).
[226] No. E2008-00535-SC-R11-CV Filed May 24, 2009 Session.

Chapter 32:
Morbidity and Mortality Conference: What Is Discoverable

Another form of the peer review process occurs at the Morbidity and Mortality conference, which most departments of surgery conduct on at least a monthly basis. Morbidity and Mortality (M&M) is a great learning experience because, while it is good to learn from your mistakes, you can also learn a lot from someone else's mistakes.

The discussions at M&M are often heated, personal, and critical. The presenter often gets very defensive and sometimes angry when questioned about their actions on the case they are presenting. The discussions are frank and open. Only physicians are allowed to attend—not even medical students are allowed. Unfortunately, plaintiff's attorneys are now trying to get the information discussed at these conferences hoping to find incriminating information not in the medical records or, even better, an admission that a screw up occurred.

The benefits of this type of conference are to learn from one's mistakes or from the mistakes of colleagues so that the same mistakes are not repeated and the advancement of surgical knowledge can occur. These discussions are the hallmark of the conference and need to be open and critical. Frank discussions are unlikely to occur if there is fear that the records of the meeting could be used by a plaintiff's attorney in a malpractice action. The advancement of knowledge that is a product of this type of conference would grind to a halt.

The state of Tennessee recognizes the importance of the peer-review committee and the legislature has passed a law which protects those discussions from discovery. The peer-review discussions "...shall be privileged communications subject to the laws pertaining to attorney-client privilege."[227] It's hard to say if the M&M conference has the protection of a peer-review committee. There are cases that highlight how some of the courts are dealing with this issue.

In *Weekoty v. United States*,[228] Mr. Weekoty died while under the care of a United States Health Service physician. The case was discussed at their M&M conference and the plaintiff's attorney made a motion to compel the release of the records to the plaintiff. The Magistrate granted the motion ordering that the documents related to the meeting be released. The United States appealed the verdict. The Appeals Court reversed the decision of the Magistrate holding that, "The material sought by Plaintiff's Motion to Compel is protected by the self-critical analysis privilege, perhaps more properly called the medical peer review privilege, and is neither subject to discovery nor introduction at trial."[229] However, not all courts agree with the conclusions of this case.

In *Syposs v. United* States,[230] the plaintiff tried to obtain all of the peer review records of the defendant, Dr. Lorenzo Teruel. The court agreed with the plaintiff, holding that "these records must be presented to Plaintiff as this Court declines to recognize a medical peer review privilege," at least as it applies to the records generated by the peer-review committee. In its opinion, the court felt that the protections were for the peers who were doing the review and the *privilege* was designed to keep them from being sued by the person they were reviewing.

The *Syposs* court noted that the hospitals failed to "provide any reason to believe some physicians would not provide candid appraisals of their peers absent the asserted privilege."[231] The court also stated that "Congress, in providing protection for those involved in peer review, did not establish a privilege for most documents created in the process."[232] As you can see, we have two different courts in different jurisdictions coming to very different conclusions regarding who and what is protected in the Morbidity and Mortality conference.

In 2005, the United States Congress passed a law called the Patient Safety and Quality Improvement Act of 2005. One of the major goals of the law was to encourage health care providers to present their errors without fear of reprisal. The idea was to improve *quality of care* for all patients, which is an important public policy interest. Under the law, physicians would be able to voluntarily submit errors to a patient safety organization which would be certified by the Department of Human Services (DHS). The DHS would be responsible for creating a searchable database of medical errors which could then be analyzed, to hopefully develop new care systems and best practices that would lead to a decrease of similar type errors in the future. The patient safety organization where the errors would be reported to would have the responsibility to develop and disseminate information with respect to improving patient safety.

Even though the Patient Safety Act seems like a good law to enhance patient safety, there is a legitimate fear that reporting what would otherwise be privileged information would lead to the loss of the privilege, making the defense of a lawsuit more difficult. If the patient safety organization is truly a regulatory agency, then precedent would seem to indicate that all privileges would be lost as to information reported to that agency. An example would be the Securities and Exchange Commission (SEC) for which corporations must report to for such issues as insider trading. Case law agrees that the privilege is waived as to the information reported to the regulatory agency and this would seem to be precedent as to the medical peer-review privilege.

As is true with most laws, there are exceptions. In the Patient Safety Act, the privileged information that is generated at a peer review meeting may be used in a criminal proceeding if the information would not be reasonably available from other sources. A judge in a criminal proceeding may require an in camera determination to see if the privileged information contained relevant information of a criminal act. In this type of situation, the Secretary of Health and Human Services may have to disclose the information.[233] Criminal Law takes precedence over Civil Law in this situation.

At this point you are probably thinking that this "criminal" exception would not apply to a physician being sued for malpractice. Unfortunately, you are wrong. Even though malpractice law is civil in nature, it is not unheard of for criminal issues to be raised in a malpractice action. If this occurs, the exception to the privilege would be applicable. There are cases on record where the line between malpractice and a criminal act is blurred.

An eight-year-old boy died during routine ear surgery. The anesthesiologist was charged with manslaughter and criminally negligent homicide. He was found to be innocent of these charges but he lost his license to practice medicine.[234]

A surgeon was found guilty of second-degree murder after he performed a second trimester abortion and the patient bled to death from a lacerated cervix.[235]

Most are familiar with the case of the Duke Lacrosse players who were unfairly prosecuted by a District Attorney (DA) who was later charged with prosecutorial misconduct. It can happen to physicians, also.

The case of Rosalyn Scott shows how a good surgeon can have her career irreparably harmed by a prosecutor who has a political agenda. A Los Angeles County sheriff was shot multiple times in the line of duty. He was transported to the Level 1 Trauma Center at Drew University where surgeons operated for nine hours. Dr. Scott, the vice chair of surgery at that institution, was consulted but she was not the operating surgeon. After 36 hours in the intensive care unit, the patient died.

Based on an anonymous tip, the District Attorney decided to investigate the case as a homicide rather than malpractice. He presented the evidence to a Grand Jury but the Grand Jury didn't agree with him and they refused to hand down an indictment. The DA then contacted the Medical Board with the recommendation that the licenses of several physicians, including Dr. Scott, be revoked. The Medical Board agreed with the DA and revoked the licenses. The Board found that the physicians were liable for *gross negligence* – meaning that they were liable for a "conscious, voluntary act or omission in reckless disregard of a legal duty and the consequences to another party..."

The Surgical Community, faced with an uproar of protest, had experts review the case and those experts found that the Board's charges were unfounded. Despite the independent review, it took the Board two years to rescind the charges.[236] Even though the charges were dropped, significant harm was done to a surgeon's career and reputation.

There are other exceptions to this peer-review privilege. For example, civil rights issues may take priority. A whistle-blower action where the provider of the information has suffered an adverse employment action such as loss of employment, failure to promote, or failure to provide any other employment benefit for which the individual would otherwise be eligible, would also trump the privilege. Another example would be in a criminal proceeding where a defendant would be entitled to any evidence in his favor. In these situations, the information requested would have to be provided to the requesting party.

Immunity from suit does not mean the peer reviewer has *immunity* from disclosure. The public has a need for relevant facts in *litigation* and the facts of the peer review may be relevant to the *litigation*. Since some courts have not found objective evidence supporting the view that confidentiality is necessary for the peer review process to achieve the public's interest in improving the quality of health care, they will allow the documents associated with the peer-review process to be *discoverable*.

Attorneys rarely think of the beauty of the law or its rational development. They are primarily concerned with the needs of their clients and how the law can be applied — or changed — to accomplish their client's goals. If they want information that you believe is privileged, they will still do everything in their power to get it.

Even if you believe the information you have generated in the peer-review process is privileged, you cannot just ignore a subpoena or other request for the information. In the Federal Rules of Civil Procedure, Rule 26(b)(5) mandates that the party objecting to a discovery request must identify and describe the privileged information and materials being withheld. The information that needs to be revealed includes an admission that the document exists, identification of the person who created the document or knows who did, the time the document was created, and the purpose for the existence of the document. Obviously, this identification must be done in such a way as to not reveal the underlying protected information. If the information is unintentionally revealed, you have likely lost the privilege through your own incompetence.

Even if the court recognizes the *privilege*, the people identified in the disclosure may be called upon to testify as to the facts of the case. This recognizes that facts are always *discoverable* and cannot be hidden by the cloud of a *privileged* communication.

If the *privilege* is recognized, it can be waived if the information is knowingly and voluntarily disclosed. An example of this is a defendant, who while being deposed, testifies that the peer-review acknowledged that he was not negligent. By opening this door, the plaintiff is now allowed to walk through to see what the peer-review committee had at its disposal so as to come to that conclusion.

What if there is an unintentional waiver of the privilege? This could occur if the information is sent to opposing counsel attached to records that are not privileged. Courts handle this type of *inadvertent waiver* in different ways. One approach is to hold that the *privileged information* can never be waived. In this situation the court will say that the disclosure can never constitute a waiver because there was no *subjective intent* to disclose the information. Other courts have a *strict accountability* approach which holds that an *inadvertent waiver* is a *fully effective waiver* of the *privilege*. This is a pretty harsh approach and it puts the blame fully on the disclosing party in hopes that all parties will be vigilant and careful, or else.

Most courts use a *balancing of the circumstances* test which looks at various factors such as the precautions taken to prevent *disclosure*, the time it took for the disclosing party to recognize the error, the scope of the production of materials, the extent of the disclosure, and the overriding interest of fairness and justice. This is probably the most even-handed approach but it can still result in loss of the *privilege* so it would be best to not release the information in any way, shape, or form unless the court rules that you must.

At least 46 states have *statutes* that protect the work product of medical review committees. These laws are to protect the committee members from liability and protect the proceedings, e.g., the records, materials produced, and materials considered. Although the *statutes* are somewhat protective, they will not prevent parties present at a peer-review committee from testifying at a deposition or a trial regarding information not relating to the committee proceeding itself. Remember, facts are always *discoverable* and cannot be hidden.

All people involved with the peer-review process should check with their legal counsel to determine how these records are being viewed in their courts so that they can take appropriate steps to protect these documents; or at least be careful of the words they use in the documents themselves.

Vocabulary

Weekoty v. United States
Syposs v. United States
gross negligence
Immunity
discoverable
inadvertent waiver
privileged information
subjective intent
strict accountability
fully effective waiver
balancing of the circumstances

Citations

[227] TCA sec. 63-6-219(e).
[228] *Weekoty v. United States*, 30 R.Supp.2d 1343 (D.N.M. 1998).
[229] Id.
[230] *Syposs v. United States*, 63 F.Supp.2d 301 (W.D.N.Y. 1999).
[231] Id.
[232] Id.
[233] Section 922(c) of the Patient Safety and Quality Improvement Act of 2005.
[234] USA Today, Oct. 19, 1998, Section D, 1-2.
[235] New York Times, Sept. 13, 1995, Section B, 3.
[236] LA CMA Physician, Sept. 1997, 29-34.

Chapter 33: Rules of Professional Responsibility for Lawyers

Law students are required to take a course on Professional Responsibility. Once they are admitted to the state bar, they have to abide by a certain set of rules which are modeled after *The Model Rules of Professional Conduct* of which all states have their version. Lawyers need to understand the seriousness of abiding by these rules. The licensing bodies and the courts of the various states will enforce these rules and the sanctions can be serious and include the loss of the license to practice law if these rules aren't followed. One chapter of these rules deals with the lawyer as an advocate. These are the main rules that pertain to a medical malpractice action as this is the role that the lawyers are playing in these proceedings.

Plaintiff's attorney is an advocate of the plaintiff and Defendant's attorney is the advocate of the defendant. The first rule in this chapter, Rule 3.1, states that a lawyer should not bring forth a frivolous claim. He must first do a reasonable inquiry as to the basis in law and fact to justify the proceeding. "What is required of lawyers, however, is that they act reasonably to inform themselves about the facts of their client's case and the law applicable to the case and then act reasonably in determining that they can make good faith arguments in support of their client's position."[237]

The lawyer does not have to believe that his client will win the case, but it will be frivolous if he cannot make a good faith argument on the merits of the action.[238] A frivolous case will be thrown out of court.

Another rule (Rule 3.2) attempts to keep the litigation on track. It states that the attorney must do what he can to expedite the litigation; however it may not be uniformly enforced as evidenced by cases that have taken years to resolve. This Rule is supposed to keep things moving so that the court does not get overwhelmed with cases that drag on forever. If a lawyer is being paid an hourly fee, there is a financial reason for him to drag out the litigation until the funds dry up. Rule 3.2 is meant to curb that type of behavior.

Rule 3.3 is about candor towards the tribunal. This rule requires that the lawyer not lie to the court as to the facts of the case or to the law that applies. This rule includes the pre-trial discovery process.

Lawyers are deemed to be *officers of the court* and as such, they must provide the court with the law that pertains to the case at hand even if the law is contrary to their client's side.[239] In other words, the lawyer cannot just back up his argument with the *statutes* and case law that are supportive of his position—he is obligated to point out contrary law and argue why that law is not applicable to the case at hand or he must make a *good faith* argument as to why that law should be overturned by the court. However, the rule only requires that the lawyer disclose *contrary law* that is applicable in your jurisdiction. He is not obligated to state *contrary law* from another state or country.

However, it's unreasonable for an attorney to depend on opposing counsel to raise *adverse authority* in the controlling jurisdiction. The attorney must disclose *adverse authority*. This seems to be helping the opposing party—and it is, but the idea is to help the Court come to a fair decision on the case. The best way to have a just decision is for the Court to be presented all of the legal arguments that may be applicable to the facts of the case. This is an example where the attorney may not be acting in the best interests of his client but obligations to the *tribunal* take precedent.

The rules don't allow an expert witness to be paid a fee that is contingent on the outcome of the case. A lawyer who agrees to a contingent fee arrangement with an expert witness will be in violation. Under Rule 3.3 (h), a lawyer shall not "offer an inducement to a witness that is prohibited by law; or pay, offer to pay, or acquiesce in the payment of compensation to a witness *contingent* on the content of his or her testimony or *the outcome of the case.*" However, it is permissible to "compensate an expert witness on terms permitted by law. The common law rule in most jurisdictions is that it is improper to pay an occurrence witness any fee for testifying and it is improper to pay an expert witness a contingent fee."[240]

What happens if an expert testifies that he is charging a *contingent* fee? In one particular case, the opposing attorney went on to the next question without batting an eye. He knew the credibility of the witness could be attacked in court by reading back the answer that he gave at the deposition. One can only imagine the embarrassment of the Plaintiff's attorney who had hired this witness knowing that the credibility of the witness had taken a hit and there was nothing he could do at that time to fix the problem. Yes, there is the possibility the attorney didn't know the contingent fee for a witness was against the rules, but a responsible attorney would know this fact.

So what type of payment would be proper for an expert witness? Section (h) says that the following payments would be proper: "(1) expenses reasonably incurred by a witness in attending and testifying; (2) reasonable compensation to a witness for that witness's loss of time in attending or testifying; or (3) a reasonable fee for the professional services of an expert witness."[241]

Attorneys can be paid on a *contingency* basis. State law will usually specify if there is to be a percentage of award cap. Under the Rules of Professional Conduct, it is only written that the contingent fee must be *reasonable*.[242] The list of things taken into account in determining *reasonable* is long and, some believe, open to interpretation.[243]

If a fee is to be *contingent* on the outcome of the case, the agreement must be in writing and signed by the client. The fee agreement must state how the fee is to be determined including the percent going to the lawyer in the event of settlement, trial, or appeal. The agreement must also explain how expenses are to be deducted—if at all—before or after the contingent fee is to be calculated.[244] Hopefully, the plaintiffs are knowledgeable when they sign on to this type of fee agreement and have full understanding.

Often, attorneys will ask questions to surprise the person on the stand, but their appropriateness comes under question. In one case, the Plaintiff's attorney started his questioning by asking about the time frame of an affair the resident allegedly had with the patient, who was now deceased. All of the defendants and their attorneys had no knowledge of an alleged affair which, at the very least, would have been unprofessional on the part of the resident. The resident denied having the affair, but the question did shake him up.

This type of questioning may be improper. Under Rule 3.4 section (e), a lawyer shall not: "in trial, (1) allude to any matter that the lawyer does not reasonably believe is relevant or that will not be supported by admissible evidence." Though this was a deposition and not a trial, the rules probably still apply because those involved in the deposition are under oath and answers must be given as if a judge and jury were present. The deposition testimony can be read in court for the right reasons so it makes sense that the rule should apply in a deposition.

Counsel needs to determine what evidence they will present. They must decide if the evidence is admissible under the rules of the court, the laws of the State, and the Rules of Professional Responsibility. If a lawyer believes that the evidence is questionable as to admissibility, the usual course of action is to have a pre-trial hearing or a conference with the judge and opposing counsel with the jury not present. The Court will then make a decision as to whether or not the evidence will be let in and the opposing counsel will then be on his toes to make a timely objection if he feels the court's decision is incorrect. In fact, some lawyers will violate the rules in hopes that the opposing attorney will be asleep at the wheel and not raise an objection. If the adversary fails to object, it is quite likely that the evidence will then be allowed to stand under a *raise or waive* rule. There is concern as to whether or not this skirting of the rules is ethical.

"The Tennessee Supreme Court in *State v. Smith*,[245] held that a trial court generally has no duty to exclude evidence or to provide a limiting instruction when a case is tried to a jury, in the absence of a timely objection, and a party may consent to the admissibility of evidence that is otherwise prohibited by the Tennessee Rules of Evidence, so long as the proceedings are not rendered so fundamentally unfair as to violate due process of law."

Lawrence A. Pivnick, a Professor of Law at the Cecil C. Humphreys School of Law in Memphis makes a case that lawyers should not rely on the *raise or waive* rule and should instead "voluntarily self-police his or her conduct and refrain from offering evidence that he or she does not reasonably believe is admissible absent the use of the *raise or waive rule*, particularly in cases where the adversary party is not represented by counsel.[246] In summary, 'two wrongs should not make it right.'"[247]

The American College of Trial Lawyers agrees with Professor Pivnick. They state, "A lawyer should not attempt to get before the jury evidence which is improper. In all cases in which a lawyer has any doubt about the propriety of any disclosures to the jury, a request should be made for leave to approach the bench and obtain a ruling out of the jury's hearing, either by propounding the question and obtaining a ruling or by making an offer of proof."[248] At this point in time, courts are divided as to what should be done by a lawyer who wants to bring in evidence that he suspects is objectionable. Following Professor Pivnick's advice would help with fundamental fairness.

Rule 3.4 makes it a requirement that a lawyer shall not state a personal opinion on the credibility of a witness, the culpability of a civil litigant, or the justness of his case.[249] It seems that many lawyers are able to skirt this rule by using questions instead of statements. For example, an attorney may say things like, "You would lie to protect your friend, wouldn't you?" His message to the jury is the witness is not credible. By not stating the witness is lying, he isn't violating any rules, but some see this as a pretty thin line which to walk. However, there aren't many courts that give much more than a verbal admonishment in the way of enforcing this rule because the attorney is really vigorously helping to present his client's case using any tools available to him.

These rules can't be used to bring a civil action against an opposing attorney. In the preamble and scope of the rules, it's clear that "[t]he Rules are designed to provide guidance to lawyers and to provide a structure for regulating conduct through disciplinary agencies. They are not designed to be a basis for civil liability. Furthermore, the purpose of the Rules can be subverted when they are invoked by opposing parties as procedural weapons."[250] The bottom line is that a lawyer who violates a rule or rules of *professional responsibility* will be subject to a disciplinary hearing from which he may be punished, but he will not be subject to a civil suit by an opposing lawyer or party.

Vocabulary

officers of the court
good faith
contrary law
adverse authority
tribunal
contingency
raise or waive
State v. Smith
professional responsibility

Citations

[237] Tennessee Rules of Professional Conduct; Rule 3.1 comment [2].
[238] Id.
[239] Id. Rule 3.3: Candor Toward the Tribunal. Under section (a), "a lawyer may not knowingly (1) make a false statement of fact or law to a tribunal; or (2) fail to disclose to the tribunal legal authority in the controlling jurisdiction known to the lawyer to be directly adverse to the position of the client and not disclosed by opposing counsel."
[240] Comment [4] Rule 3.4: Fairness to Opposing Party and Counsel section (h).
[241] Rule 3.4 section (h).
[242] Rule 1.5(a).
[243] Id.
[244] Id.
[245] *State v. Smith,* 24 S.W.3d 274 (Tenn. 2000)
[246] Lawrence A. Pivnick, *Offering Objectionable Evidence – Does an Adversary's Failure to Object Make the Practice Right?* Tennessee Bar Journal, Volume 46, no. 17, December 2010. p.19.
[247] Id. p. 24.
[248] American College of Trial Lawyers, Annotated Code of Trial Conduct 18(g)(Oct. 2005) as cited by Professor Pivnick in his article page 24.
[249] Rule 3.4(e)(3) in Tennessee Rules of Professional Conduct effective January 1, 2010.
[250] Paragraph 21 of the Scope of the Tennessee Rules of Professional Conduct, effective January 1, 2010.

Chapter 34: Removing Medical Malpractice from the Courts

Once a medical malpractice claim is filed, it is not unusual for the case to drag on for years until it is resolved. A cardio-thoracic physician along with a neurosurgeon were sued for medical malpractice for a trauma case they were involved in 1996. A defense verdict was finally obtained after a jury trial in 2013. During the passage of time, the first judge died. The second judge assigned to the case had to recuse herself since she knew one of physicians. The plaintiff's attorney had been pushing for settlement, but the physicians refused as they felt the case was without merit and they did not want to be listed in the National Practitioner Data Bank (NPDB) which could have occurred if a payment had been made on their behalf by their malpractice carrier.

Because of the costs involved in pursuing a case along with the uncertainty of the results, alternative methods to resolve disputes have come into vogue with the goal of avoiding litigation costs and coming to a monetary solution quickly. This could have benefits for both sides of the dispute. However, as more suits are settled using the alternative methods of dispute resolution, one of the undesirable consequences is that courtroom skills of the trial lawyers will be downgraded. As with anything, the more you practice your craft, the better you become.

In 2010, there were only 384 jury trials in Tennessee civil courts; this was about a thousand fewer cases than a decade prior.[251] In 2008, there were only 5,325 civil and criminal jury trials in U.S. District courts as compared to 6,839 in 2000 and 9,844 in 1990.[252] Kathryn Barnett, a trial lawyer in Nashville, said, "If you don't try cases, then it's difficult to understand the importance of all the steps along the way."[253] There are positives and negatives to settling a malpractice case either by trial or by an alternative method. You and your attorney need to decide what is best for you.

Not everyone has bought into the trend for alternative dispute resolution. Joe Jamail, one of *Forbes* magazine's richest people in America, said, "The move to replace jury trials with mediation and arbitration is actually an effort by elitists in our society to control how disputes are decided."[254] Mr. Jamail is the famed trial lawyer who represented Pennzoil in its lawsuit against Texaco in 1985. His contingency fee award was estimated to be in the $400 million range on the case that settled for $3.3 billion; the jury had actually returned a verdict for Pennzoil for $10.53 billion.[255]

Mr. Jamail feels that the decline in trial cases is actually detrimental to the legal profession. "By not trying the small cases, the lawyers don't get the courtroom experience. When the huge, bet-the-company cases come along, there are only a handful of trial lawyers who can handle it."[256]

If you find yourself on the wrong side of a lawsuit, be suspicious of your attorney if he seems to be pushing you to settle. He may not have the requisite experience to see your case through a jury trial. Remember, if you settle you still may be required to notify the National Practitioner Data Bank and that information will follow you through your career. The settlement could have negative consequences if you try to move to another job and it may even affect you during your routine re-credentialing and re-privileging processes at your present location.

Some malpractice carriers may push for a settlement if they estimate that the costs of defending the case will be substantially higher than the cost of the settlement. Other malpractice carriers may agree to not settle without the agreement of the practitioner.

It is not surprising that physicians will fight to keep their malpractice carriers from settling a case that they feel is defensible. A settlement could lead to the physician being reported to the National Practitioner Data Bank which could have far-reaching consequences.

Any time a practitioner has to go through a privileging and credentialing process, whether it is to gain privileges at a new hospital or to renew privileges at a hospital he has been practicing in, he will have to report any new listings in the NPDB. This self-reporting is a usual requirement in the credentialing process. Even if he decides to try and keep new listings in the NPDB from the privileging committee, he is likely to be found out as this committee is required to query the NPDB on its own. This could have serious consequences for the provider as the committee may decide to not grant or renew privileges.

It is a matter of truthfulness. Practitioners depend on the truthfulness of others taking care of a patient so as to formulate a judgment on the best plan of treatment. If those in the medical profession can't depend on the veracity of their peers while caring for the patients, then this could affect quality of care. If a physician is not truthful, especially when it comes to patient care, what else could they do that is not ethical and moral? Many believe that these untruthful practitioners should not have privileges and should probably be reported to the appropriate medical board. It is generally the medical board that can take disciplinary action against the practitioner.

Administrative Agencies

There is ample evidence to support the creation of agencies whose function would be to investigate, and if necessary, provide compensation to those who have been injured through malpractice. In the Worker's Compensation model, a worker injured on the job does not have to sue his employer in order to be compensated for his injury. The employer benefits by not having to face a high damages award. Both parties have given up their *due process rights* but they both have gotten something of value in return. The courts have ruled that these types of dispute resolution are constitutional.

The Veteran's Administration has a model in place where this type of system is already working in the malpractice arena. The health care system for our veterans comes under the Federal Tort Claims Act (FTCA). The FTCA was put into effect in 1946. It outlines the legal steps that must be taken by those who allege they have been injured by negligence or wrongful acts by those who are employees of the federal government. Physicians who are VA employees fall under this Act so allegations of malpractice by VA physicians must be filed against the United States—not against the particular physician.

A plaintiff must exhaust his administrative remedies before he can file a malpractice action in court. Under the FTCA, the action must be filed in a federal court. If a plaintiff files a malpractice claim in state court against a VA physician, it will be thrown out for lack of jurisdiction and a lot of time and energy by the plaintiff's attorney will be wasted.

Under the FTCA, all malpractice claims filed against the United States must meet specific procedural requirements. For example, once the claim is filed, the United States has six months in which to investigate the claim. If at the end of the six months, the Veterans Administration has not made an acceptable offer to the plaintiff, the plaintiff would then be allowed to file the complaint in federal court.

There are drawbacks for plaintiffs. By taking the claim and mandating it be filed in the federal court system, it immediately puts lawyers who are not experienced with the federal system at a disadvantage. Remember, most malpractice cases come under state courts which must follow the common law of the state. Even though the federal court in which the case is filed will have to follow the common law of the state in which the alleged malpractice occurred due to the Erie doctrine, the procedures that must be followed will come under federal law, not state.

The Federal rules of Civil Procedure may be very different from the rules of procedure for the state. Filing times may be different, discovery rules may be different, and the rules of evidence may be different. These differences can put lawyers who are not experienced with the federal system at a disadvantage and, if the Rules are not followed, the case may be thrown out before it is even heard.

The United States Attorney's Office will have the lawyers that defend the United States of America on these claims; they are very comfortable working in the federal courts which may put them at some advantage.

Under the discovery process in the federal courts, both sides will need to reveal, even without being asked by the opposing party, all materials relevant to the case. This can include medical records, tax returns, social security records, and affidavits of experts. Both sides will have the opportunity to interview witnesses under oath at depositions.

Under the Federal Tort Claims Act, the United States can require the injured plaintiff to undergo an independent medical exam to confirm the nature of the claimed physical injuries. The Act also requires that if the case is tried, it must be in front of a Federal judge, not a jury. A Federal judge is less likely to be influenced by emotion than a jury. Of course, without exceptions, there are no rules. You can never be certain what will happen with any particular judge.

On occasion, the United States may decide to pay a settlement to the plaintiff rather than go thru the process of a trial. If a payment is made, the VA must then decide if the practitioner involved has to be reported to the NPDB. There is a group in the VA Central Office in Washington, D.C. that makes this decision. The practitioner is allowed to make an argument that he was not negligent in which case he should not be reported. He can also request that a peer-review be made on the facts of the case which could support his side.

If the VA Central Office decides that the payment was made for strategic reasons and was not due to any malpractice on the part of the practitioner, they can elect to not report the practitioner to the NPDB.

Following is an example of a report of a peer-review on a case settled with a payment being made to the plaintiff. The review was to determine if the clinician should be reported to the NPDB. Personal information and dates have been changed to so as to maintain confidentiality of the process and the people involved.

Dr. WWW was asked to review the medical records of Patient X so as to perform a peer review of Dr. A, and make an assessment of reporting to the National Practitioner Data Bank (NPDB).

Mr. X was a long-time patient at the VAMC in Memphis who was being taken care of for a variety of medical problems. This review focuses on a below-knee amputation that was done for complications of gangrene of the foot. The Office of Regional Counsel had determined that the VA was negligent in failing to consider revascularization of the lower extremity and to consult a vascular surgeon which they concluded was "a significant factor that contributed to the amputation of the foot." As a result, a payment of several thousand dollars was made to Mr. X.

The facts of the case are as follows. Mr. X was being cared for by VAMC Memphis for multiple medical problems which included diabetes, hypertension, nicotine dependence, and bipolar disorder. He was seen by the Podiatry Service for treatment of a left foot wound that was assessed to be a diabetic ulcer and not due to ischemia. He was referred to the General Surgery service for further evaluation and treatment. On numerous occasions, he was noted to have palpable pulses in the dorsalis pedis and posterior tibialis arteries. These pulses were documented by several physicians right up to the day of the amputation. He was also noted to have developed a wet gangrene of the 4th and 5th toes of the foot for which a transmetatarsal amputation with debridement of the plantar surface was done. At the conclusion of that procedure, it was documented that hemostasis had to be actively pursued with the electrocautery.

A week later, further debridement of the left foot had to be done for progression of the gangrene. Debridement was brought back to viable tissue and again "hemostasis was obtained" implying that there was a blood supply to the area of the debridement.

Several post-operative notes written by several physicians documented good pulses and capillary refill of the foot in question.

The patient was seen by the Plastic Surgery service and those surgeons felt that the foot had a good granulation base which could take a split thickness skin graft.

Unfortunately, the infection progressed with both soft tissue and bone involvement. In an effort to save the patient's life, a below knee guillotine amputation was done six weeks after the first amputation. The amputation incision was closed a week later and the wound healed well.

Several general surgeons were involved in this patient's care and none of them felt that the area had a questionable blood supply.

Based on Dr. WWW's review of the medical records of Mr. X, he came to the following conclusions:

(1) The decision to award a settlement to Mr. X was incorrect. The preponderance of the evidence supports the position that the blood supply of the left foot was adequate and there was no need to get a Vascular Surgery consult. All of the attending surgeons involved in the case did not see a need for a Vascular consult and the notes in the medical record support that conclusion. Failure to consider a consult from a vascular surgeon was not a significant

factor contributing to the amputation of the lower extremity;

(2) There was no breach of the standard of care by Dr. A. With the presence of wet gangrene, the patient needed to have the toes amputated and the foot debrided regardless of the blood supply to the foot. The operative notes all described blood flow to the surgical field and, in fact, the BKA flap healed well—supporting the fact that the blood supply to the area was adequate. Dr. A did what a reasonable surgeon would do if faced with the same or similar circumstances;

(3) Dr. A was performing within his scope of practice;

(4) The patient's physical exam and his complaints were consistent with infection, not ischemia;

(5) Dr. A should not be reported to the NPDB as there was no breach of the standard of care in regards to Mr. X.

So who would be best in determining monetary awards for patients alleging medical malpractice? It may depend on knowledge base when it comes to who will function better—administrators or juries. Those with scientific and/or medical training would be able to understand the medical issues better than an untrained juror and thus, less likely to award outrageous amounts to the patient or family, but they might be more inclined to hold the practitioner accountable for errors that an unlearned jury might be inclined to ignore if they were convinced that the practitioner was, at least, minimally competent and appeared to be a caring individual. Keeping disputes out of court would lead to more timely settlements; a payout would probably be less. However, simple legal procedures may lead to the filing of more suits. Any patient with a bad outcome, not necessarily the result of malpractice, would be more likely to file a claim.

Getting plaintiff attorneys out of the process seems like an inherently good idea but the plaintiff's bar would likely fight this idea tooth and nail and their political clout should not be underestimated.

Removing the stigma of being reported to the National Practitioner Data Bank would go a long way to having physicians be more inclined to settle malpractice cases where they are culpable as opposed to fighting to the often bitter end so as to avoid being reported. However, there is doubt the politicians would be willing to do away with this data base as many of our legislators—most of whom are attorneys by training—feel that it would be giving bad doctors a free pass.

They have a valid point. There are bad doctors and they should be identified and held accountable. However, it may be better if accrediting state agencies, such as medical boards, would be given the authority to do this. In this way, physicians would be judged by a truer jury of their peers. Unfortunately, history has shown that doctors have not been very good at policing their own; a sea change in the disciplinary process would need to occur if this administrative justice system were to become operational.

Arbitration

Arbitration is a means of settling a dispute where the adverse parties agree to have their conflict decided by a person that they have jointly chosen. This is one of the ways of resolving a dispute outside of a courtroom setting. By using the informal setting of arbitration instead of the more formal and procedure-oriented court system, time and costs may be decreased. This is not to say that arbitration is cheap—it can be quite costly. For example, if an arbitrator charges $250 per hour, then two to three weeks of arbitration will cost up to $30,000. Since it's unlikely that the plaintiff can afford this cost, then everyone is still looking at malpractice carriers and plaintiff's attorneys to foot the bill.

While arbitration is like a trial before a judge without the jury being present, there are important differences. Witnesses may testify and evidence may be presented. The arbitrator will listen and then render a verdict. They may or may not get independent experts and their review of the evidence may not be very exhaustive. The basis of their decision is not required to be revealed. Because the basis of the decision may be vague, an appeal of an adverse award is not likely to be successful unless the appellant is able to show the arbitrator was acting fraudulently or was biased—both of which can be hard to prove as there may be no written record like there would be in a court proceeding. In arbitration proceedings, there is no court reporter taking notes.

At least fifteen states have tried arbitration. Few patients agreed to sign up and those that did tended to fight the agreement if they were on the losing side of the conflict. New York had a system of arbitration to assess damages in cases where the defendant conceded liability. Since not many defendants were conceding, the system molded from disuse.

Why would anyone consider arbitration considering the shortcomings? The answer is two-fold. There is the likely decrease in the costs of litigation and there is the fact that some health care organizations may require arbitration in return for lower premiums.

Mediation

Mediation provides a more informal setting for settling a malpractice action. In this situation, a neutral intermediary meets with the opposing parties at a venue different from the formal, procedure-bound courtroom. There is no jury and there is no judge although it isn't unusual for the mediator to have been a judge at one time. At the start of the mediation session, both parties are brought together in the same room where they are allowed to present the issues as they see them. The parties are pretty much free to present their theories of the case and they don't need witnesses. There are no restrictions on the evidence presented and, in fact, the statements may not even be true. Since the testimony is not under oath, there is no risk of perjury for not being truthful. However, when the testimony of one of the parties is not truthful or is distorted in an unfair manner, the opposing party will probably be angered and less likely to settle.

After the issues have been presented, the litigants and their attorneys are separated—usually they are put in different conference rooms—and the mediator then goes between the parties bringing various offers and counter offers back and forth. If the parties have been forced into mediation by the court, there may not be any offers to begin with and the mediation may end quickly, with no resolution.

The mediation process is meant to find a compromise between the two parties and takes away the risk that one of the litigants will lose in a court of law. It is not surprising that mediation does not work unless both parties are willing to compromise from the start. This begs the question as to why the litigants would be together in a mediation session when compromise is unlikely. The answer lies in the prerogative of the judge assigned to the case. He may order a mediation session before he is willing to set a trial date in hopes that he can avoid going to trial with its attendant expenses in time and money. If the judge orders the litigants to try mediation, they have little choice but to do it.

Strategically speaking, it may be worthwhile to go to mediation even if you strongly believe in your position and have no intention of compromising under any circumstances. If the opposing party is looking to compromise, they may present valuable information to you during their opportunity to present their theories. You may learn their strategy and take steps to counter it at a later time, such as at trial.

This is what happened in a recent case when a physician sued for malpractice was forced into a mediation session by the court; he and his attorney felt strongly the plaintiff had no case. During the plaintiff's presentation, he made claims from deposition testimony that were, in fact, wrong. The defendant and his counsel felt the plaintiff and their counsel were not up on the facts of the case and this encouraged the defendant and his team to proceed to a trial where the true facts would come out. They didn't reveal their strategy since it would only allow the plaintiff to better prepare to counter the defendant at the trial.

When the mediator presented a settlement number from the plaintiff, the defendant and their counsel remained silent. The mediator was waiting for a counter offer and he would have waited a very long time if the attorney had not informed him that there would be no offers unless plaintiff's offer was to drop the case. This stance only angered the plaintiff who shortly thereafter tried to amend his complaint from *negligence* to *gross negligence*. This amended complaint could have allowed for higher damages, maybe even beyond the malpractice carriers coverage limit. This is a strategy used by plaintiffs to intimidate defendants to settle. It did not work in this case.

Mediation may work when both parties are amenable to settle. This may be the case if the risks of defending the case are very high or if the costs of defending the case exceed the costs of the proposed settlement. Most physicians do not want to settle even if the costs of defending are high since these costs are on the malpractice carrier. Also, any settlement will still need to be reported to the National Practitioner Data Bank. The carrier may have the power to settle despite the physician's wishes depending on what the coverage entails. The best malpractice coverage allows the physician to have the final say — the carrier may then have to defend even if the costs of defending outweigh the costs of the settlement. There will be no report to the NPDB if the defendant practitioner wins the case.

Collaborative Practice

Collaborative Practice is a relatively new mechanism of alternative dispute resolution. In this process, the parties all agree up front that they will not litigate to solve their dispute. The parties of the dispute, including medical malpractice, agree to share all information freely in an effort to come to a settlement before going to court. The attorneys in this type of process have a delicate balancing act in that they have to meet the needs of their client while at the same time working with both sides so as to come to a mutually agreeable conclusion. If the process is not successful, all of the attorneys must withdraw from the case as they now have information from both sides which would put them in a conflicted position if they were to continue in the representation.

The advantages of *collaborative dispute resolution* are the decreased costs, less time involved in coming to a resolution, the ability of the parties to have more control over the case since a judge and jury are not involved, and the possibility of coming to an unconventional resolution — which is very unlikely to happen in a court where money damages are the usual solution. Collaborative law is not likely to work where the parties really do not like each other. The underlying anger may be such as to make another form of dispute resolution or litigation preferable.

People have compared collaborative law to mediation without the neutral third party. The clear disadvantage of the collaborative process is when the parties find themselves deadlocked because the benefit of the thoughts and observations of the third party are not available to get things back on the right track. If the Collaborative Law process doesn't resolve the issue, another form of alternative dispute resolution like mediation or arbitration can still be tried. If all else fails, the courts may have to be the final arbiter.

There are very few medical malpractice cases that lend themselves to this type of resolution because there is often a great deal of ill-will on both sides in this type of controversy. Lawyers who participate in this type of process need to be educators, advisors, and creative problem solvers as opposed to warriors. It is more likely to work if the parties are trying to keep someone from being hurt, like children in a divorce proceeding. Since the physicians are intent on keeping their names out of the National Practitioner Data Bank, it is unlikely they will agree to any kind of settlement negotiations so long as they are convinced that they did nothing that amounts to negligence.

Vocabulary

due process rights
Arbitration
Mediation
Collaborative Practice
collaborative dispute resolution

Citations

[251] http://www.nwtntoday.com/news. Published in The Messenger March 2, 2011. See also The Tennessean, http://www.tennessean.com
[252] Id.
[253] Id.
[254] Joe Jamail www.abajournal.com/magazine/article/joe_jamail posted March 1, 2009.
[255] Id.
[256] Id.

Chapter 35: Health Courts

In another effort to cut the costs associated with litigating a malpractice case, the new health care legislation passed in 2010 has provided money for the states to experiment with different methods of solving the disputes. One of the more intriguing ideas is to develop a new court system dedicated totally to malpractice cases. These courts, called health courts, are not a new idea.

The idea of setting up a separate series of courts that would specialize in resolving medical malpractice cases has been previously debated in Congress. Sen. Enzi (R-WY) and Sen. Baucus (D-MT) proposed setting money aside for states to test health care courts. Sen. Cornyn (R-TX) proposed allocating money for health courts but he would not deny injured patients the right to a jury trial.

It is not just the Senate that has looked into this new court system. Rep. Thornberry (R-TX) proposed a grant system to allow the states to establish health courts. With the passage of President Obama's health care plan, somewhere embedded within the 2,400 pages is money to try out the health court concept. It is just a matter of time before this legal experiment begins.

The move to look for new ways to resolve medical malpractice issues is cost driven. The premiums for malpractice insurance are very high. As discussed previously, judgment awards can be very high and the cost of *defensive medicine*, ordering tests and doing procedures that may not have been necessary for the patient's care but were done by the physician so that he could claim he did what he could to avoid a bad result, have also helped drive health care costs up.

The health court system has some good ideas but in order to better understand the possible benefits, you need to look at some of the main problems of the present system. Only 2% of patients who are injured by negligent care ever file a malpractice claim.[257] The elderly and the poor are even less likely to sue.[258] Going to court is like rolling dice. Much of the outcome is based on chance. Most patients who are harmed by medical errors are not compensated. Physicians are responsible for billions of dollars spent on unnecessary tests which drive up the cost of health care. These tests are ordered so as to better defend a potential malpractice suit and are really not for patient care. With a jury system, the juries cannot set precedent and jury decisions are often inconsistent with similar types of cases coming to very different results. Many argue that proper *standards of care* should be for the judges to decide, not the juries. And, as previously stated, with court proceedings often unpredictable, emotionally draining, and often inefficient with some cases dragging on for over ten years, many plaintiffs and defendants don't have the stamina or the finances to see their case through to the end.

State health courts would be designed to avoid these problems. Specialized judges would be appointed who would make rulings on *standards of care* as a matter of law. Experts would be hired by the court rather than hired by the plaintiff or defendants. There will be a *liberalized standard for negligence* which will be defined as a mistake or medical treatment falling outside a *range of good practice*. There will be no need to prove fault. Proceedings would be expedited, patient access would improve, there would be limits on non-economic damages which would be based on the severity of injury, and those limits would be set by an independent commission created by Congress.

It is thought that the health court system would lead to quicker and more reliable justice. It is also hoped to lead to improved patient safety and lower costs for health care. Compensation for the patient would be uniform, based on the injury. Ideally, patients with similar injuries would be compensated the same.

Under the health court system, the plaintiff would first need to file a claim which would then be reviewed by a health court review board. If the board believed that the injury was clearly due to malpractice, the claim would be paid according to a schedule of benefits. These obvious meritorious claims would have an expedited payment. These events are classified as *accelerated compensation events* (ACE). Examples of ACE would be giving penicillin to a patient with a known penicillin allergy, amputating the wrong extremity, or leaving a clamp inside the operated patient.

In situations where the board feels that the injury was too small to justify an award they would have the authority to dismiss the claim. If the board feels that they do not have enough information they can send the case forward for a health court trial presided over by the aforementioned specially trained judges who would have back-grounds and training in science and/or medicine. It's surprising that legislators might look for judges who are not trained in the law, but this thinking "outside the box" could be a great boon to malpractice cases and their outcomes. Lawyers for the parties would be allowed at the trial but there would be no juries. There would be a *liberal legal standard* for awarding compensation to the injured party.

A plan described by the Progressive Policy Institute would have the judges appointed by the state governors. Questions still remain to be answered to how much specialized training these judges would need to preside over health court cases. It is also unclear at this time who could apply for this position from the pool of nurses, PhDs, MDs, DOs, etc. Answering how much medicine a health court judge would have to know or how much legal experience they would need would help answer many questions about how to appoint a health court judge.

The Health Court would be allowed to commission expert witnesses of the Court's choice. Judges would rely on the experts in order to make binding determinations as to causation, standards of care, compensation, and other related issues. The experts would have to be neutral which would be more likely than if they were hired by one of the parties and getting monetary compensation.

Injury would be defined as the result of a mistake that should have been prevented. Also, the *injury* would not have occurred if *optimal care* had been given. This new standard has been called an *avoidability standard* and is obviously easier to prove than the previous *negligence standard*. By this new standard, the plaintiff would have to prove that the injury would not have happened if *optimal care* had been given.

Under the plan, if *liability* is found, *damages* would be awarded by the court which would have to use a *schedule of benefits* that covers both *economic* and *non-economic damages*. The *schedule of benefits* would be developed through a *consensus process* involving research into similar awards in the United States and abroad. The method of compensation, although a novel idea in the malpractice setting, is similar to the compensation found in worker's compensation cases. In this new system, *non-economic damages* would be determined by a tiered system based on the severity of injury. The schedule would be adjusted annually on the federal level and then would be used by the health courts in the states.

Compensation Models

Worker's compensation, vaccine injury compensation, tax courts, and the National Labor Relations Board are just a few of the examples of compensation models that have worked in the past. They provide strong evidence this type of compensation could work as well for malpractice cases if these systems are tailored to the needs of the Health Court System.

Studying the similarities as well as the differences of these models as compared to the needs of the Health Court System would make application less problematic. These previous systems are all based on a *no-fault* model which is different from what is envisioned for the Health Court

System. They are based on *federally created public rights*, not *long-standing state common law rights*. For example, *negligence* is a *long-standing common law cause of action* and as such, makes the jury requirement a strong *private right*. All of the existing models take the Seventh Amendment of the United States Constitution out of play.[259]

Another factor these previous compensation models have in common, which is different from that envisioned for the Health Court System, is they all have *strict liability standards* which provide *compensation* for any injured person whether *negligence* is involved or not. In these models, there is no *intent* to have a *deterrent function* which is built in to the Health Court System. With no intent to have a deterrent function, the monetary awards will, probably, be lower than they are in the present tort system.

Other Courts

The National Childhood Vaccine Injury Act (NCVIA) of 1986 was an attempt to relieve the drug manufacturers from liability from complications of vaccines that were deemed to be important for public health. The Vaccine Court, as it was called, was set up so families who had been injured by vaccines would be compensated in a non-adversarial forum. This was also a *no-fault compensation* program. The Secretary for Health and Human Services had the discretion to *foreclose on a claim* – meaning he could deny the claim, and he often did. Cases could linger for years and most of the claimants lost. In fact, only about 36% of the claims were *adjudicated* and none of them included autism cases which numbered in the thousands.

Although the program was a no-fault system, people could only recover damages if the injury was in the table of medical conditions set up by the Department of Health and Human Services (HHS). The definitions set up by HHS changed in 1995 when some conditions were eliminated and some were redefined in such a way as to make it more difficult for the claimant to win. As a result, this system failed to meet its mandate as an alternative for dispute resolution.

The autism cases, a potentially significant problem with the NCVIA, were recently resolved by the United States Supreme Court in *Bruesewitz v. Wyeth*.[260] Several thousand plaintiffs alleged that vaccines were causing autism in children. There was no reasonable scientific data to support the association so it was not one of the injuries listed in the Injury Table. Plaintiff's attorneys tried an *end around* by bringing suit in the state courts on *products liability grounds*. Their hope was to claim that the vaccines were defectively designed or made which would allow suits under a theory that could avoid the requirements of the NCVIA.

In *Bruesewitz,* the Court upheld rulings of the lower courts which held that federal law preempts suits for unsafe design of vaccines. The Court felt that the Food and Drug Administration (FDA) could determine if a vaccine's design was safe and the FDA should not be second guessed by lay juries who would have to rule on evidence of a highly technical nature. Not surprisingly, some plaintiffs feel that the vaccine compensation law does not do enough to protect patients from injuries which may be vaccine related. However, the Supreme Court decision does support the strong public policy of vaccinating our children; it is also a strong incentive for manufacturers to keep producing the needed vaccines and doing research necessary to develop new ones.

The Air Transportation Safety and Stabilization Act of 2001 was a compensation fund set up by Congress for the victims of the September 11, 2001 terrorist attacks. The Act provided for automatic compensation for the small group of claimants. Again, this was a *no-fault* system and was instituted to avoid the massive litigation that would have been brought against airlines, the World Trade Center, New York City, the Federal Government, and numerous other entities the number of which would only have been limited by the imagination of plaintiff's attorneys. Unfortunately, the rules of this Act have come under attack for *unfairly* excluding some victims and *inadequately* compensating others.

There are other examples of the government trying to take some forms of litigation out of the courts. The government has debated making compensation automatic for victims of asbestos. This system would have been *no-fault* and would have allowed for judicial review of the awards. It is unknown if this compensation would be construed as *fair* because, so far, the system has been rejected based on budget grounds.

Health Courts may work. Physicians seem to like the idea as do the insurance companies. Politically, both the Republicans and the Democrats generally like the concept. Not surprisingly, it's the Plaintiff's Bar and the American Bar Association who have come out against the concept because it could mean less award(s) for the plaintiff should they win their case. The American Bar Association (ABA) argues, "[the ABA has] a strong history of firmly supporting the integrity of the jury system, the independence of the judiciary and the right of consumers to receive full compensation for their injuries, without arbitrary caps on damages."[261]

In February 2006, the ABA adopted a resolution opposing the creation of Health Courts. Here are some interesting facts: (1) 60% of the cost of the current medical malpractice system goes to lawyers and court costs; (2) more money goes to the lawyers than the patients that have been harmed by medical malpractice and; (3) the ABA ignores the precedent set by the other specialized courts that are in existence and functioning well.

The ABA believes that the Health Courts would take away the injured patients' right to a jury trial which is guaranteed under the 7th Amendment without providing a system that offers equal or better protection. It is unclear how they arrived at their conclusion. The ABA is afraid that the compensation system would be susceptible to undue influence by powerful entities like the insurance industry. They are also concerned that the proposed payout schedule is, in fact, a *de facto cap* on *non-economic damages*. Instead, they would prefer *sensible reforms* of the present existing *state court tort systems*. It begs the question as to what they would consider to be *sensible*.

Another key argument brought forth by the ABA is that a Health Court System violates the *principles of federalism*. The courts would *pre-empt* constitutional guarantees to trial by jury without the required *quid pro quo* of eliminating the injured party's burden of proving fault. This, along with the fact that several states have found the caps on damages to be unconstitutional, makes it a long shot that the courts will ever be instituted.

I think the present proposals set forth in favor of the Health Court System will be deemed unconstitutional. Before the Health Court System has a chance for acceptance, the burden of proof must be removed from the plaintiff and *non-economic* caps need to be addressed. A strict liability system, like worker's compensation, may work. Procedural safeguards should be put in place and the judges should be Article 3 judges who serve for life. This would make it less likely that lobbies of insurance companies, hospitals, and lawyers would have much influence. An appeals process using the Federal Appeals Courts and, eventually the Supreme Court may need to be in place.

If the Health Court system is eventually deemed to be unconstitutional, then a constitutional amendment would be a possibility. This would require 2/3 of both houses or 2/3 of the legislatures of the states to propose the amendment which would then have to be ratified by ¾ of the states; not an easy task.

Vocabulary

defensive medicine
standards of care
liberalized standard for negligence
range of good practice
accelerated compensation events
liberal legal standard
avoidability standard
negligence standard
schedule of benefits

consensus process
no-fault
federally created public rights
long-standing state common law rights
private right
strict liability standards
deterrent function
no-fault compensation
foreclose on a claim
adjudicated
Bruesewitz v. Wyeth
end around
products liability grounds
inadequately
de facto cap
non-economic damages
state court tort systems
principles of federalism
pre-empt
quid pro quo

Citations

[257] New England Journal of Medicine vol. 324; p. 370-6 (1991).
[258] *Medical Error: What do we know? What do we do?* Jossy-Bass, 2002.
[259] The Seventh Amendment deals with the right to have a jury trial in Suits at common law.
[260] *Bruesewitz v. Wyeth* 131 S. Ct. 1068 (2011). The 3rd U.S. Circuit Court of Appeals upheld the dismissal of the suit against Wyeth because a residual seizure disorder which was on the original table of disorders that would be compensated was removed from the table in 1995, one month prior to the family bringing their claim. If the Court had allowed the suit to be filed, it would have opened up the field of vaccine litigation to over 5000 autism cases. This could have affected our nation's vaccine supply which could have led to a public health emergency.
[261] Janice Mulligan, Chair of Standing Committee for Medical Professional Liability.

Chapter 36:
Going Bare

Going bare is the strategy to avoid malpractice suits by assigning most of your worldly possessions to someone you trust and then foregoing malpractice insurance altogether. This practice is most prevalent in Florida where in 2004 it was estimated that over 3,000 of the 89,000 licensed physicians were without malpractice coverage.[262] Since some specialties have yearly premiums that are well over $200,000 per year, this strategy makes sense from a financial standpoint. The reasoning is that plaintiff's attorneys will be reluctant to go after defendants who clearly do not have the assets, or insurance, to pay off any judgments that they may be liable for. If a physician is without assets or insurance, offering the plaintiff a modest settlement might be acceptable in light of the fact that if they refuse, they would get nothing.

This strategy made some sense when a physician could claim a Chapter 7 Bankruptcy which would allow him to use the Bankruptcy court to do away with any financial liabilities and start over. Their credit rating would take a hit for a while, but most physicians could probably survive, especially if they could maintain their income. However, recent changes in Bankruptcy law have made it unlikely that a physician would be allowed to go Chapter 7. Under the new laws, there is a financial integrity test whereby the person claiming bankruptcy would not be allowed to use Chapter 7 if they still had a substantial income—most physicians would not qualify. If there still was a substantial income, the claimant would have to file under Chapter 13. A Chapter 13 bankruptcy does not discharge the debt. Instead, a five or ten year payment plan would be set up so that the creditors would be paid off. These creditors would include the plaintiffs if you were to lose the malpractice action. Future income would be at risk where it would have to be used as part of the payment plan and wages could be garnished.

Another problem of *going bare*, at least in Florida, was *tort reform* passed in 2003. As part of the reform, the physician who had a judgment against him was required to pay up to $250,000 per claim or have a payment plan in place within thirty days of the judgment or his medical license would be suspended. The law also required that the physician would be liable for this $250,000 for up to three claims in one year. All of a sudden, the physician would be liable for up to $750,000 per year or risk losing his license.

The Florida tort reform also had a *three strikes rule* which meant that the practitioner who had three judgments against him would likely lose his license. Most physicians would want to fight against this eventuality which would require them to hire legal representation and pay the legal fees. If they had malpractice insurance, their carrier would hire an attorney that they know was experienced in malpractice and they would pay the legal fees, which can be substantial. *Going bare* would mean the physician would have to hire his own attorney who may or may not be so experienced in this area of the law.

The other major risk of *going bare* is to have the person you have assigned all of your assets to—this would usually be the spouse—decide to sue for divorce and leave you with nothing. Since almost one half of all marriages in the United States end in divorce, this risk is substantial. Because of the obvious risks involved in *going bare*, this strategy is a risky way to manage possible malpractice liability.

Darryl Weiman

Vocabulary

Going bare
tort reform
three strikes rule

Citation

[262] www.msnbc.com/id/5234637/

Chapter 37: Conclusion

Lawyers who are involved in medical malpractice cases, especially those on the plaintiff's side, claim that the present *tort system* is the best way to pursue justice so that those who have been injured by medical negligence can be fairly compensated. They will argue, with some justification, that the medical profession has failed to monitor the health care providers and, as a result, incompetent providers have not been identified and weeded out.

There is presently no data that supports any claims of the current *tort system* improving the quality of health care. However, the system may be a deterrent to poor care as physicians and others practice *defensive medicine* so as to better defend themselves if they are sued. With a jury system, the juries cannot set precedent and jury decisions are often inconsistent with similar types of cases coming to very different results. Many argue that proper *standards of care* should be for the judges to decide, not the juries.

There is data that physicians are ordering more tests and doing more procedures because of fear of malpractice allegations, but the tests add to costs and the procedures have their own risks which may actually increase the chance of harm to the patient. The added costs of *defensive medicine* have been estimated to run into the billions of dollars per year. No one knows how much harm the extra procedures and tests have done nor is it known if they have from time to time helped make a diagnosis that otherwise would have been missed.

One of the goals of *tort reform* is to decrease the costs of health care by cutting down on the costs of the added tests and procedures, but there is no good data that this goal will be realized. As the mindset of the present health care providers has been set for years, how likely is it that they will suddenly change the way they practice if, for example, limits are placed on pain and suffering? Lawyers who argue that the current *tort system* is meant to improve the quality of care are being disingenuous. The system may lead to fewer intentional and negligent acts, but those cases are probably few and far between. The majority of medical negligence cases never even make it into the *tort system*. The patients involved are never compensated and the medical *tortfeasors* get away with the negligence.

Many plaintiff's attorneys will reject cases they feel will be difficult to prove or where the potential damage award is too low for them to justify their time and expense to pursue the *remedy*. Where is the justice if only a small number of injured patients can make it into the system with legal representation? There is also the significant issue of the present system punishing many innocent health care providers. Lawyers have a tendency to name every provider in the medical record so as to not miss any of the potentially liable parties. If the system works as it is supposed to, the innocent providers will eventually be dismissed from the suit but not until the system has given them a financial beating. They will have to get an attorney for their defense and they will need to spend time reviewing the medical records and educating their counsel on the medical issues.

The physician defendant who has been sued will be wary, even fearful of his patients. He will order more tests and do more procedures so as to be better able to defend any future suits even though there are added costs and risks of complications for everything he does.

Lawyers do not understand why doctors take a medical malpractice suit so personally. They do not understand what an ordeal it is to have your judgment called into question in such a public manner. Suits filed in the court system will be in the newspapers with the physician's name printed in black and white for all to see. No matter how the case turns out, some damage has already been done and for a physician, perception is very important to their reputation.

Even if the physician's malpractice carrier opts to settle for a lesser amount than the projected costs of litigation, the physician's name will be submitted to the NPDB and this occurs without any determination on the negligence issue. This part of the system on its face is unfair. There shouldn't be a black mark in the Data Bank without a determination on the negligence issue. This NPDB listing may affect the physician's future privileging and credentialing at his present workplace and it may affect his ability to get a new job in another location.

It is not required that you go to a law school or visit a court library in order to get some basic information to help you understand the legal issues of your case. It is amazing how much law can be learned over the Internet. Do a simple online search with the topic you are interested in studying, but limit yourself to your particular state. You can even use advanced searches to get the case law in your jurisdiction that pertains to your situation. Remember, case law from other jurisdictions may be helpful to you in understanding the legal issues but they usually do not have any legal authority in your state. Therefore, if you are truly interested in obtaining a thorough analysis of any of the issues discussed above, there is no better way to do it than to study case law pertaining to the topics in your particular state.

Since medical malpractice is usually resolved in a state court, it would be best to study the common law of your jurisdiction. Be warned, even if you find a case in your jurisdiction that may be on point and in your favor, it does not mean that the case is still *good law*. Tell your attorney what you have found and ask him to let you know if any case and its outcome that you find similar to your situation is still accepted or if it has been subsequently overturned. Your attorney has quick ways (not available to you) to find out this information.

Very often, your malpractice carrier will provide you with a competent lawyer but you need to be sure that the lawyer is working for you and not the carrier. If he is working for the interests of the carrier, you should go ahead and find your own attorney to represent your interests; it will definitely be worth the costs.

It is vital for physicians to become involved in the process of attaining malpractice reform. For too long, physicians have sat on the sidelines while reform was debated and legislated by politicians who were either lawyers themselves or beholden to plaintiff's lobby. Physician leaders need to learn the law. They need to be knowledgeable, agile, and adaptive as the law is constantly changing. Physician leaders need to be flexible so as to deal with a wide range of adversaries and scenarios.

The tides in health care are changing faster than ever before. Even just a few years ago, no one would've imagined Congress would pass legislation that would force citizens to buy health care insurance which would have conditions that must be covered whether the buyer wanted them or not. The fact that Congress could levy a heavy tax on those who choose not to buy this mandated insurance was once unthinkable. Now Congress has mandated 16,000 new IRS employees to police this new law. The new health care law also requires the formation of 157 new boards and commissions to further decide what the legal requirements of the law will be.

Twenty states brought suit claiming the new health care legislation was unconstitutional as it exceeded the powers of Congress under the Commerce Clause. Other Federal Court judges deemed the law constitutional again claiming the power from the Commerce Clause. The Supreme Court ruled that the mandate to buy health insurance is constitutional, but only under the taxing power of Congress; Justice Roberts said it was not a Commerce Clause issue. No matter what the ruling, this legal battle is likely to go on for years and it is time for physicians to learn what they need to know so as to participate in the process from a position of strength.

The law is dynamic. It is constantly changing depending on the minds of sitting *appellate court* judges and the legislative and executive branches of the government. Opinions can change as can *statutes*. One of the goals of this book is to present physicians a starting point to better understand the fluid nature of medical liability so that they will be better positioned to voice their opinions with some basic fund of knowledge so as not to be at the mercy of those who practice law for a living. Medical doctors are generally very smart people. They should not be made to feel inadequate when under attack in a court of law. I hope this book will help level the playing field for those in the medical profession.

If there is a final message to give it is this: never, never, never lose your cool in court or when being questioned at depositions. Always be respectful of the opposing attorney no matter how much he tries to get you to lose your temper. Facts will always win out over put-downs, innuendos, and unjustified allegations. Facts are the basis of any persuasive argument. As John Adams—a noted attorney before he became President of the United States—said, "Facts are stubborn things."

Lawyers charge a lot of money as do many expert witnesses.[263] If you are a medical expert witness, how much you charge will come out at trial. If you charge an exorbitant amount, unreasonableness will be in the mind of the judge and the jury. They may then conclude that more than your time is being paid for.

Perception is important. Always answer truthfully. If you don't know an answer, say so. Don't make up an answer just to support your case. Stay away from fancy words and medical terms. Educate the jury. If you're the one being sued, there's no one who knows your particular case better than you do. After all, you're the one who examined the patient, assessed the data and instituted the treatment. If you used your best judgment and that judgment was reasonable, it can go a long way in winning your case.

Being sued for malpractice can be extremely stressful. One of the ways to help handle this stress is to learn as much as you can about the legal process. I hope this book will help you on your journey in learning some malpractice basics. Unfortunately, malpractice litigation is one of the prices of doing the business of taking care of patients. Despite this unpleasantness, taking care of patients is one of the most honorable callings in our society.

Since a trial can be compared to war, remember the words of the Chinese philosopher, Sun Tzu: "So it is said that if you know others and know yourself, you will not be imperiled in a hundred battles..."[264] Prepare for your battle with a good attorney. Know the facts of your case and practice proper courtroom behavior.

Medical Malpractice: A Physician's Guide

> One of the goals of this book is to present physicians a starting point to better understand the fluid nature of medical liability so that they will be better positioned to voice their opinions with some basic fund of knowledge so as not to be at the mercy of those who practice law for a living.

"Knowledge is good."[265]

Darryl Weiman

Vocabulary

tort system
defensive medicine
standards of care
tortfeasors
remedy
good law
appellate court
statutes

Citation

[263] Some neurosurgeons charge $1,500 per hour to testify as an expert witness. These same experts are known to charge over $900 per hour to review the medical records. This should not come as a surprise as some lawyers have also broken the $1000 per hour fee barrier. Of course this does not include the lawyers who have earned several times that rate working on a contingency basis.
[264] The Art of War. Sun Tzu. Translated by Thomas Cleary. Shambhala, 1991. Page 24.
[265] *Animal House*. The movie.

The Author

Darryl S. Weiman, M.D., J.D. is a Fellow of the American College of Surgeons and a member of the American Association of Thoracic Surgeons. He is a graduate of Northwestern University where he majored in Biomedical Engineering. Dr. Weiman did his medical school training at Saint Louis University.

After medical school, he did his General Surgery residency at the University of Chicago and his Cardiothoracic residency at Long Island Jewish Hospital.

While maintaining an active practice in cardiothoracic surgery at the University of Tennessee Health Science Center, Dr. Weiman obtained a legal education at the Cecil C. Humphreys School of Law at the University of Memphis. He passed the Bar Exam for the State of Tennessee.

Dr. Weiman continues to be a Professor of Surgery at the University of Tennessee Health Science Center and is the Chief of Surgery at the VA Medical Center in Memphis. Although he does not practice law, he does research on health care issues and speaks and publishes on some of these topics.

Dr. Weiman is married to Kathleen Weiman and has two daughters, Johanna and Millicent, who are both getting ready for college.

Acknowledgements

With love to my wife, Kathleen, and my daughters, Johanna and Millicent. Their patience, encouragement, and inspiration were invaluable through the years spent in law school, doing research for, and writing this book.

To Victoria Houseman Bromley who edited the first drafts of the book to make the writing understandable to the non-lawyer, and for reorganizing the sequence of chapters to clarify the applicable legal process and associated issues.

To Glen Aubrey and the team at Creative Team Publishing who were willing to take on this project despite the paucity of work in this area and not being sure if the intended audience would even be interested.

To Justin Aubrey for his logo and cover designs.

To Randy Beck for the website design and instructions on marketing to get the existence of this book out to interested parties.

To my parents, whose emphasis on education helped in forming my career; this has not been an easy road.

To Kyle Wiggins and Steve Barlow, fellow law school students who were willing to help the unconventional heart surgeon who was juggling an active surgical practice while trying to meet the academic requirements of the school.

To my medical colleagues who insisted that this work be done to help level the playing field in the process and intricacies of malpractice law.

Citations

[1] Waters JW. A Surgeon's Little Instruction Book. Quality Medical Publishing, Inc., St. Louis, Missouri, 1998.
[2] Black's Law Dictionary, Seventh Edition, Bryan Garner editor-in-chief.
[3] 509 U.S. 579(1993).
[4] *Frye v. United States*, 54 App. D.C. 46, 47, 293 F.1013,1014 (1923).
[5] Id.
[6] Id.
[7] Federal Rules of Evidence, Rule 402.
[8] Federal Rules of Evidence, Rule 702.
[9] *Cardwell v. Bechtol*, 724 S.W.2d 739, 754 (Tenn. 1987).
[10] *Westmoreland v. Bacon, M.D.*, No. M2009-02643-COA-R3-CV Filed January 31, 2011.
[11] Id. at 5.
[12] Id at 7.
[13] Id. at 8.
[14] Id.
[15] In the Court of Appeals of Tennessee at Nashville, May 13, 2010, No. M2009-01860-COA0R3-CV Filed August 25, 2010.
[16] Id. p.5.
[17] Id.
[18] Id.
[19] Id.
[20] Id. p. 9.
[21] Tenn. Code Ann. section 29-26-122.

[22] *Graniger v. Methodist Hospital Healthcare Systems, Inc.,* No. 02A01-9309-CV-00201, 1994 WL 496781 (Tenn.Ct.App.)
[23] Id.
[24] *Johnsey v. Northbrooke Manor, Inc.,* No. W2008-01118-COA-R3-CV.
[25] Id.
[26] *Katrina Martins, et al. v. Williamson Medical Center,* No. M2010-00258-COA-R3-CV (Tenn.Ct.App. 2010).
[27] Id.
[28] Id.
[29] *Holt v. City of Memphis,* No. W2000-00913-COA-R3-CV, 2001 WL 846081 (Tenn. Ct. App.).
[30] Id.
[31] *Mooney v. Sneed,* 30 S.W.3d, 304, 307-08 (Tenn. 2000).
[32] *Holt v. City of Memphis,* 2001 WL 846081 (Tenn. Ct. App.)
[33] *Peete v. Shelby County Health Care Corp.,* 938 S.W.2d 693, 696 (Tenn.Ct.App. 1996).
[34] Id.
[35] Black's Law Dictionary, Bryan Garner, editor-in-chief.
[36] *Ybarra v. Spangard,* 154 P.2d 687 (Cal.1944).
[37] Tenn.Code Ann. Section 29-26-115.
[38] Id.
[39] *Gresham v. Ford,* 241 S.W.2d, 408 (Tenn. 1951).
[40] Id.
[41] *Hurley v. Eddingfield,* 59 N.E. 1058, (Ind. 1901).
[42] *Millard v. Corrado,* Mo. App.E.D (1999)
[43] Id.
[44] Id.
[45] Id.
[46] Restatement (Second) of Torts, section 324A.
[47] *Kilpatrick v. Bryant,* 868 S.W.2d 594, 602 (Tenn. 1993).
[48] Id.
[49] *Taylor v. Jackson-Madison County General Hospital,* 231 S.W.3d 361, 374 (Tenn. Ct. App. 2006)(citing *Kilpatrick v. Bryant,* 868 S.W.2d 594, 602 (Tenn. 1993).
[50] Id. at 375-76.
[51] *Palsgraf v. Long Island Railroad.* 248 N.Y. 339; 162 N.E. 99
[52] Id.
[53] It is sometimes said that surgeons may be wrong but they are never in doubt.
[54] No. M2009-01730-COA-R9-CV- Filed June 23, 2010.

[55] Id. at p.2.
[56] Black's Law Dictionary, Seventh edition, Bryan Garner, editor-in-chief.
[57] Article IV, Rule 401. Definition of "Relevant Evidence" in Tennessee Rules of Evidence.
[58] Federal Rules of Evidence Rule 802.
[59] Federal Rules of Evidence Rule 801(d).
[60] Id.
[61] Id.
[62] www.the-injury-lawyer-directory.com/negligence_chart.html
[63] Black's Law Dictionary, Bryan A. Garner, editor-in-chief, Seventh Edition.
[64] *Eckert v. Long Island R.R. Co.*, 43 N.Y. 502 (1871).
[65] *Baltimore & Ohio R. Co. v. Goodman*, 276 US 66 (1927).
[66] *Alexander v. Kramer Bros. Freight Lines, Inc.*, 273 F.2d 373 (1959).
[67] *Butterfield v. Forrester*, 11 East 60 (1809).
[68] Id.
[69] *Brown v. Kendall*, 60 Mass, (6 Cush) 292, (1850).
[70] Id.
[71] *Martin v. Herzog*, 126 N.E. 814 (1920).
[72] *Solomon v. Shuell*, 457 NW 2d 669 (1990).
[73] Id.
[74] *Smithwick v. Hall & Upson*, 59 Conn. 261 (1890).
[75] *McIntyre v. Balentine*, 833 S.W. 2d 52 (Tenn. 1992).
[76] Id.
[77] Id.
[78] Under the discovery rule, the statute of limitations for medical malpractice starts to run when the plaintiff discovers, or reasonably should have discovered the occasion, the manner, and the means by which a breach of the standard of care that caused the injuries occurred and the identity of the person who caused the injury. *Stanbury v. Bacardi*, 953 S.W.2d 671,677 (Tenn. 1997).
[79] *Matz v. Quest Diagnostics Clinical Laboratories, Inc.*, WL 22409452 (Tenn.Ct.App. 2003).
[80] *Stanbury v. Bacardi*, 953 S.W.2d at 677.
[81] *Matz v Quest Diagnostics Clinical Laboratories, Inc.*, WL 22409452 (Tenn.Ct.App. 2003).
[82] 963 S.W.2d 726 (Tenn. 1998).
[83] *McIntosh v. Blanton*, 2004 WL 1869977 (Tenn.Ct.App.). 164 S.W.3d 584, (Tenn.Ct.App. 2004).
[84] Id.

[85] Id.
[86] Id.
[87] Personal communication with Dr. Muhlbauer.
[88] *Lou Ella Sherrill et al. v. Bob T. Souder, M.D. et al.* No. W2008-00741-SC-R11-CV-Filed October 28, 2010.
[89] Black's Law Dictionary. "Damages are the sum of money which a person wronged is entitled to receive from the wrongdoer as compensation for the wrong." Frank Gahan, *The Law of Damages 1 (1936).*
[90] 517 U.S. 559, (1996).
[91] Id.
[92] Id.
[93] Id.
[94] 532 U.S. 424(2001).
[95] *United States v. Bajakajian,* 524 U.S. 321(1998).
[96] 538 U.S. 408(2003).
[97] Id.
[98] Id.
[99] Id.
[100] Tenn Code Ann. Section 29-26-119.
[101] Ola B. Smith Lecture at the University of Virginia School of Law, March 23, 2004.
[102] ABA Journal, May 2010, p. 16-17.
[103] Id.
[104] Id.
[105] Black's Law Dictionary, Seventh Edition, Bryan Garner, editor-in-chief.
[106] Black's Law Dictionary, Seventh Edition, Bryan Garner, editor-in-chief.
[107] *Batson v. Kentucky,* 476 U.S. 79 (1986).
[108] *Powers v. Ohio,* 499 U.S. 400 (1991).
[109] *Edmonson v. Leesville Concrete Co.,* 500 U.S. 614 (1991).
[110] *Georgia v. McCollum,* 505 U.S. 42 (1992).
[111] *J.E.B. v. Alabama,* 511 U.S. 127 (1994).
[112] *Purkett v. Elem,* 514 U.S. 765 (1995)**.**
[113] Laala Al Jaber, Google Transforms Jury Selection Process, ABA Journal. www.abajournal.com/news/article/internet_transforms_jury_selection_process posted February 18, 2011.
[114] 12 Angry Men, the movie.

[115] Federal Rules of Evidence number 615.The Exclusion of Witnesses. This rule states, "[a]t the request of a party the court shall order witnesses excluded so that they cannot hear the testimony of other witnesses, and it may make the order of its own motion. This rule does not authorize exclusion of (1) a party who is a natural person, or (2) an officer or employee of a party which is not a natural person designated as its representative by its attorney, or (3) a person whose presence is shown by a party to be essential to the presentation of the party's cause, or (4) a person authorized by statute to be present."

[116] ABA Model Rules of Professional Conduct Rule 3.4(b) states "A lawyer shall not...offer an inducement to a witness that is prohibited by law." The comment to this provision explains, "With regard to paragraph (b), it is not improper to pay a witness's expenses or to compensate an expert witness on terms permitted by law. The common law rule in most jurisdictions is that it is improper to pay an occurrence witness any fee for testifying and it is improper to pay an expert witness a contingent fee."

[117] The Federal Rule of Evidence 703 says, "facts or data that are otherwise inadmissible shall not be disclosed to the jury by the proponent of the opinion or inference unless the court determines that their probative value in assisting the jury to evaluate the expert's opinion substantially outweighs their prejudicial effect."

[118] For example, the Federal Rule of Evidence 803(6); Records of regularly conducted activity. A memorandum, report, record, or data compilation, in any form, of acts, events, conditions, opinions, or diagnoses, made at or near the time by, a person with knowledge, if kept in the course of regularly conducted business activity, and if it was the regular practice of that business activity to make the memorandum, report, record, or data compilation, all as shown by the testimony of the custodian or other qualified witness, or by certification that complies [with other rules] or a statute permitting certification, unless the source of information or the method or circumstances of preparation indicate a lack of trustworthiness.

[119] Thomas A. Mauet, <u>Trial Techniques</u>, Sixth Edition, p.9, 2002.

[120] *Cathy Chapman, et al., v. James Lewis, M.D., et al.* No. E2009-01496-COA-R9-CV (Tenn.Ct.App).

[121] Id.

[122] Id.

[123] Tenn. Code Annotated section 20-9-303.

[124] *Hitaffer v. Argonne Co.*, 183 F.2d 811 (D.C. Cir. 1950).

125 Judgment notwithstanding the verdict, also called judgment non obstante veredicto (JNOV for short) is a judgment entered for one party even though the verdict was originally given to the opposing party. Black's Law Dictionary, Seventh Edition, Bryan Garner, editor-in-chief.
126 Additur—"a trial court order, issued usu. with the defendant's consent, that increases the damages awarded by the jury to avoid a new trial on grounds of inadequate damages; the term may also refer to the increase itself, the procedure, or the court's power to make the order." Black's Law Dictionary, Bryan Garner, editor-in-chief.
127 Remitittur—"the process by which a court reduces the damages awarded by a jury verdict; a court's order reducing an award of damages." Black's Law Dictionary, Bryan Garner, editor-in-chief.
128 Black's Law Dictionary, Seventh Edition, Bryan A. Garner, editor in chief. "An error or defect of judgment or of conduct; any deviation from prudence or duty resulting from inattention, incapacity, perversity, bad faith, or mismanagement."
129 Black's Law Dictionary, Seventh Edition, Bryan A. Garner, editor in chief.
130 John Salmond, *Jurisprudence* 364 (Glanville L. Williams ed. 10th ed. 1947) in Black's Law Dictionary, Seventh Edition, Bryan A. Garner, editor in chief.
131 Institute of Medicine, To Err is Human: Building a Safer Health System 1 (Linda T. Kohn et al. eds., National Academy Press 2000).
132 Noam Sher, <u>New Differences Between Negligence and Strict Liability and Their Implications On Medical Malpractice Reform</u>, *Southern California Interdisciplinary Law Journal,* Vol. 16:335 (2007).
133 American College of Surgeons. Expert Witness Affirmation, 2004.
134 Id.
135 Id.
136 Id.
137 Id.
138 Federal Rules of Evidence Rule 703 states in part, "The facts or data in the particular case upon which an expert bases an opinion or inference may be those perceived by or made known to the expert at or before a hearing. If of a type reasonably relied upon by experts in the particular field in forming opinions or inferences upon the subject, the facts or data need not be admissible in evidence in order for the opinion or inference to be admitted." Most, if not all states have a similar rule for their courts.
139 American College of Surgeons Expert Witness Affirmation, 2004.
140 Blacks Law Dictionary Pocked Edition, 1996, p. 244.

141 American College of Surgeons Expert Witness Affirmation, 2004.
142 Id.
143 Id.
144 Federal Rules of Evidence Rule 703 as above.
145 American College of Surgeons Expert Witness Affirmation, 2004
146 Id.
147 Id.
148 Blacks Law Dictionary Pocket Edition, 1996, p.131
149 Under U.S.C. section 1512(e) which states "In a prosecution for an offense under this section [witness tampering], it as an affirmative defense. . . that the conduct consisted solely of lawful conduct and that the defendant's sole intention was to encourage, induce, or cause the other person to testify truthfully."
150 American College of Surgeons Expert Witness Affirmation, 2004
151 ABA Model Rules of Professional Conduct comment to Rule 3.4.
152 Usually the state's highest appellate court.
153 Rule 702, Tennessee Rules of Evidence.
154 *Frye v. United States*, 293 F. 1013 (D.C. Cir.1923)
155 2001 Advisory Commission Comment to Rule 702 of the Tennessee Rules of Evidence.
156 955 S.W.2d 257 (1997).
157 Rule 26 in the Federal Rules of Civil Procedure.
158 Rule 26(b)(4)(B) of the Federal Rules of Civil Procedure.
159 Rule 26(b)(4)(C) of the Federal Rules of Civil Procedure.
160 *Erie Rail Road Co. v. Tompkins,*304 U.S. 64 (1938).
161 Martha A. Field, Federal Common Law, The Oxford Companion to the Supreme Court of the United States, 2nd edition, p. 321, 2005.
162 *Johnson v. Richardson,* No.W2009-02626-COA-R3-CV-filed August 12, 2010.
163 Id.
164 Id.
165 *Johnson v. Richardson* No. W2009-02626-COA-R3-CV –filed August 12, 2010.
166 Id.
167 Id.
168 *Canterbury v. Spence,* 464 F.2d 772 (D.C. Cir. 1972).
169 Id.
170 Id.
171 *Cardwell,* 724 S.W.2d at 749.
172 EMTALA Statute: 42 USC 1395 dd.

[173] EMTALA Statute: 42 USC 1395 dd.
[174] 895 F.2d 1131 (6th Cir. 1990).
[175] 289 F.3d 1162 (9th Cir. 2002).
[176] 95 F.3d 349, 351 (4th Cir. 1996).
[177] 291 F.3d 757 (11th Cir. 2002).
[178] CMS letter to State Survey Agency Directors to explain enforcement policies published in the Federal Register/Vol. 68, No. 174, pg. 53222 on September 9, 2003, effective November 10, 2003.
[179] Sara Rosenbaum, The Nation, October, 16, 2008.
[180] *Heimlicher v. Steele and Dickson County Memorial Hospital.* www.iand.uscourts.gov/e-web/decisions
[181] 16 F.3d 590 (4th Cir. 1994)
[182] A pericardial effusion is fluid in the space between the pericardium and the heart.
[183] *Danks v. Maher,* 177 So.2d at 417-418 (La. App. 1965)
[184] Id.
[185] 298 S.W. 2d 761, 767 (Tenn. App. 1956).
[186] Id.
[187] Black's Law Dictionary. 1996
[188] The standard of care for medical malpractice is what a reasonable practitioner of the same specialty would do if faced with the same or similar circumstances. In Tennessee, the locality rule would also apply.
[189] *Allen v. United States,* 164 US 492 (1896).
[190] Id.
[191] *The People v. Robert Gainer, Jr.,* 566 P. 2d 997 (1977).
[192] Id.
[193] Id. Footnote 22.
[194] http://juryboxblog.blogspot.com/2009/06/dynamite-charge-might-blow-up-in-judges.html
Edward Schwartz, June 16, 2009.
[195] Black's Law Dictionary, seventh edition.
[196] Id.
[197] 18 USC sec. 286, 371.
[198] 18 USC sec. 101.
[199] 18 USC sec. 1341.
[200] 18 USC sec. 1343.
[201] 18 USC sec 1956, 1957.
[202] 42 USC sec 1320(a)-7b(b).
[203] 18 USC sec 1347.
[204] 18 USC sec 669.

[205] 18 USC sec 1035 and 42 USC sec 1320a-7b(a).
[206] 18 USC sec 1518.
[207] 18 USC sec 1956(a)(1).
[208] 111 F.3d 934 (D.C. Cir. 1997).
[209] *United States v. Pani*, 717 F.Supp 1013 (S.D.N.Y. 1989).
[210] *United States v. Lorenzo*, 768 F.Supp 1127 (E.D. Pa 1991).
[211] *Peterson v. Weinberger*, 508 F.2d 45 (5th Cir. 1975).
[212] Tenn. Code Ann. Section 63-6-219 (TPRL). Subsection (d) grants immunity to participants in the peer review process.
[213] Id. Subsection (e).
[214] *Lee Medical Inc. v. Beecher*, No. M2008-02496-SC-S09-CV filed May 24, 2010.
[215] *Lee Medical* at 525.
[216] *Groller v. Methodist Medical Ctr. Of Oak Ridge*, 1989 5 WL 151498, (Tenn. Ct. App. Dec. 13, 1989).
[217] Under the federal law, the hospital will need to meet the requirements of a patient safety organization which is designed to improve quality of care and patient safety by compiling and analyzing medical data. If they meet the requirements, the records generated will be privileged under the federal law.
[218] Tennessee Rules of Evidence Rule 501.
[219] Tennessee Code Ann. Section 63-6-219(c).
[220] No. E2005-01043-SC-S09-CV — Filed May 14, 2007.
[221] 234 F.R.D. 617 (2005)
[222] Tex. Health & Safety Code section 161.032
[223] 42 U.S.C. sections 11101 et seq. For a more complete discussion see American Medical Association, Physicians Guide to Medical Staff Organization Bylaws (2008).
[224] No. E2008-00535-SC-R11-CV-filed May 24, 2010 In the Supreme Court of Tennessee at Knoxville, Sept. 3 2009 Session
[225] Tennessee Code Ann. Section 63-6-219(e).
[226] No. E2008-00535-SC-R11-CV Filed May 24, 2009 Session.
[227] TCA sec. 63-6-219(e).
[228] *Weekoty v. United States*, 30 R.Supp.2d 1343 (D.N.M. 1998).
[229] Id.
[230] *Syposs v. United States*, 63 F.Supp.2d 301 (W.D.N.Y. 1999).
[231] Id.
[232] Id.
[233] Section 922(c) of the Patient Safety and Quality Improvement Act of 2005.

[234] USA Today, Oct. 19, 1998, Section D, 1-2.
[235] New York Times, Sept. 13, 1995, Section B, 3.
[236] LA CMA Physician, Sept. 1997, 29-34.
[237] Tennessee Rules of Professional Conduct; Rule 3.1 comment [2].
[238] Id.
[239] Id. Rule 3.3: Candor Toward the Tribunal. Under section (a), "a lawyer may not knowingly (1) make a false statement of fact or law to a tribunal; or (2) fail to disclose to the tribunal legal authority in the controlling jurisdiction known to the lawyer to be directly adverse to the position of the client and not disclosed by opposing counsel."
[240] Comment [4] Rule 3.4: Fairness to Opposing Party and Counsel section (h).
[241] Rule 3.4 section (h).
[242] Rule 1.5(a).
[243] Id.
[244] Id.
[245] *State v. Smith,* 24 S.W.3d 274 (Tenn. 2000)
[246] Lawrence A. Pivnick, *Offering Objectionable Evidence — Does an Adversary's Failure to Object Make the Practice Right?* Tennessee Bar Journal, Volume 46, no. 17, December 2010. p.19.
[247] Id. p. 24.
[248] American College of Trial Lawyers, Annotated Code of Trial Conduct 18(g)(Oct. 2005) as cited by Professor Pivnick in his article page 24.
[249] Rule 3.4(e)(3) in Tennessee Rules of Professional Conduct effective January 1, 2010.
[250] Paragraph 21 of the Scope of the Tennessee Rules of Professional Conduct, effective January 1, 2010.
[251] http://www.nwtntoday.com/news. Published in The Messenger March 2, 2011. See also The Tennessean, http://www.tennessean.com
[252] Id.
[253] Id.
[254] Joe Jamail www.abajournal.com/magazine/article/joe_jamail posted March 1, 2009.
[255] Id.
[256] Id.
[257] New England Journal of Medicine vol. 324; p. 370-6 (1991).
[258] *Medical Error: What do we know? What do we do?* Jossy-Bass, 2002.
[259] The Seventh Amendment deals with the right to have a jury trial in Suits at common law.

[260] *Bruesewitz v. Wyeth* 131 S. Ct. 1068 (2011). The 3rd U.S. Circuit Court of Appeals upheld the dismissal of the suit against Wyeth because a residual seizure disorder which was on the original table of disorders that would be compensated was removed from the table in 1995, one month prior to the family bringing their claim. If the Court had allowed the suit to be filed, it would have opened up the field of vaccine litigation to over 5000 autism cases. This could have affected our nation's vaccine supply which could have lead to a public health emergency.

[261] Janice Mulligan, Chair of Standing Committee for Medical Professional Liability.

[262] www.msnbc.com/id/5234637/

[263] Some neurosurgeons charge $1,500 per hour to testify as an expert witness. These same experts are known to charge over $900 per hour to review the medical records. This should not come as a surprise as some lawyers have also broken the $1000 per hour fee barrier. Of course this does not include the lawyers who have earned several times that rate working on a contingency basis.

[264] The Art of War. Sun Tzu. Translated by Thomas Cleary. Shambhala, 1991. Page 24.

[265] *Animal House*. The Movie.

Index

A

Abrams v. US	7
Accelerated compensation event (ACE)	414
Adams, John	11
additur	235
admissible	112
Advanced Cardiac Life Support (ACLS)	83
affidavit	94, 104, 105
affirmative defense	175, 195, 207
Affordable Care Act (ACA)	340
Air Transportation Safety and Stabilization Act	419
Alabama Great Southern RR v. Caroll	334
Alexander v. Kramer Brothers	125
Allen charge (see Dynamite charge)	
Allen v. United States	322
answer	35
arbitration	402, 403
Austin v. American Association of Neurological Surgeons	252

B

Baltimore & Ohio v. Goodman	125
Batson v. Kentucky	161, 162
beyond a reasonable doubt	67, 68
best evidence rule	198
BMW v. Gore	147, 148, 149
Borrowed Servant Doctrine	307, 309, 310, 311
Bravo v. Sumner	277
Brown v. Kendall	126
Bruesewitz v. Wyeth	418, 419
Bryan v. Rectors	300
Bryant v. Adventist	299, 300
burden of persuasion	68, 175, 218
burden of proof	85, 87, 175
Bush v. Gore	159
Butterfield v. Forrester	126

C

Canterbury v. Spence	281
Captain of the ship	307, 309, 310, 311
Carpenter v. Klepper	277
case in chief	175, 195, 209
causation	36, 37, 39, 49, 55, 86, 87, 88, 138, 178, 221, 251
cause of action	53, 56, 130, 139, 141, 224, 270
Cardwell	45, 46
cause challenge	161
Certificate of good faith	53
certiorari	39
civil procedure	100, 101

Chapman v. Lewis	214
clear and convincing	67, 68, 314
closing argument	213, 214, 216, 217, 218
Collaborative practice	407, 408
comparative fault	128, 129, 130, 219
comparative negligence	128, 129, 130, 291
compensatory damages	150
complaint	97, 98
conflict of laws	331, 332, 336
contiguous	275, 276
contingent fee	253, 382, 383
contributory negligence	123, 124, 125, 126, 127, 128, 130, 333
Cooper v. Leatherman Tool	148
counter claim	175, 209
cross examination	115, 118, 180, 181, 182, 183, 184, 187, 199, 202

D

damages	129, 145, 146, 225, 416
Danks v. Maher	310
Daubert v. Merrell Dow	37, 40, 42, 43, 257, 258
declarant	104, 115, 116, 119
defamation	352
demonstrative evidence	188
de novo	149
deposition	101, 105, 106, 107, 108, 107, 111
dicta	271
direct examination	176, 202
directed verdict	175, 191, 279
disclosures	264, 266
discovery	36, 97, 100, 106

Discovery rule	132, 134, 138
diversity of citizenship	270
do not resuscitate	300
due process	36, 98, 100, 148-151, 393
duty of care	72, 73, 77
duty owed	71, 221
Dynamite charge	321, 323, 324

E

Eckert v. Long Island RR	124
Edmonson v. Leesville Concrete	162
Emergency doctrine	316
emergency medical condition	297
EMTALA	77, 295-304
Erie v. Tompkins	268, 270, 327, 330
evidence	112, 114
exemplary damages	66
expert testimony	53
Expert witness affirmation	247

F

False Claims Act (FCA)	341
fault	239
Federal Tort Claims Act (FTCA)	393-395
Frye v. United States	39, 40, 258
forum shopping	272, 332
foreseeability	75, 88-90, 314
fungibility	45
futile care	303, 304

G

Garza v. Scott-White	359
general acceptance test	41-43
Georgia v. McCollum	162
going bare	425-427
Good Samaritan rule	313-315, 317-318
Graniger v. Methodist	54
Gresham v. Ford	64
gross negligence	65, 67, 68, 154, 239, 314, 318, 373, 406
guilty	33

H

Harry v. Marchant	301, 302
Health Courts	411-417, 420-422
hearsay	114-116, 189, 201
Heimlicher v. Steele	303
Hensley v. Cerza	47
Herbst, Arthur	275, 276
Hitaffer v. Argonne	225
holding	39, 271
Holt v. City of Memphis	56, 57
Hurley v. Eddingfield	71

I

impeach	118
informed consent	281, 284-292
In re Baby K	303
instruction conference	211, 212

interrogatories	101-103, 358, 359
invoke the rule	165

J

Jamail, Joseph	390, 391
Johnson v. Northbrooke	55
Johnson v. Richardson	276, 277
judgment	84
judgment as a matter of law	191
judicial notice	190
jury consultants	163
jury selection	159

L

last chance letter	99
Law of agency	224
Law School Admission Test	5
leading	182
learned treatise	118
Lebron v. Gottlieb Memorial	154, 156
Lee Medical v. Beecher	353-355
legal cause	37, 86
Lex Loci Delecti	334
liability	34
locality rule	35, 82, 223, 226, 275, 277
loss allocation	34
loss of consortium	224, 225

M

malpractice, medical	33, 34, 98, 339
Martin v. Herzog	127
Martins v. Williamson	55
material	328
Matz v. Quest Diagnostics	133
McDaniel	45
McDaniel v. CSX	258
McIntosh v. Blanton	136
McIntyre v. Balentine	129
mediation	403-406
Millard v. Corrado	73
Miller v. Birdwell	93
ministerial act	288
Mooney v. Sneed	57
morbidity and mortality conference	351, 354, 367-368
motion to dismiss	56

N

National Childhood Vaccine Injury Act	417, 418
National Practitioner Data Bank	389, 391, 392, 396, 397, 401-406, 408, 432
Negligence	33, 52, 55, 56, 58, 59, 61, 62, 224, 242, 251, 252, 260, 282, 356
no fault	416-420
non obstante veridicto	235
notice	53, 54, 98

O

objections	196-206, 211, 215
obstruction of justice	252
opening statements	169-173
open the door	265
ordinary damages	151
ordinary negligence	271

P

pain and suffering	145, 146, 152-154, 226
Palsgraf v. Long Island Rail Road	88
patient centered standard	287
patient dumping	295
Patient Safety Act	370
peer review	351-357, 361-363, 367-369, 371, 373, 374, 376, 377
Peete v. Shelby County	58
People v. Gainer	323
perjury	327-329, 343
peremptory challenge	161, 162
Peterson v. Weinberger	345
Physicians At Teaching Hospitals	342, 343
pleadings	35
Powell v. Community Health Systems	362
Powers v. Ohio	161
practitioner (health care)	57
prejudicial	201, 202
preliminary instructions	164
preponderance of the evidence	67, 68, 221
prima facie	58, 173, 191

probative 201
projection 214-216
proximate cause 37, 86, 224, 241, 251
professional disclosure standard 287
professional responsibility 387
prosecutorial discretion 347
punitive damages 67, 145-151
Purkett v. Elem 162

Q

qui tam 343, 344
quid pro quo 421

R

Raise or waive rule 385
Real evidence 188
Reasonable degree of medical certainty 86, 87
reasonable fee 267
rebut 187
rebuttal 209, 210, 218
re-direct 187
rehabilitate 187
relevant evidence 112, 114
relief 98
remedy 35, 240, 431
remittitur 154, 155, 236
res ipsa loquitur 58-61
Rescue doctrine 127
Restatement (second) of Torts 76
right to privacy 282, 283

Rule 402	40
Rule 701	48
Rule 702	40, 41
rules of evidence	40, 112
Rural Education v. Bush	311

S

served	35
service	98, 99
Scott, Rosalyn	372, 373
Shadrick v. Coker	134, 135, 141
Sherrill v. Souder	138
Smithwick v. Hall	128
Solomon v. Shuell	127
speculation	190
standard of care	34, 36, 57, 58, 62-65, 81-83, 85-87, 94, 137, 221-223, 239, 243, 249, 251, 260, 261, 275, 277, 346, 351, 413, 415, 430
Stark law	341, 347
state actor	98
State Farm v. Campbell	150
statement against interest	119
State v. Smith	385
statute of limitations	99, 130-133, 135-140, 333
statute of repose	53, 54, 99, 140-141
stipulations	187, 189
Stratienko v. Chattanooga Hamilton	357
strict liability	241-245
substantive	270
surrebutal	209
sustain	114, 196
substantially assist	37

summary judgment	38
Syposs v. United States	369

T

Taylor v. Jackson Madison County	87, 88
Thorton v. Southwest	298
three strikes rule	427
tolling	134
tort	33
trier of fact	36, 68, 112, 116, 188, 239, 249, 250, 264
Twelve Angry Men	164
two schools of thought	64

U

undue prejudice	46
United States v. Krizek	342
United States v. Lorenzo	344
United States v. Panni	344

V

voir dire	160, 163

W

Weekoty v. United States	368
Westmoreland v. Bacon, MD	44
wrongful conduct	137

Products and Services

Products:

Dr. Weiman has authored two books, available through his website: www.MedicalMalpracticeAndTheLaw.com.
1. *Medical Malpractice – A Physician's Guide to Navigating the Minefield of Medical Malpractice Law*
2. *Fundamental Issues in Health Care Law: Facts for the Health Care Professional – A Lecture Series*

Services:

Dr. Weiman has written and offers a timely lecture series that addresses essential topics in Health Care Law. The lecture series contains 13 talks, each designed to effectively communicate the facts a health care professional needs to know.

The topics are:

1. Stark 1 and Stark 2
2. Doctrine of Informed Consent
3. EMTALA
4. Expert Witness
5. FTCA and NPDB
6. Health Care Talking Points
7. Health Courts
8. Introduction to Law
9. Morbidity and Mortality Conferences
10. Regulation of Provider Conduct
11. Resident Files; Are they discoverable?
12. Themes for a malpractice defense
13. Theresa Schiavo: How a surgeon lost his chance to become president of the United States

Dr. Weiman has presented as a visiting professor on numerous occasions. You are invited to contact him through his website, to arrange your lecture presentations, and for more information.

www.MedicalMalpracticeAndTheLaw.com

CPSIA information can be obtained at www.ICGtesting.com
Printed in the USA
LVOW06*2318100714

393660LV00002BB/2/P